IF IT'S PREDICTABLE, IT'S PREVENTABLE

MORE THAN 2,000 WAYS TO IMPROVE THE SAFETY AND SECURITY IN YOUR SCHOOL

TED HAYES, CSP, MSE
SCHOOL SAFETY AND SECURITY CONSULTANT

ENDORSED BY:

LITTLE CREEK PRESS®
A DIVISION OF KRISTIN MITCHELL DESIGN, LLC

Mineral Point, Wisconsin USA

Little Creek Press®
A Division of Kristin Mitchell Design, LLC
5341 Sunny Ridge Road
Mineral Point, Wisconsin 53565

Editor: Nancy Pfotenhauer
Book Design and Project Coordination: Little Creek Press

Limited First Edition
Novmember 2013

Printed in Wisconsin, United States of America.

For more information or to order books:
hayes.schoolsafety@gmail.com or www.littlecreekpress.com

Library of Congress Control Number: 2013950059

ISBN-10: 0989643166
ISBN-13: 978-0-9896431-6-0

This publication contains the opinions and ideas of its author. It is intended to provide helpful and informative material on the subjects addressed in the publication. It is sold with the understanding that the author and publisher are not engaged in rendering personal or professional services in this publication. This publication is not a substitute for professional services, which should be sought before adopting any of the suggestions of this publication or drawing any inferences from it. The author and publisher specifically disclaim any liability, loss, or risk, personal or otherwise, which is incurred as a consequence, directly or indirectly, of the use and application of any of the contents of this publication.

The author alone is responsible for statements of fact, opinion, recommendations, and conclusions expressed. Publication in no way implies approval or endorsement by M3 Insurance Solutions, Inc., or by its directors and officers, or its employees.

Front cover photo: © Luckydoor | Dreamstime.com

TABLE OF CONTENTS

This key represents the 'key' ideas of each chapter.

ACKNOWLEDGEMENTS

Apart from my efforts, this book was developed with the support and encouragement of many. I take this opportunity to express my sincere gratitude to those who assisted in the successful completion of this book.

I would like to express my greatest appreciation to my M3 Insurance teammates — Mike Victorson, Julie Redders, Mark Meeks, Julie Meeks, Kevin Miller, Pam Queoff and Chris Halverson. I thank you for your professional knowledge and assistance.

I would like to thank Nancy Pfotenhauer, my remarkable editor and Kristin Mitchell and the team at Little Creek Press, my publisher, for their guidance and tireless efforts in formatting and developing this book.

A big thank you to Eric Brooks, photographer, who graciously provided the pictures within my book.

Thank you to the Wisconsin Sheriffs and Deputy Sheriffs Association for their support and endorsement of this book.

Lastly, a special thank you to my best friends — John Fink, Darrel Hoene and Phil Love — you have always been there for encouragement and in times of need.

"Always plan ahead.
It wasn't raining when
Noah built the ark."

— Richard Cushing

ENDORSEMENTS

I just finished reviewing your book draft, and have to say that I am grateful for the opportunity to do so. I would not have expected to find all of the areas of my responsibilities as a Safety Coordinator and Facilities Director in one single publication. I was taken aback to find the amazing amount of pertinent information available in your book, and how easy a read it is.

I recently began the annual ritual of updating our school district's "Emergency Response Plan," and found it a breeze after reading your book. The way you categorized the "Table of Contents," and the detail of your years of experience with regard to the topics is priceless. I would strongly recommend all Facilities and Safety Coordinators take the time to read this comprehensive book. I would even go a step further, and recommend school district Administrators read this book, to help them understand better, the reasons for implementing the safety measures we put in place. I have already begun avoiding, minimizing, and transferring a portion of the liability we carry.

Gary Siegman, Director of Buildings and Grounds,
Whitefish Bay (WI) School District

It's Predictable, It' Preventable **by Ted Hayes — as a read — it's incredible!** Every administrator, teacher and other staff member should have a copy of this book. It is a superb, comprehensive guide and reference document that contains an extensive compilation of knowledge and expertise. I have worked with Ted Hayes for many years in benign circumstances and in crisis. He is the go-to guy, experienced, calm, and level-headed. I want him on my team. In my decades of military service I have also worked in other benign and crises situations, the experiences of which often transferred to what we faced in public schools. Point being, I have seen many of these practices work and can without reservation say that everyone will benefit from reading this book.

One cannot help but gain ideas and insight covering all facets of school safety, security, and liability operations that will be invaluable. Let's face the truth; we know that there will always be some future negative event impacting our lives. With this book as a resource and with the guidance of common sense proactive people in our schools, we stand a much better chance of averting a really bad day.

Thomas R. Owens, Ph.D., Director of Business Services,
Stevens Point (WI) Area Public School District

FOREWORD

By Mike Victorson, President and CEO, M3 Insurance

As a father, I know the joy that comes from watching my children learn and grow. I feel their excitement when they come home from school brimming with stories, and their pride as they read or sing or build something new. And I also know the overwhelming desire to keep them safe. It's an instinct I share with parents everywhere.

Every day as our kids head off to school, we assume they'll be home at the end of the day. We count on teachers and staff to protect them as if they were their own, and we believe our kids are in reliable hands. The unfortunate truth, however, is always right beneath the surface of our assumptions and expectations. Whether natural or man-made, bad things happen to good people.

Reading this book makes it clear to me that (to the extent we can) we are obligated to plan ahead to keep our schools safe. We must work together to identify specific safety and security exposures at our schools and develop plans to prevent them from happening. My colleague, friend, and author of this book, Ted Hayes, has been doing just that for more than 25 years.

Ted's "real" title is Senior Risk Manager at M3 Insurance; it's an honor to have him on the M3 team. But what his title doesn't tell you is that over the years he's taken it upon himself to document thousands of ideas and best practices he's observed on school visits with the idea of sharing them with anyone willing to take up the mantle of safety. While it's true his role at M3 centers around risk management strategies and liability concerns as they relate to clients' insurance coverage and premiums, Ted's greater concern is personal.

Like me, Ted is a father. And like me, he has always counted on his children being safe at school. Ted tells us that the real work is recognizing, reducing and eliminating accident and injury exposures and security threats at our schools before they happen, and less on determining the course of action once they do. He is vigilant about asking the tough questions and tracking dangers of all shapes and sizes in our ever-changing culture and environment so plans can be ready when needed.

In producing this book, Ted has taken decades worth of handwritten notes and compiled them into a reference guide of sorts. It's been a labor of love. This go-to manual helps administrators predict, and then prevent bad things from happening. It provides quick and easy brush-ups, quick hitting topics for staff meetings and orientation material for new employees. It also addresses best practices for when a crisis does occur, because even the most well prepared schools face emergency situations at one time or another.

I am humbled to have the opportunity to introduce Ted's book, and I'm confident I can speak for parents everywhere as I acknowledge him for his time, passion and commitment to doing the right thing for our children.

"By failing to prepare, you are preparing to fail."

- Benjamin Franklin

INTRODUCTION

It's not a secret, at one time or another your school district struggles to develop proactive and effective risk management programs to address the ever changing multitude of school safety and security concerns.

Besides the many required compliance programs, your school district must address employee and student accident and injury concerns, life safety requirements, crisis prevention needs, workers' compensation issues, auto liability questions and public liability exposures. Do not overlook the potential legal concerns, where your school district may be held liable if it does not make a good faith effort to provide a safe, secure, and hazard free learning environment for your students.

It's important your school district recognizes that a risk management program is above all a *human concern* — the absolute safety and security of your staff and students is paramount. The real work is recognizing, reducing, and eliminating accident/injury exposures and security threats within your school district. These tasks need to be planned and implemented by those who know your schools the best — school staff, your insurance company, local law enforcement, emergency medical personnel, and the school community.

Working together, your district can successfully *plan ahead* and identify your specific safety and security exposures to develop a proactive risk management plan.

The development of your comprehensive school risk management program should involve the following steps:

• Identify and assess your district's specific exposures that may result in an accident, an injury, property damage, or an act of violence.

• Select and implement the best risk management strategies to address these exposures.

• Monitor your results and make improvements or modifications when and where necessary.

For the majority of your school risk management concerns, accurate risk exposure identification is critical. No matter the activity, constantly ask the following questions:

- Are our school activities 'age appropriate' for the students involved?

- Do we provide the proper supervision that is required for the activity?

- Do we understand the risks that are inherent to the activity?

- Does our school district have proper insurance coverage for the activity?

- Have we developed emergency plans for each activity?

- Have we identified the exposures and risks that our students will be exposed to?

- Have we thought about how significant the risks are and if they are worth taking?

- What will our school district do to reduce or eliminate these risks?

- Have the identified risks materialized in the past? If so, how frequently and what was the result?

- What are other school districts doing to manage these same types of exposures or risks?

- And possibly the most important question of all — if these students were my own children, what would I do?

When I convene with school administrators to discuss viable school risk management strategies, there are three basic strategies to review:

- Your school district can **avoid** the risk.

- Your school district can **reduce** the risk.

- Your school district can **transfer** the risk.

Let's review each of these strategies in greater detail:

Risk Avoidance

After completing a thorough risk assessment of the exposure, risk, or activity, your school district may determine that the best thing to do is to eliminate the risk and avoid the activity altogether.

A real life example of risk avoidance is not allowing your school employees to participate in a potentially high injury risk activity such as a donkey basketball game. Another example is saying 'no' to a community group that asked to use your baseball diamond for a softball tournament where alcohol would be served.

Risk Reduction

Ask yourself if the exposures or activity can be modified to reduce the risk to your school district. An example of risk reduction is the requirement that all students must wear the proper personal protective equipment whenever they are in the technology education shop area. Another risk reduction example is requiring additional supervision at the big football game against your cross town rival which hundreds of spectators are expected to attend.

As the name implies, risk reduction is conducted to reduce the risk of an activity.

Risk Transfer

Your school district often makes the decision to use vendors, subcontractors, or private companies to provide services for activities outside the direct control of the school district.

Examples of risk transfer include using a charter bus company to transport students for a field trip or hiring a subcontractor to perform everyday cleaning of your schools.

With most of these risk transfer situations, the planning, instruction, and supervision of the activity is out of the direct control of your school district. It's important that your district ensures that the required expertise and certification is provided and that the appropriate insurance coverage is in place to address any potential liability concerns.

Improving the overall safety and security of your school district using these risk management strategies is not a new idea. All school districts practice risk management in some manner, often on a very informal basis.

Whatever risk management strategy is favored, your school district, staff, and students are best protected by conducting and maintaining a planned, well-documented hazard mitigation process that fulfills your district's legal obligation to maintain an appropriate standard of care.

Appropriate Standard of Care

An appropriate standard of care stresses that your school district employees must always **"act as a careful or prudent parent would act in a particular situation."** Over my many years of my school risk management consulting, I have stressed those words "act as a careful or prudent parent would act," hundreds of times to school administrators and teachers.

Repeatedly stress to your school staff that, *"acting as a careful or prudent parent would act"* does not mean acting as a careful or prudent **teacher** or a reasonable **person** would act. It clearly means **acting** as a careful or prudent **parent** would act if faced with the same situation or circumstances.

Instruct your school employees that the 'careful and prudent parent' standard of care depends upon a variety of factors such as:

• The number of students involved in the activity.

• The nature of the activity.

• The age of the students involved in the activity.

• The competency and capacity of the students involved in the activity.

• The degree of skill and training the students have received.

• The nature and condition of equipment involved in the activity.

And let's never forget that as an educator, your school district's duty of care may apply in a variety of settings including:

• In the classroom.

• On school grounds or on the playground.

• On excursions or field trips.

• Before and after school hours.

• During the transportation of students.

• Off school property if it is a school sponsored activity.

Developing and maintaining a reasonable and appropriate standard of care can be a monumental task for your school district. That is why developing a step-by-step plan to implement your comprehensive school risk management program is so very important.

When developing your risk management plan and reviewing the exposures faced by your school district on a daily basis, always keep these two questions in mind:

• Is the outcome of the activity, whether good or bad, **predictable**?

• And, if the outcome is bad, is it **preventable**?

If your answer is **'yes'** to either of these questions and something bad does occur, your district may be determined to be negligent… and negligence often is payable!

Because of these concerns, for the past quarter of a century, I have assisted school districts like yours in selecting and implementing the best and most appropriate risk management strategies. My job is to help you recognize, reduce, and eliminate your potential workers' compensation, auto, property, and general liability exposures that may result in an accident, injury, or monetary loss involving your school district.

Over the years, I have consulted to school districts on all parts of the school risk management spectrum — small school districts, large school districts, schools with detailed risk management plans, and schools with little or nothing when it comes to addressing safety and security concerns.

Early on in my consulting career, I began documenting the good school risk management ideas and best practices in a notebook — my permanent record of the best and brightest safety and security ideas that I observed throughout our Wisconsin schools. A few years ago, I began reviewing this notebook as well as the many school risk management articles that I had authored. It was time to pull this information together and write this book. It is my wish that the hundreds of best practices discussed in this book will assist your school district in recognizing and addressing potential hazards and exposures before something bad (or costly) occurs.

IF IT'S PREDICTABLE, IT'S PREVENTABLE focuses on those issues that present the greatest frequency (number of incidents and claims) and severity (monetary cost of claims, serious injury) exposure to your school district.

Not all of these school risk management best practices are mine the majority of these best practices were learned from working with some of the best school safety coordinators, buildings and grounds supervisors, principals, coaches, and administrators that our state has to offer.

For your convenience, I've divided *If It's Predictable, It's Preventable* into five major sections:

SECTION ONE: **School Security Best Practices** addresses the many risk management best practices that can be directly applied in your school buildings and classrooms — best practices that will reduce the chance of a violent incident, school shooting, or other crisis from taking place in one of your schools.

SECTION TWO: **School Safety Best Practices** addresses the best practices to reduce your district's exposure to staff and student accidents and injuries.

SECTION THREE: **School Liability Best Practices** addresses the relevant general liability exposures and best practices faced by your school district on a daily basis.

SECTION FOUR: **School Insurance Best Practices** addresses a number of insurance best practices that your school district must review to ensure adequate insurance coverage is provided for your actions, exposures, risks, and activities.

SECTION FIVE: **School Fleet Liability Best Practices** deals with the fleet exposures that every school district faces but often overlooks.

It is my sincere desire that you keep this book handy and use it as a reference guide to continually *plan ahead* when questions arise regarding certain school safety and security exposures of your school district.

"Expect the best, plan for the worst and prepare to be surprised."

– Denis Waitley

SCHOOL **SECURITY** BEST PRACTICES

Just like every other parent, I want to believe that my school district is safe and doing everything humanly possible to maintain a secure environment for my children during the school day.

Even though it appears that every day we read about another school bullying incident, a violent crime on school grounds, or a deadly shooting, the truth is, the assiduous efforts of our school employees and emergency responders continue to provide an extremely safe environment for our children.

Unfortunately, the chance your school district will someday be affected by a crisis — whether it is natural or man-made — is very real.

A natural disaster such as the tornado that destroyed the schools in Joplin, Missouri can strike your community with little or no warning. Man-made disasters such as violent school shootings continue to occur in all corners of our country. Thousands of times each day, students are bullied and harassed by classmates, cyber-bullied on the internet or targeted by malicious rumors and threats — issues that just may be the match that lights the powder keg of a violent act within one of your schools. And let's never overlook the often forgotten but ever present fear of terrorism.

1 **I realize that it's never popular to say, but we need to stop believing that our schools are public facilities — forever open for our community members and visitors to visit and use with little or no security controls.** Every community has individuals who have thought about disrupting your school day by targeting one of your schools with some type of violent act. Now is the time for every one of your schools, no matter how large or how small, to develop sound crisis prevention plans, implement these plans, then practice these plans... then practice them some more.

If you have attended one of my crisis prevention presentations, you heard me state that all school employees need to be ready to 'act not react' when it comes to dealing with a school crisis or emergency. Ensuring your principal, teacher, custodian, or volunteer aide knows exactly what to do in a crisis situation may be the difference between life and death for themselves, a fellow school employee, or one of your students.

Your school district's preparation for a crisis is a never ending task. On a positive note, the chances that your school district will ever have to deal with a shooter in your hallways or an actual bomb hidden in your school are quite low — but in case you do, you want to be prepared to act immediately and effectively.

The best practices discussed in this 'Security' section will assist you in evaluating what your school can do to reduce the potential risk, frequency, and severity of an emergency or a crisis. Review these best practices and implement those which make your school a better place for our children to learn.

2 **Don't be one of the many school districts that wait until a crisis occurs to plan their response.** An effective crisis plan addresses what your school district will do before, during, and after a crisis. Planning for a crisis ahead of time provides the best chance to eliminate or reduce the damage caused by a crisis.

Remember these tips when developing your crisis plan:

PREDICT — Think outside of the box and attempt to anticipate everything that could possibly go wrong with your school operations.

POSITION — Clearly determine what your district's position will be on these issues.

PREVENT — Institute proactive crisis preventive measures.

PLAN — In case your prevention doesn't work, prepare a plan for dealing with the crisis.

PERSEVERE — Follow your crisis plan and stick to the positions you have taken. See the crisis through in a thorough and professional manner.

EVALUATE — If your crisis plan is enacted, review the results to determine if there are additional steps that can be taken to prevent the crisis from happening again.

"Everyone has a plan — until they get punched in the mouth."

— Mike Tyson

After a Crisis Occurs

After a crisis occurs, your number one goal is recovery. This is the time to re-establish your school's infrastructure and return to the 'business of learning' as soon as reasonably possible. Quickly returning to the classroom doesn't always ensure that your students are ready to address learning tasks, but restoring the educational routine is critical in leading your students through their emotional crises.

3 **Constantly inform your students, their families, and the media.** After a crisis occurs, be very meticulous in communicating the steps that are being taken to ensure student safety and security.

4 **Educate families and community members regarding the support services your school district is providing and the appropriate community resources that are available.** Make sure your messages to your students are always age appropriate.

5 **Address the cultural and language differences when developing your district's crisis communication materials.** Emails, letters, and other communications may need to be translated into languages other than English, depending on your community.

6 **Appraise the emotional needs of your students and staff.** Identify those individuals who may need intervention by the school counselor, school psychologist, social worker, or other mental health professional.

7 **Long before a crisis occurs, arrange for appropriate interventions by school or community-based service providers.** Determine the services available for families who may need to seek treatment for their children or themselves. Appropriate group intervention may be beneficial to students and staff experiencing less severe reactions to your crisis. Any group interventions should be age appropriate.

8 **Allow your students to talk about what they felt and experienced during the traumatic event.**

9 Contemplate providing crisis stress management during class time. Your goal is to allow students to talk about what they felt and experienced during the traumatic event in a caring and trusting environment.

10 Understand that your younger students may not be able to fully express their feelings verbally. Young students may benefit from participating in creative activities such as drawing, painting, or writing stories.

11 Conduct daily debriefings for staff, responders, and others who assist during crisis recovery. These debriefings can help your staff cope with their own feelings of confusion and vulnerability.

12 Allow for as much time as needed for your staff and student emotional recovery. Depending on the event, an individual may take months or even years to recover.

Armed Students in School

A teacher's worst nightmare is the suspicion that a student may be carrying, concealing, or possessing a weapon in school or worse, their classroom. Talk with your staff members about the procedures for addressing armed students.

13 Your students, parents and guardians must clearly understand that possession of any weapon will result in removal from the school and could result in prosecution. This is a great topic to address during student assemblies, parent-teacher conferences, and with parent mailings/emails.

14 Instruct all of your staff members to immediately report (to the principal) a student suspected of possessing a weapon on school property.

15 If the weapon is believed to be a gun, carefully consider whether an attempt to confiscate the weapon can be safely performed without endangering others.

Share these gun confiscation procedures with your staff:

16 **Confiscate a weapon only if it is absolutely safe to do so.**

17 **Do not make contact with the student; instead immediately contact law enforcement.** Ask law enforcement to respond in a low-key manner so as to not startle the student.

18 **Never attempt to retrieve the weapon if it is believed to be in a locker or other location.** Again, wait for law enforcement to arrive. A police officer will know how to unload a loaded gun so it does not accidentally discharge in the school building.

19 **Do not attempt to discipline or restrain the student before the police get there.**

20 **Use a student messenger to send a note to the office if you believe someone is concealing a weapon in the classroom.** Try to provide as much information as possible such as:

• The student's name.

• The exact location of the student in the classroom.

• Unique identifiers such as description of clothing.

• The type of weapon that is suspected.

• The room number.

• The approximate number of students in the classroom.

• Any other useful information.

⚿ 21 Learn to recognize some of the warning signs that a student may be carrying or concealing a weapon on their body:

- During a routine security check or confrontation with the student, the individual is seen feeling their body to ensure the weapon is in place.

- Look for a sag in the individual's jacket or coat. The pocket of the jacket where the weapon is stored may hang lower than the other side.

- The individual's clothing appears out of place — they are wearing clothing that appears too warm for the weather. The clothing may provide a hiding space for a weapon.

- The individual uses just one hand to perform routine tasks. This is an attempt to keep one hand free to handle the weapon.

- The individual wears just one glove. Again, one hand is left free to handle a weapon.

- A part of the weapon is visible. The barrel of a gun may be seen protruding from beneath a coat, the tip of a knife can be seen sticking out of a sleeve, etc.

- The individual walks with an unnatural gait — not swinging their arm on the side of the body where the weapon is located. They may be holding a weapon in place to prevent it from falling.

- The individual 'palms' the weapon in the palm of their hand in preparation for ready use.

- The individual turns their body away from a school authority figure to hide or protect a concealed weapon. This is a practice commonly called 'blading.'

Biological and Chemical Threats

What seemed impossible just a few years ago, in fact has become a very real serious concern. A biological or chemical attack within your community may have devastating effects on your school district. Even though the likelihood of an attack seems beyond belief, there are a number of best practices that your school district should consider:

22 **Institute procedures to recognize and address suspicious packages or items delivered to your school.** The U.S. Postal Service can provide information on suspicious packages, mail, and anthrax concerns.

23 **Never allow any of your students to open the school mail.** Mail opening should be conducted by only one school employee in an area that is segregated from all open areas and students.

24 **Require your school employees to always wear protective gloves when opening the school mail.**

25 **Ensure that the maintenance staff and the principal know how to quickly shut down your school's ventilation system if an airborne contaminant is suspected or present.** An airborne contaminant that is allowed to spread quickly throughout your building's ventilation system could have deadly results for a large group of students and staff.

26 **At all of your schools, develop lockdown and evacuation procedures for biological and chemical threats.** It is possible to have a simultaneous lockdown of one area of your school building while evacuating other parts of the building — both a lockdown and an evacuation may need to occur at the same time.

27 **Develop 'Shelter-in-Place' plans to as part of your lockdown and evacuation plans.** Identify the safe areas (preferably with no windows) in your school buildings to relocate staff and students. I encourage you to meet with your local fire, law enforcement, HAZMAT, and emergency management officials for advice on developing 'Shelter-in-Place' controls.

28 During a teacher in-service presentation have your county emergency management agency review biological and chemical terrorism concerns and controls as they relate to your school.

29 Develop your district's emergency plans with your school district, neighboring districts, and the broader community in mind. You may need to rely on neighboring school districts for resources, such as additional buses to quickly transport your students.

30 Contact your local emergency management agency to review their community emergency plans. They may be planning to use your school buses or facilities during a major emergency.

Bomb Threats

I once read that 'there has never been a bomb explosion in a United States school where a bomb threat was called in beforehand.' This may be a comforting thought, but it is not something we can use to develop your school's bomb threat procedure.

The presence of an explosive device and/or the reception of a bomb threat are situations that your school personnel must be ready to confront in a calm and professional manner. Although the vast majority of bomb threats turn out to be pranks, they still must be taken seriously to ensure the safety and security of your students, staff, and visitors.

The majority of school bomb threats are delivered by phone although a bomb threat can also be written, emailed, or verbally communicated.

Sadly, bomb threats are occurring on a more frequent basis every year in our schools. For whatever reason, it appears individuals are getting satisfaction from calling in a bomb threat to cause fear, disruption, and chaos. Why do these individuals call in bomb threats to our schools? Here are a couple of reasons to consider:

THE THRILL OF DISRUPTION. The individual calling in the bomb threat enjoys the 'power' they wield when one phone call can shut down their school for an entire day. Students get to leave school, the police are called to the scene and the media broadcasts the big story — everyone's day is disrupted. The thrill of "I caused all of this disruption" is very real and exciting for the caller.

ONE LESS DAY OF SCHOOL. Calling in a bomb threat means a day away from school — doesn't it just make sense that the majority of bomb threats occur when the weather is nice?

THEY WON'T CATCH ME. The chances of catching a bomb threat caller are minimal unless they slip up or don't know what they are doing when using a phone or the internet. It's a very dangerous prank that has a minimal chance of getting caught. Like my good friend retired Everest Metro (WI) Police Chief Dan Vergein once told me, "Catching someone who calls in a bomb threat is like catching smoke with a net — it ain't gonna happen."

31 **Meet with your police department and telecommunications representatives to determine the equipment needed to trace incoming calls to your school.** The new trend today is to send bomb threat messages via the internet. Those sending internet bomb threat messages aren't stupid — their messages are virtually untraceable. Not very comforting, but it is reality.

32 **At the beginning of the school year, get the message out loud and clear that your district will trace all bomb threats that come in to any of your schools.** Getting this message out may detract some from making such threats.

33 **If your school district is fortunate enough to trace the origin of a bomb threat, the police must push for conviction.** The media must get the message out that the bomb threat caller/sender was apprehended and swift justice is being sought.

34 **No matter how a bomb threat is received, call the police immediately.**

35 **Ask the police to respond to your school's bomb threat with a low key approach.** This means unmarked police cars and plain clothes officers if at all possible. Don't provide the bomb threat caller/sender the added 'thrill of disruption.'

The following is a partial list of best practices that should become part of your district's procedures in the event a bomb or bomb threat is received:

36 **Ensure each school's receptionist has a bomb threat/harassing phone call checklist that is readily accessible.** A bomb threat and harassing phone call checklist should be distributed to all staff members. This checklist should be printed on brightly colored paper, laminated and kept next to all main office school phones.

37 **While the caller is speaking to you on the phone, fill out your 'Bomb Threat Checklist.'** An example of a bomb threat checklist is included at the end of this chapter and many other examples can be found on the internet.

38 **Ensure that the 'Bomb Threat Checklist' is filled out completely and accurately.**

39 **Stay calm and indicate your desire to cooperate with the bomb threat caller.** Never antagonize or challenge the caller.

40 **Obtain as much information as possible from the bomb threat caller.** Prolong the conversation as long as possible and ask their permission to repeat any instructions to make sure they were understood.

41 **Attempt to determine the caller's familiarity with your school facility.**

42 **Identify any background noises which may be indicators of where the call is coming from.**

43 **Never hang up the phone.** If you need assistance, use hand signals to get the attention of a co-worker. If this isn't possible, use another phone to call for immediate assistance.

44 By landline only, immediately call '911', other school administrators, and principals.

45 If a student is receiving the bomb threat call, instruct them to give the phone to an adult to resume the conversation if at all possible.

46 Determine if the bomb threat is credible by immediately consulting with school administration and your police department. If the bomb threat is credible, the building must be evacuated.

47 Do not allow the use of portable school or public safety radios, cellular phones, digital phones, or any other electronic devices. These devices may have the capacity to detonate an explosive device.

48 Instruct everyone to not turn the lights on or off but have them remain in their current position.

Threat Level Determination

The following are some factors to assist your school district in the determination of the bomb threat level. These factors are to be used only as a guide in conjunction with all of the other available information.

49 If the caller was vague in their threat, simply stating that there is a bomb, provides no specifics, and hangs up the phone quickly — the threat level is probably low. Their probable motive was to cause disruption to your school day.

50 If the caller provides details such as the size, type, or location of a bomb — the threat level may be considered medium. In a medium level bomb threat, the caller usually stays on the line longer and states their motive for the bomb.

51 A high level bomb threat caller is very detailed, describing the type, power, location, or time of detonation. The caller may stay on the line longer or may make multiple calls. The caller may also exhibit advanced knowledge of bombs. In addition, the caller may make demands such as publicity, money, etc.

52 Maintain multiple evacuation sites to prevent the caller from placing an explosive device in the area where students gather during a bomb evacuation. Each school's potential evacuation sites should be rotated on a periodic basis to prevent a caller from focusing on just one evacuation site.

If a Bomb Evacuation Occurs

53 Immediately and rapidly evacuate all students and staff to your pre-determined evacuation areas.

54 Ensure that handicapped and special needs students receive immediate evacuation assistance.

55 Ask your school staff to complete a rapid visual check of their classrooms and building as they exit. Any suspicious or unusual items should not be touched and must be reported immediately to the police.

56 Establish a command post at least 400 feet from any of the school buildings.

57 Ensure your command post is away from any vehicles, waste containers, mail boxes, or any objects that could conceal a bomb.

58 School staff should never use walkie-talkies or cell phones to communicate. Employee runners should be used to communicate to the staff and students at the various evacuation sites.

59 **Instruct your students to take their personal belongings with them when they are evacuating the school.** There will be no stopping at their lockers or at the bathroom.

60 **Instruct your students to immediately turn off their cell phones.** If a bomb is present, a cell phone signal may be enough to detonate the bomb.

61 **Never use cell phones or security radios at the evacuation assembly site.** As mentioned earlier, staff members should utilize 'runners' to communicate with the command center.

62 **When you reach the evacuation assembly area, take roll of your students and continue to supervise your class.**

63 **Remain at least 400 feet away from buildings until the "all clear" announcement is given.** Ensure your students are kept in open areas away from vehicles, other buildings, waste containers, etc.

64 **Move students to a pre-determined off grounds evacuation area if it appears that the search will take an extended period of time or if weather conditions are a concern.**

65 **If your school buses are used to transport students, make sure the buses are inspected for suspicious items prior to allowing students to board.** Students should never be allowed to leave the evacuation assembly area unless instructed by a school staff member or transported to another safe location.

66 **Instruct your staff members to keep a log of students' movements and note the new location in the event of transport.**

Conducting a Bomb Search

67 Develop a systematic bomb search plan to search your school building.

68 Simply stated, look for an object that doesn't belong. A bomb can look like an ordinary object, such as a knapsack, briefcase, or lunch box. Be aware of objects that do not belong or one that someone does not claim, such as an unattended briefcase. Your police department can provide pictures of homemade bombs.

Divide the building into sections and assign each section to search teams as follows:

69 Teachers will search their immediate classroom. I stress the importance of locking the classroom door when the room is not occupied by a staff member. If the room is never left unoccupied, it will make your search for a bomb that much easier.

70 Physical education teachers will search the gymnasium, locker rooms, and hallways near these areas.

71 Librarians will search the library, storage rooms, and any related areas.

72 Cafeteria personnel will search the kitchen, cafeteria, and food storage areas.

73 Custodians will search custodial areas, storage rooms, equipment rooms, stairwells, the auditorium, and the building perimeter including trash cans/dumpsters.

74 Administrative personnel will search administrative areas, hallways, and any empty classrooms.

75 Administrators and school resource officers will search bathrooms and hallways as well as assisting in searching areas not already searched.

76 Administrators will be assigned specific sections of the school to be sure all areas have been searched.

Search Team Search Procedures

77 Use two person search teams whenever possible.

78 Search team members should stand in middle of room and listen for any unusual noises. If there are two searchers, go to opposite sides of the room and listen.

79 During the first search, divide the room into two levels. First search the floor and all areas up to window sill height or three feet above the floor.

80 During the second search, search areas from three feet high to the top of the searcher's head. Move in a circular motion around room, coming back to the starting point.

81 During the third search, search from the top of the head to the ceiling level.

82 During the fourth search, search the ceiling and structural supports, the window air conditioning units, and the light fixtures.

83 At the completion of a room search, where no suspicious item was found, the searcher will place a sheet of paper on the outside of the door or on the outside doorknob marked with a half "X." When law enforcement or administration completes their search of the same room they will complete the "X" thus marking that the room in question was searched and is clear.

If A Suspicious Item Is Found

84 **Never approach, move, or touch any suspicious item. Report the exact location and an accurate description of the object to the police.** At this point the incident becomes a police matter and control of the scene transfers to law enforcement.

85 **Identify the danger area and immediately evacuate the building.** Be sure evacuation takes place away from the danger area and at least 400 feet from the building.

86 **Never allow anyone to re-enter the school building until the police inform you that it is safe to do so.** At the conclusion of a bomb threat evacuation:

87 **Account for all of your students and report any missing students to your administration.**

88 **Meet with law enforcement personnel to critique the incident to determine improvements, if any, that may be required to properly execute the bomb threat procedure in the future.**

Here is an example of a 'Bomb Threat Checklist.' As I mentioned earlier, many other checklists can be obtained by simply searching the internet.

Bomb threat questions to ask the caller:

• When is the bomb going to explode?

• What is the material involved?

• How much material is involved?

• Where is it right now?

• What does it look like?

• What kind of device is it?

• What will cause the device to function?

• Did you place the device? Why?

• Are there any additional devices?

• What is your name and address?

BOMB THREAT CHECKLIST

Exact Message Received:

Name of Person Receiving Call:

Time:

Date:

Callers Identity:	Male Female	Adult Juvenile	Approximate Age:
Origin of Call: (if you can tell or ask)	Local Long Distance Phone Booth	Residence Cell Phone Internet	Internal (from within the building)
Vocal Characteristics:	Loud Soft Pleasant	High Pitch Deep Raspy	Intoxicated Other
Speech:	Fast Slow Distinct	Distorted Nasal Slurred	Stutter Lisp Other
Language:	Excellent Good	Fair Poor	Foul Other
Accent:	Local Not Local	Regional Foreign	Other
Manner:	Calm Angry Emotional Laughing	Rational Irrational Belligerent Righteous	Coherent Incoherent
Background Noises:	Machinery Trains Street Office Machines	Quiet Music Voices Party Atmosphere	Bedlam Animals Other

Bullying and Harassment

Let's face facts, bullying is a cowardly form of violence that is all too common throughout our schools. It has somehow been considered an inevitable (and uncontrollable) part of adolescence. Too often bullying occurs out of the presence of adult supervision, via the internet and cell phones, or in front of adults who fail to stop it.

Bullying creates a 'fear climate' among your students, restricting their ability to learn and participate in school activities. It's also no secret that bullying in schools is a significant factor in the majority of violent acts or school shootings that have occurred.

For this reason, it's important that your school employees, parents and community members know how to recognize and intervene in reducing bullying behavior in your schools. When schools send a clear hard-line message that no form of bullying will be allowed, the safety and security of the learning environment is improved for everyone.

89 Teach your staff the signs that a child is being bullied in your school. These signs include but are not limited to:

- Social and interpersonal skills may be lacking.

- Lack of a sense of humor.

- Victims are made fun of or pushed around by the bully.

- Bullied students don't stand up for themselves easily.

- Their body language often says, "I am a victim" — hunched shoulders, head low, little eye contact.

- Noticeable physical differences — overweight/underweight, disabled, may show unexplainable bruises or scratches on their body.

- Noticeable emotional differences — sudden mood swings, passive or shy.

- Overly sensitive to comments, cries easily, aggressive or disruptive in class, blames self for problems.

90 Teach all of your staff to recognize the warning signs of a bully. These signs include, but are not limited to:

- Bullies often view their surroundings as hostile or negative with little hope of improvement.

- Bullies lack adequate supervision. No one has taken the time to straighten them out — teach them right from wrong.

- Get to know the parents. Oftentimes a bully is bullied at home.

91 Determine the level of bullying and harassment that takes place throughout your schools and the community. Take the time to meet periodically with law enforcement — these meetings will reveal valuable information for both school and law enforcement personnel.

92 Teach your school employees who the students are that are involved in bullying and harassment, when it most often takes place, and where it occurs in your school.

93 Develop and enforce a strong anti-bullying policy. Anti-bullying policies and rules are needed to protect your school district from potential liability as well as to provide a safe environment for your students. Ensure that your policy is based on your community and school needs.

94 Develop a written policy that restricts students from loitering in school parking lots, hallways, bathrooms, and other areas where bullying could occur. The policy should be reviewed with students at the beginning of the school year and periodically thereafter.

95 Ensure that all school staff and students understand the expectations and consequences if the anti-bullying policy is violated. Bullying and harassment is a great topic to address during the first day of classes during an all school assembly.

96 **Clearly define the different types of bullying and harassment conduct that are prohibited.** All school employees, students and parents/guardians should be expected to comply with your school's anti-bullying/harassment policies.

97 **Plainly define the actions that will be taken against those who violate your school's anti-bullying/harassment policies.**

98 **Make sure students have an easy way to confidentially report incidents of bullying, harassment or other related conduct.**

99 **Understand your school district's responsibility to receive bullying and harassment reports/complaints and provide guidance for investigating and addressing these reports/complaints.**

Ensure that:

• Prompt investigations are conducted on all reports/complaints.

• Identified timelines for responding to complaints are followed.

• Policies and procedures are in place to ensure persons who file complaints or those who cooperate in investigations are not retaliated against.

• Appropriate actions are taken against those persons who violate your school district's bullying and harassment policy and support and concern is provided for persons who are the victims of bullying, harassment, or other forms of unapproved conduct and behavior.

• Steps are taken to prevent further bullying, harassment or other related behavior.

• Documentation of investigations and follow up actions occurs.

100 Review and update the school district's anti-bullying/harassment policies and procedures on a regular basis to ensure they are being implemented properly. Good times to review policies and rules are at the beginning of the school year, during in-service training or on return from vacation breaks.

101 Remember to review your policies and procedures with part-time employees, aides, custodians, bus drivers, volunteers, and substitute teachers. Educate your community's parents, day care providers, teachers, and law enforcement personnel about bullying and its long term effects.

102 Your school must always stress your zero tolerance for bullies.

103 Ensure teachers are made aware of who the bullies are in your school. The majority of bullying occurs when there is little or no supervision. Let your bullies know they are being watched.

104 In the classroom, teach your students to honor their feelings. If someone makes them feel uncomfortable, it is probably a warning sign.

105 Teach your students to report any bullying or harassment to a responsible adult, school staff member, parent, or police officer.

106 As simple as it sounds, teach students how to ask for help.

107 Teach your students how to become 'tough targets.' Instruct students to walk with confidence, head up, eyes straight ahead, and long strides.

108 Instruct your students to always walk with others. There is strength in numbers.

109 Tell your students if they are told by a bully "don't tell" — the proper thing to do is to tell.

110 When an act of bullying is related to hate crimes, immediately refer the individual to law enforcement.

111 **Never blame a student if they are bullied. If they confide in you that they are being bullied — believe them.** Kids may be embarrassed to tell someone if they are being bullied — you have to ask them.

112 **Parents should not instruct their children to fight back.** Remember, the bully is almost always bigger and stronger.

113 **Parents should not confront the bully's parents.** They may be the root cause of the bullying behavior — confrontation may make the situation worse.

114 **Don't promise a student that you will keep a bullying situation a secret.** Parents can help, your school district will help.

115 Beginning in elementary school, teach classes on how to improve assertiveness and friendship skills.

116 **Get your community involved in your school.** Ask parents and grandparents to volunteer in the classroom, supervise in the hallways, cafeteria, and at after school events.

117 **Make it a point to "pinch the bully."** All serious violent behaviors must be immediately reported to the police.

Bus Security

Every day in this country, school buses transport millions of students to and from school, athletic events, and field trips. A violent incident transpiring on a school bus is a crisis scenario often overlooked by the majority of school districts. For too many schools, there's the belief that an effective bus security plan just cannot be developed. The truth is simple — your school district must be proactive in your bus safety efforts by planning and practicing for the various emergencies that may occur on one of your school buses.

Bus Crisis Planning

118 **Develop bus crisis plans with school administration, your police and sheriffs departments, and local emergency medical responders.** Your plan should address crises such as fires, weather emergencies, serious vehicle accidents, school evacuations, and hostage situations as well as terrorist activities.

119 **Your bus drivers, school administration, law enforcement, and emergency responders must train together.** Everyone needs to know their role and how others will respond during a bus crisis.

120 **Ask your local law enforcement, SWAT teams, and emergency responders to periodically conduct emergency training exercises on your buses.**

121 **Develop alternative bus evacuation routes from each of your schools, events, and facilities.** Alternative evacuation routes may be used if roads are closed, blocked, damaged, or if there is a substantial amount of traffic congestion.

122 **Make sure your district's transportation manager, super-visors, and bus drivers are trained as to their role in your school district's crisis prevention program.**

123 Be prepared to quickly mobilize your bus services for any incident when drivers are not normally scheduled. This may include a mid-day school evacuation or a bus accident occurring late at night.

124 Mutual aid agreements should be developed with nearby school districts if additional buses are needed for mass or rapid mobilization of your students and staff.

125 Practice for a variety of 'what if' bus emergency scenarios. There are a multitude of emergencies that your bus drivers should be trained to recognize and address.

126 Hold periodic meetings with school administration and your bus drivers to discuss problem students, discipline concerns, and other related issues.

Driver/Bus Security Controls

127 Maintain accurate and up-to-date passenger lists and route sheets for all your school buses. These lists should be maintained for all bus trips that take place before, during, and after school.

128 Always forbid any unauthorized persons or strangers from entering or riding on your bus. If someone attempts to enter one of your buses, the driver must call '911' and your school administration immediately.

129 Require all your bus drivers to possess photo identification cards. Parents may request identification from their child's bus driver, especially if a new or substitute driver is used.

130 Make certain background checks have been conducted on all your bus drivers and bus company employees.

131 Develop a system for your bus drivers to report suspicious incidents or persons at the bus facility or on their route. Refer to the chapter regarding the recognition of suspicious people and vehicles for further information.

132 Present basic self-defense and security training for all your bus drivers.

133 Develop easy to understand crisis codes that your bus drivers can use to alert dispatch that they may have a problem or need immediate assistance.

134 Ask your bus drivers to inspect their bus for foreign objects, both inside and outside, any time it has been left unattended. This could be during an athletic event at another school district, a trip to a museum, etc.

135 Ensure that each of your school's bus pick-up and drop-off areas do not have other vehicular traffic present. Complex traffic patterns, where two different types of transportation (bus/car, bus/child, car/child) cross each other's travel path, are the 'hot spots' where a serious accident could occur. The chance of a child darting out from behind a stopped bus into the path of another vehicle is very real. The best control is to designate your bus pick-up and drop-off areas for bus traffic and nothing else.

136 Assess each of your school bus routes to identify any potential trouble spots. This may include bad neighborhoods, excessive shrubbery at drop off/pick up areas, poorly lit areas, dead end roads, etc.

137 If a bus incident or accident occurs, have one specific person designated to communicate pertinent information to your other schools, parents, law enforcement, and the media.

138 Strictly control access to all bus keys.

139 Ensure that all of your buses are equipped with two-way communication.

140 Ask your bus drivers to maintain '911' on their cell phone speed dial.

141 Install a "trouble indicator" light on each school bus that drivers can activate to alert others of possible troubles on the bus.

142 Instruct your bus drivers to never leave their bus running when it is unattended. Tell them to turn off the engine and take the keys with them.

143 Train your school bus drivers how to address on-bus conflicts such as a fight between students that occurs on the bus. Bus drivers should also be trained on what to do when confronting angry parents, strangers, trespassers, and other threats of violence.

Bus Facilities

144 Occasionally perform a security risk assessment of your facilities, including bus storage yards, garages, etc. Your insurance company's loss control department may be of great assistance in this area.

145 Restrict the access to your bus parking areas to buses only. Don't allow others to park near or walk among the school buses if at all possible.

146 When possible, park your school buses in a fenced in, illuminated parking area.

147 Whenever possible, allow access to your school bus parking area through one gate only.

148 Ask your police and sheriff's department to routinely patrol your bus parking areas.

149 Advise school employees to report any suspicious people at the bus facility or on route.

150 Maintain up-to-date student rosters, emergency contact phone numbers, and a first aid kit on each of your buses.

151 Place identifying numbers on the top of your school buses which could be seen from above during an emergency.

Cell Phones in School

The instant communication capabilities of cell phones can be an asset or a hindrance for your school district. There are many potential misuses of cell phones in your school including:

- The ability to bully or harass other students with unwanted voice or text messages.

- Texting or phoning friends during the school day.

- Cheating on tests by recording, sending, or receiving test questions and/or answers.

- Taking photos of exam answers.

- Taking inappropriate photographs of other students in areas such as the locker room or restroom.

- Calling in bomb threats which oftentimes cannot be traced by law enforcement.

- Calling others outside of the school to meet at the school to participate in a fight or a confrontation.

- The possibility that cell phones could be used to detonate a bomb if it is near or on school grounds.

- In a real emergency, excessive cell phone use may overload and cripple the cellular phone systems.

- The law enforcement view that drug deals have been made using a cell phone during school hours.

- The serious concern that during a real school emergency, large numbers of students may call their parents. Those parents may rush to the school, creating a vehicle and parent hazard for emergency service personnel.

With all of this being said, consider instituting the following cell phone controls:

152 Ban student use of cell phones except for special circumstances such as a medical need. These special circumstances should be reviewed and approved by your school board.

153 Confiscate student cell phones that are being used during the school day. Parents can explain why their child has these items in school when they come to reclaim them.

Every year, more and more school districts give in to public and parental pressure and allow cell phones to be carried by students. Carefully weigh the advantages and disadvantages — not allowing students to carry cell phones is a critical safety and security control.

154 Allow school staff members to carry their cell phones during the school day. Cell phones are the best form of immediate emergency communication.

155 Make sure your playground supervisors and large event supervisors carry their cell phones. Good crisis planning ensures that your school staff members carry their cell phones during the school day and during school events to allow for instant communication during an emergency or crisis.

Combative Students

Over the past ten years, there have been almost 3200 workers' compensation claims where combative students in Wisconsin schools have injured school employees. Workplace violence claims of this nature account for almost one-quarter of the total school related workers' compensation claims, according to a recent insurance company study.

Anyone who deals with students must understand that how we communicate with a disruptive, combative, or aggressive student can be the difference between a non-violent discussion and a physical confrontation.

Remember:

• The words we speak make up only 7% of our communication.

• The tone of our voice makes up 38% of our communication.

• Our body language makes up 55% of our communication.

For these reasons, it is important that your staff members understand the 'universal precautions' that should be taken with anyone who exhibits verbal or physical aggressive behaviors.

156 Always attempt to project a calm image to your students. Remaining calm in both your physical actions and verbal discussions with students may defuse the situation.

157 Pause and think before reacting to a combative student's actions. If the student uses inappropriate language or begins calling you names, don't react aggressively; this may only serve to escalate the student's aggression.

158 **Try not to take an aggressive student's behavior personally.** Remember, at the verbal and physical aggression stages, the student may be at a loss for self-control. Inappropriate language or body gestures may take place — don't let this bother you.

159 **Use breakaway safety lanyards if your employees wear their identification badges around their neck.** Breakaway lanyards utilize a plastic clasp or a Velcro strip that will easily open if the lanyard is caught or pulled by a combative student.

160 **Avoid wearing dangling jewelry, earrings, necklaces, etc.** An aggressive student may grab a necklace and try to choke you with it.

161 **Remove any objects from the immediate area that could be used as weapons against you.** Don't provide aggressive students easy access to weapons such as scissors, staplers, letter openers, paper weights, etc.

162 **Never allow your staff members to bring household chemicals and cleaners from home in to the school.** These hazardous substances could cause significant injury if a student were to spray them in a teacher's eyes. Your school should only purchase non-hazardous chemicals and cleaners.

163 **Before the situation gets out of control, encourage the student to go walking, out of the area, to 'let off some steam.'**

164 **When removing a student to a quiet area, don't isolate yourself with that student in a corner or behind closed doors.**

165 **During any type of confrontation, provide the student adequate personal space.** At a minimum, 18 inches to 3 feet should be maintained between the teacher and an aggressive student.

🗝 166 **If a student's behavior suddenly becomes physical, give the student a lot of personal space.** Closing in or trying to restrain the student usually ends badly and will only escalate unsafe behavior.

167 **When talking to a student, don't hover over them.** Lower yourself to the student's level; this may mean leaning on a filing cabinet or sitting on the edge of a table or desk to project a calm image.

168 **Don't startle a student with rapid or sudden body movements.** Whether you are speaking or listening to the student, attempt to slow down all of your movements. Keep yourself calm by breathing slowly, speaking slowly, moving your eyes slowly, and blinking less frequently — this portrays a level of calm.

169 **Never startle a disruptive student from behind.** Stay in the plain view of the aggressive student and present yourself in a calm, rational manner. Many teachers have been injured when a combative student was startled from behind resulting in the student striking the teacher.

🗝 170 **Do not be within arm's reach of a potentially violent or aggressive student.** Position yourself out of the student's reach — out of the 'line of fire.'

171 **Whenever possible, avoid face-to-face, eye-to-eye, toe-to-toe interaction with a potentially violent or aggressive student.**

172 **Attempt to take a 'supportive stance' towards the aggressive student.** Ensure that you are at least one leg length away, off to the side, and at angle to the student. When performed properly, a supportive stance doesn't invade the student's personal space, avoids the 'challenge position' and provides less chance of physical injury to the student or the teacher.

173 **Always angle your body away from the combative student's dominant hand.** Whenever possible, take mental notes in the classroom — does the student write with their right or left hand? A right handed writer probably has a dominant right hand. Another simple tip to remember: most people wear a wrist watch on their non-dominant hand.

174 **Always be aware of your voice — don't speak too loud or too fast.**

175 **Control your facial gestures.** Keep your facial expressions calm if at all possible. A frown or scowl may be portrayed as a feeling of dislike or displeasure. A straight facial expression may provide no evidence of interest. A wince portrays sudden dislike or pain.

176 **Maintain eye contact at all times when talking with a combative student.** The student may get a sense of confidence that you are truly listening to them. Constant eye contact will also allow you to spot some of the common head and body movements that you would have surely missed if you were looking somewhere else.

Crisis Communication

177 **Your school administrators, principals, social workers, and counselors should meet regularly with law enforcement officials to discuss troubled students, rumors, and threats of violence.**

178 **Develop communication methods for your school staff, students, families, and the media.** It is critical that you develop communication methods for all of the groups that may be directly or indirectly involved in a crisis.

179 **Use simple terminology in your crisis communication plan.** It only creates more confusion if your communication terms do not mean the same to everyone involved in responding to a crisis. Use plain language rather than codes.

180 **Determine the safest means to communicate with law enforcement and emergency responders.** For example, if students are evacuated from the building, will staff use their cell phones, radios, or student runners to relay information? Remember, there is always the concern that electronic devices (like a cell phone) can detonate a bomb.

181 **Determine your school's needs for a reverse evacuation plan.** A reverse evacuation plan is implemented if an incident occurs outside of the school building where students are present. Your staff needs to rapidly move students into the building and institute a lockdown. A reverse evacuation plan requires a great deal of rapid communication.

182 **Establish procedures for contacting off-site students and staff.** It is important that your staff knows what to do if a lockdown is initiated and a bus load of students is returning from a field trip at the same time.

183 **Require all staff members involved in off-site activities to have a way to communicate with the school.** Cell phones should be maintained by all school staff members.

184 **Develop maps and digital photos regarding the layout of your school.** Before a crisis occurs, send detailed information regarding your classrooms, hallways, stairwells, location of utility shut offs, maintenance areas, chemical storage rooms, and potential staging sites to law enforcement and emergency responders.

185 **Use care when designating your various staging sites.** Develop staging sites for treating the injured, receiving the media, and for student-family reunification.

186 **Locate your student-family reunification site far away from the media staging site.**

187 Ask law enforcement to help determine the best areas to stage the emergency responders. This should be a private area, segregated from the media and any curious onlookers.

188 Develop student accountability and release procedures. During and immediately after a crisis, you must be able to account for all students, staff members, and visitors who are in your school. If law enforcement or emergency responders believe people are missing, their response to the situation may change. For example, the risks are greater if a SWAT team thinks not all students and staff members are accounted for during an emergency lockdown.

189 Long before a crisis occurs, inform families of your district's student release procedures. Your goal is to prevent parents from coming to the crisis area immediately to pick up their children. Part of your student release procedure must ensure that students are only released to authorized individuals.

190 On a regular basis, your school's crisis team must communicate with staff members who are supervising students. Timely and accurate information should be provided to your staff before, during, and after a crisis.

191 Develop a parent-family communication plan that will be initiated during and after a crisis or emergency. At a minimum, your students' families must know that a crisis has taken place and appropriate steps are being taken to ensure their children's safety.

192 Let families know when, where, and how their children will be released as promptly and accurately as possible.

193 Keep your district's crisis plan terminology simple and easy to understand. Your terminology and notifications should be simple and the same throughout all schools in your district. For example, the code words used to notify staff of an emergency lockdown in one school should be the same code used in any other district school. You will only complicate things when complicated codes are used.

194 Develop numerous ways to communicate. Remember, during an actual crisis, your school's computers, public address announcements, telephones, and cell phones may not be operational. Backup communication plans are needed — another good reason to maintain a supply of walkie-talkies.

195 Make sure appropriate school personnel have access to your communication gear. Consider maintaining a pack that contains a cell phone and a walkie-talkie, that is easily accessible by administration.

196 Make sure your school communication systems are compatible with the emergency responder devices. Cell phones, two-way radios, and walkie-talkies need to be compatible with the emergency responder's communication equipment.

197 Ensure that your school's communication equipment does not interfere with the emergency responder's equipment.

198 Require playground supervisors, physical education teachers on the athletic field, supervisors on field trips, those supervising detention area, etc., to carry a walkie-talkie or a cell phone.

199 Install secure phone lines that cannot be monitored or scanned. During a crisis situation, this may be your only communication link to the outside world.

200 Designate a 'hot line' for crisis situations. The media can assist with getting this number to the public as the events unfold.

201 Have bullhorns available to alert students and staff of staging areas.

202 Establish an emergency call-up list for police, fire/emergency medical services, your crisis team, psychologists, and counselors.

203 Develop an alternate means of communication in the event the primary source fails.

Mass Communication Concerns

As a school administrator, directing a school district is comparable to taking care of a family of thousands; you're pulled in a million different directions trying to juggle the duties that keep everything running smoothly. There are never enough hours in the day or dollars in the district budget to do everything you would like to do. And yet, every student and staff member of your school district is important to you when an emergency strikes or a crisis takes place, nothing matters but keeping everyone safe and secure.

204 Developing an effective mass notification system is one of the best ways to ensure the safety and security of your students and staff. It provides security, brings simplicity and cohesion to the bustle of the school environment, and saves money by consolidating your existing systems. Most importantly, it saves lives.

205 Use a mass notification system that can be activated by the push of a button. Instead of an already distressed staff member having to find a PA system microphone, figure out how to use it, and come up with an effective message on the spot, use a system that will broadcast a pre-recorded message as easily as touching a panic or duress button.

The benefits of this type of mass communication system include:

• An effective system allows a user to respond immediately to an emergency by sounding an alarm and broadcasting information in a clear and easy manner.

- Some mass notification systems also provide 24/7 security through alarms and messages that are programmed to be triggered by an event. If an intruder enters the school after hours, an alarm sounds and notifications are sent to law enforcement. Or, if the fire alarm is set off, a message automatically communicates instructions for evacuation. This ensures that even when you cannot be physically present, you can be sure that your staff and students are protected.

All of these security features won't do any good, though, if the system is not simple to use. Look for a system that is a good fit with the technical level of your school. There are mass notification systems on the market that are extremely easy for users of all skill levels. Some systems also integrate with a school's existing products, which enables staff members to continue to use products that are familiar to them, but also take advantage of new technologies.

206 Your school district's communication system should be simple for users to send and receive messages via a range of media and choose who receives those messages. The more channels for communication there are (i.e. desk phones, internet, cell phones, email, etc.), the easier it is to keep everyone informed.

207 Since not everyone's needs are the same in an emergency, a system that allows a user to provide detailed notification to specific audiences or locations is critical. For instance, in a situation like a water main break in the central building of a school, a user can send a message to just the people in the affected building to tell them to evacuate immediately, then send a separate message to everyone else on campus warning them to stay away from the area.

Crafting an Effective Mass Notification Message

208 In order to craft an effective mass notification message, it is important to consider the type of situation to which you are responding, what type of message you would like to send, how you will send the message, who you want it to reach, and which devices people will use to receive your message. The flow chart below illustrates the order in which you should approach crafting a mass notification message.

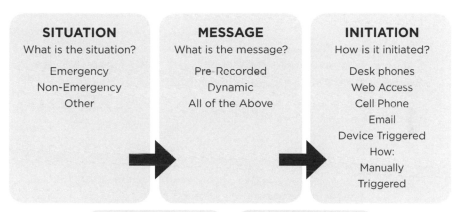

SITUATION
What is the situation?

Emergency
Non-Emergency
Other

MESSAGE
What is the message?

Pre-Recorded
Dynamic
All of the Above

INITIATION
How is it initiated?

Desk phones
Web Access
Cell Phone
Email
Device Triggered
How:
Manually
Triggered

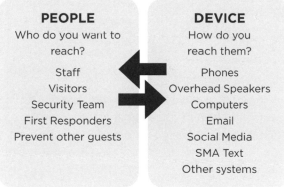

PEOPLE
Who do you want to reach?

Staff
Visitors
Security Team
First Responders
Prevent other guests

DEVICE
How do you reach them?

Phones
Overhead Speakers
Computers
Email
Social Media
SMA Text
Other systems

209 The format and tone of your message should fit the situation.

210 Be sure to first distinguish between an emergency, non-emergency, or other situation. You wouldn't scream out the day's schedule, nor would you shrug and calmly state that there is a fire in the building.

211 Once you know the situation, determine the type of message that would be the best fit. There are four main types of messages:

212 Pre-recorded messages are recommended for emergency preparedness. They are recorded ahead of time and allow a user to convey a message quickly and effectively, even if she or he is under duress. These can often be triggered by a panic/duress button.

213 Dynamic messages are good for an emergency that is in progress. A dynamic message includes up-to-date, specific or changing information such as date, time, location, and weather advisories. Dynamic messages are often used in conjunction with pre-recorded messages to customize existing information.

214 Ad Hoc messages can be used for a general announcement or emergency in progress. Ad Hoc messages are recorded on-the-spot. The user has the option of re-recording the message until he or she is satisfied.

215 Live messages are intended for immediate announcements. The message goes out as the user says it. These kinds of messages are similar in format to a PA system announcement.

216 Once you have crafted your message, decide which medium you will use to send it. An effective mass notification system will allow you to initiate a message from a variety of media, such as desk phones, the internet, cell phones, e-mail, and a panic/duress button. Some also allow a user to send a manual message or a message that is triggered by an event.

217 Determine who will receive your message. Do you want to reach everybody in your school or only a certain wing? Is the message intended for students? Staff? Parents? Will you need to alert first responders or other outside help? Make sure you have a clear idea of who you are communicating with.

218 Think about how people will receive your message. The more channels you use the better the chance you will reach your intended audience. It is important to find a mass notification system that allows you to send to many different endpoints, such as phones, overhead speakers, computers, email, social media, SMS text, etc.

Some school administrators are afraid to spend money on a mass notification system but an effective system can actually save money by integrating easily with your school's existing bell and clock, PA, and other systems. Instead of managing several separate systems that each have their own network, your network administrator or maintenance person can manage everything with just one network. He or she can draw from her/his existing knowledge instead of having to learn a completely new process.

It can be difficult to keep your entire school district safe. Implementing an effective mass notification system is a huge first step. The security, simplicity, and cost-effectiveness of a mass notification system will give you peace of mind and keep your staff and students protected.

I would like to thank Singlewire Software for assisting with the content of this chapter. Singlewire Software develops and supports innovative software centered around secure, fast, and reliable emergency notification. To learn more, visit www.singlewire.com or contact them at 608.661.1140 or www. singlewire.com/talkwithus.

Voice and Hand Signals

Voice and hand signals that your staff and students can easily recognize and understand can be important mechanisms of communication during an emergency or crisis situation. Some signals that teachers may use include:

219 A teacher waving their arms back and forth over their head means to follow the teacher in a certain direction.

220 A teacher moving their arms up and down with palms toward the ground directs students to get down on the ground wherever they are at the time.

221 A teacher pushing palms out and moving the arms forward and back signals the students to stop where they are and to stand absolutely still.

222 A teacher waving their arms from side-to-side in front of the body signals students to move away from the center of the area and to take shelter toward the edges of the area.

Phone Listings

223 Decide who will be included on your school's crisis phone listing. The list may be larger or smaller than the one listed here:

- '911'
- Law Enforcement (Police/Sheriff).
- Medical Service (EMS/hospital).
- County Emergency Management.
- Central Office/District Administrator.
- All other district schools.
- Department of Natural Resources.
- Utility Companies.
- Media (television/radio).
- School web page developer.

224 For any event, your phone listing must be readily available. Laminate the numbers on the teacher's attendance clipboards. All of the numbers must be on speed dial if at all possible.

225 When one of your district schools initiates their crisis plan, all of your schools must initiate their crisis plan (at least to some degree).

Consider this scenario: if a violent situation occurs at the high school, chances are there are high school students who have siblings attending the junior high or elementary schools. Parents will be contacting these 'unaffected' schools to check on the safety of their child or even to remove their child from school for the day.

Additionally, in the same scenario, teachers from other schools may respond to the high school to check on staff members who are friends, relatives, or spouses, as well as to offer further assistance. Maintaining calm at these 'unaffected' schools is critical during a violent incident when your crisis plan is implemented.

226 Make your local media your ally in a crisis situation. Provide the media with an accurate appraisal of what is occurring: radio, television, and the internet are the fastest ways to get critical information out to your community.

The media will ask for information such as: what occurred, a non-emergency phone number to call, the hospital where the injured have been transferred, the location of the evacuated students, the location of the student pick up area and parent staging area, etc. Be honest, and the media will respond.

227 Maintain a variety of communication channels within your school district. Open two-way communication channels must exist between:

• The school district office and all of your schools.

• Top administration and all school employees.

• The school district and law enforcement/emergency service agencies.

• The school district and the community.

Computer/Internet Concerns

Every day, your schools must address the challenges and legalities of computer and internet use. Your district must address a variety of serious issues such as virus contamination, illegal copying, and network security just to name a few.

There are a number of best practices to consider when protecting the district's confidential information and the educational interests of your students.

228 **Have your staff and students sign computer/internet acceptable use policies (AUPs).** Your AUP should contain a statement outlining the district's philosophy regarding the use and educational value of using a computer and the internet.

The acceptable use policy should clearly state:

- That using the school's computer/internet is a privilege and not a right.
- What is and is not acceptable computer/internet use as well as a disclaimer releasing the school from certain liabilities.
- The guidelines and penalties for violating the agreement.
- How, when, and where students will have access to the internet.

229 **Ensure your AUP clearly lists the computer/internet actions which are not allowed.** This may include copyright violations, commercial use, and behavior expectations — such as using good 'netiquette.'

230 **Monitor network transmissions, such as emails and visited websites of your students and staff.** The goal is to minimize viruses or other destructive situations that could pose security concerns.

231 **Ensure your AUP is reviewed and signed by the student, their parent or guardian, and a school district representative.** All involved parties must understand their obligations and that their computer/internet rights can be revoked if there is misuse.

232 Ensure firewalls are in place to prevent students and staff from downloading inappropriate or unsafe information to the school computer.

233 Understand the limitations of computer firewalls. Most firewalls provide little or no antivirus protection for your school computer systems. This can be corrected by installing proper antivirus programs.

234 Ensure your school's network administrator understands computer security and network protocols. When you purchase a firewall system, all of the 'locks' are set to 'open' and must be correctly configured.

235 Regularly download antivirus updates and scan systems regularly. The majority of antivirus programs are good at preventing invasions from known threats. Unfortunately, research indicates that over 1,000 new viruses are detected every month.

236 Install antivirus software on your school's computer network, your email system, and individual classroom computers.

237 Tell your staff and students to refrain from downloading anything from unknown sites, opening suspicious or unrecognized email attachments, or using peer-to-peer file sharing.

238 Follow the proper protective security protocols when installing your wireless network. This includes immediately changing the generic administrator password and turning off the router's broadcasting of the network's name.

239 Consider adding Wi-Fi Protected Access (WPA) encryption software to make penetration of your network more difficult.

240 Develop and enforce a policy that requires staff and students to utilize lengthy passwords that include numbers, special characters, and both upper- and lower-case letters.

241 Ensure that your staff and students aren't leaving password reminders in obvious places such as under the keyboard.

242 Consider extra computer system security such as forced delays that prevent hackers from testing multiple passwords during short periods of time.

243 Install computer software to limit data access and track data usage. This may help in keeping private, confidential information within the school district.

244 Prohibit your computer users from downloading free software, submitting sensitive information online, or opening email attachments from unapproved sources.

245 Educate students and staff members that downloads and certain email attachments can deliver viruses that will damage school computer systems. The worst case scenario would compromise the school computer network security, opening student and staff personal information to hackers.

246 Ensure appropriate filtering software is used to keep students and staff safe from inappropriate information. Filtering software restricts access to certain websites, often based on unacceptable keywords or phrases. On a side note, recognize that some filters may restrict students and staff from visiting legitimate websites if they contain sensitive keywords or phrases.

247 Make sure your district's computer policy addresses web publishing restrictions. These web restrictions usually address security and confidentiality concerns oftentimes centered around publishing the photos and/or names of students.

248 If student photos are to be published on a school web page, it should be with first names only and require parental permission.

249 At the beginning of the school year, sponsor a 'family technology night' where parents/guardians can see your school's computer facilities and programs. This is also a great time to have parents and guardians sign their student's AUP.

250 Develop internet safety and security presentations for your students. These programs can demonstrate safe internet use, evaluation of acceptable websites, only opening emails from trusted sources, etc.

251 Review internet safety and security controls during parent-teacher conferences and through school newsletters and emails. With the explosion of the Facebook phenomenon, students today spend a great deal of their free time on the internet. We've all read the stories where internet bullying and harassment contributed to violence in schools and even student suicides. Your school district can play a major role in educating parents of the dangers of the internet.

252 Instruct your staff to always log off from classroom computers when not in use and ensure that all passwords are locked. These controls are needed to prevent unauthorized access to your school's server and the user's personal information.

253 When computers are left in a classroom, require locking cables that will secure the laptop to a desk, table, or other large, heavy object.

254 Educate parents to use blocking software or parental controls that are available through their internet service provider. Use of these controls is a start, but don't expect this to totally block a child's access to inappropriate material.

255 **Educate parents to locate the computer in a high traffic area of the home.** Locate the computer in the kitchen or the living room or anywhere but the child's bedroom. It will be much more difficult for a child to visit inappropriate websites if an adult is watching.

256 **Talk to your students about the dangers of using the internet.** Not everyone out there is a nice person. Instruct them that there is much more to the internet than chat rooms.

257 **Parents must always maintain their child's on-line account.** It's a parent's right to randomly check a child's e-mail and visited internet sites.

258 **Educate parents to never provide children with their internet passwords.** Request the same restrictions of friends' parents.

259 **Encourage parents to always log-on to and log-off from the internet for a child.** This may be a way to check the history of where they have been.

260 **Stress the importance of parents spending time with their children on-line.** Parents should ask their children to show them how to get to their favorite sites.

Crisis Plan Development

261 **Realize that the majority of school shootings were not resolved by law enforcement.** In reality, the majority of these incidents lasted twenty minutes or less with the shooter committing suicide or being stopped by school faculty or fellow students.

During a crisis is the time to follow your district's crisis plan, not to make it up from scratch. This section summarizes some of the major best practices gathered from experienced school security experts to remember when called on to implement your crisis plan.

262 **If your school district does not have a crisis plan, develop one right now.** Don't waste any time, the next major crisis could occur at your school.

263 **If you do have a crisis plan in place, review it, update it, and practice it regularly.**

264 **Your crisis plan needs to address a variety of crisis events and hazards (both natural and man-made).** These include:

- Natural disasters (earthquake, tornado, hurricane, flood).
- Severe weather.
- Fires.
- Chemical or hazardous material spills.
- Bus crashes.
- School shootings.
- Bomb threats.
- Medical emergencies.
- Student or staff deaths (suicide, homicide, unintentional, or natural).
- Terrorism.
- Outbreaks of disease or infections.

265 **Develop a plan to communicate your crisis plan with families, your community, and the media.**

266 **In advance of a crisis or emergency, write template letters and press releases so your school staff will not have to compose them during the confusion and chaos of the crisis event.** It's easier to tweak small changes rather than to begin from scratch.

267 **Always expect the unexpected.** Regardless of how much time and effort was spent on crisis planning, the members of the crisis team should know that there will always be an element of surprise and accompanying confusion when a school is confronted with a crisis.

268 Each teacher's crisis plan and supplies must be readily available. Often, teachers have a difficult time finding their classroom crisis plan when it is needed during an emergency. That's why I recommend a brightly colored crisis plan that is clipped on a brightly colored clipboard — blaze orange or lime green — something that is easy to find.

269 Make sure there are a number of school employees who are trained to provide emergency medical services as well as basic first aid. Simply having first aid kits on site is not enough. Your emergency medical responders should have emergency kits at their fingertips.

270 Within each school, designate an area where emergency medical services can treat the injured. This area should be away from the media and onlookers and have parental access controls.

271 Never delay contacting emergency responders such as police, fire, or EMS personnel. A common mistake is to delay or not even call emergency responders; believing the situation can be handled in-house. Believe me, it's better to have emergency responders at your school when it is determined that their services are not needed.

272 During a crisis or emergency, your school administration needs to project a calm, confident, and professional image. Your leadership style will assist others in responding in a calm manner.

273 Don't simply 'cut and paste' from other school district's crisis plans. Other district's plans can serve as a model, but develop your crisis plan to address your specific exposures.

274 No matter the size of the school, a crisis team should be developed at each school. Who would know better how and what types of crises may occur, than staff members of that particular school?

275 Ensure each school's crisis team has a clear understanding of the safety and security resources that are available through the school district and your community.

276 Meet with your neighboring school districts to review and compare how they would respond to various emergency situations.

277 Use common vocabulary in your crisis plans. It is critical that school staff and emergency responders know each other's terminology. This means using a common vocabulary for communication regarding evacuation, lockdown, and other actions. Additionally, the vocabulary should be the same among the schools within your district.

278 Use plain language to announce the need for action, for example, 'evacuate' rather than 'code blue.' With plain language everyone in the school building including new staff, substitute teachers, and visitors will know what type of crisis is taking place and what type of response is needed.

279 Ensure your crisis plan addresses incidents that may occur off school grounds. This may include field trips, overseas trips, or away athletic events.

280 Provide your school district's crisis plan to local law enforcement, fire, and emergency medical services for their review and approval. Plans should be reviewed and approved by emergency personnel prior to implementation. Learn what kind of response you can expect from emergency response agencies. It is important to work with your community's law enforcement and emergency personnel since they have the training in this area — unlike most school districts.

281 Clearly identify the level of response needed — armed intruder, gun in locker, hostage situation, tornado, suicide, etc. Many crisis plans that I have reviewed do not address all the potential crisis situations that could occur.

282 Ensure your crisis response plan addresses events taking place after normal school hours.

283 Provide law enforcement and other appropriate emergency agencies with pass keys to your schools.

284 Install a master key lock box at the main entrance for emergency personnel.

285 Consider developing a CD or data sticks that provides site information regarding all of your schools. These materials can be distributed ahead of time to law enforcement and emergency responders so they can develop a working knowledge of your schools before an incident occurs.

286 Develop a password secured website that provides school site information. Law enforcement and emergency responders can access this information before an incident occurs and on their laptop computers when at the scene.

287 Develop an easy to read school crisis plan that is easily accessible and recognizable. It must address everyone in the school from top administration to teachers (including substitutes) to secretaries to food service personnel to custodians to bus drivers.

288 Color-code your crisis plan in a bright color so it is easily identifiable in an emergency situation. As I've mentioned before, the cover of your crisis plan should be of a bright color (blaze orange, lime green or bright pink) so it can be easily located during a crisis situation.

289 Ensure that all school staff members have a copy of your district's school crisis plan. This includes a detailed map of the school. Make sure that all staff members have read and practiced your crisis plan. It's too late to read the manual once the crisis has occurred. Your school employees must be trained to 'act not react.'

290 Frequently update your crisis manual. Your school district's crisis plans must be reviewed and updated on a regular ongoing basis. Changes occur every day, to your staff, facilities, and operations, and your crisis plan must change accordingly.

Good times to review and update your crisis plan are when:

• School employees are returning from summer and Christmas vacation.

• New employees are added to staff.

• Substitute teachers are present.

• New building construction or modification takes place.

• New roadways or changes in traffic patterns occur near or on school grounds.

• There is new emergency response (police/fire/EMS) management.

291 Remove all unneeded and background information from your crisis plan. The majority of the manuals that I have reviewed contain far too much wording, instruction, and unneeded information. Remember this at all times: Your crisis manual will be implemented in an emergency crisis situation. It must be written so it is easily understood at a glance. Employees must be able to find what they are looking for in seconds — they will not have time to read a lot of background information. You will not have the time to read and comprehend the crisis manual during a crisis situation.

292 Ensure that everyone understands the school crisis plan. Reporter talking to a teacher on a cell phone after a recent school shooting:

Reporter: "Does your school have a crisis plan?"
Teacher: "No, but we talked about it..."

"Who in my school must have a crisis plan?" School districts are always asking this question. The answer is really quite simple: everyone! If a violent incident occurs at your school, every school employee must immediately know their role.

Too often, when reviewing crisis plans for school districts, I discover a trend where administrators, principals, and teachers may have had crisis training. Often forgotten are key personnel such as food service, custodians, bus drivers, part-time employees, volunteers, and substitute teachers. Don't let this occur at your school.

293 **Support of a school district crisis plan comes from top management.** Your school district administrator, school board members, business manager, and principals must place crisis training at the top of their agendas each school year. Top management must also demonstrate commitment by attending the crisis training that takes place at each school within your district.

294 **Ensure that every school employee receives a copy of your crisis manual, receives hands on training, and is ready to 'act not react' if a crisis occurs.** Think for a moment, if a violent act occurred right now, who would be the first person notified within your school? The district administrator? The building principal? In the majority of the schools that had to implement their crisis plan, the office secretary was the first person contacted. If a bomb threat was called in to your school, who would answer the phone? The secretary. If a classroom teacher contacted the office to report a violent incident, who would take the call? The secretary. How much training have your office personnel received?

295 **Make crisis and violence prevention an integral component of every staff development training day.**

296 **Before the school year begins is the time to practice your crisis plan.** Don't just read the policy and assume that's good enough. Don't just simply walk through the lockdown procedures — practice 'rapid response' lockdown — this means full speed.

297 Conduct table top exercises with other schools to determine the best way to address various violent situations. Gather to review the development of each other's violence prevention programs, share new ideas, and publish violence prevention updates that will be distributed throughout your county's schools and municipalities.

298 As simple as it sounds, determine who is in charge during a crisis. Work with your local law enforcement to determine who will make decisions during various crisis situations.

299 Maintain up-to-date contact information for students. Your school needs contact information from family members, including the phone numbers where they can be reached during the day. In addition, each child should have several alternate contacts, such as a relative or family friend who would be able to pick up the child in the event of an emergency. One of the backup adults should live outside of the immediate area, if possible.

300 Consider the use of teacher crisis bags. A brightly colored teacher crisis bag should be considered for each classroom. The contents of these crisis bags should include the following items:

• A current student roster.

• Your emergency crisis plan.

• First aid supplies.

• A flashlight and extra batteries.

• Activity plans to be used for students when in lockdown.

• Paper and pens.

• A brightly colored clipboard and wax pencil (to communicate with emergency personnel through the exterior windows).

301 Remember to store the teacher crisis bags in easily accessible classroom locations out of the reach of children.

302 **Plan for your recovery during the preparedness stage of crisis planning.** It's important that all staff members understand their roles and responsibilities of crisis recovery. Your counselors may want to train your staff members on how to address the emotional needs of students and staff if a crisis occurs.

303 **Return to the 'business of learning' as quickly as possible.** The separation of students from their families when school reopens may be a difficult task.

Cyber Bullying

Cyber bullying involves the use of technology such as email, instant messaging, Facebook, etc. to harm others through deliberate, hostile, and oftentimes repeated behavior.

Currently, the majority of school districts are involved in the development of cyber bullying policies — unfortunately, little guidance is available regarding how to (or not to) respond to cyber bullying incidents.

Understand that cyber bullying may be worse than 'traditional' schoolyard bullying in a number of ways:

• Cyber bullying does not end when the child leaves school and arrives at home.

• Cyber bullies are often more vicious and hurtful than in-person bullies. They are not afraid to say things online; things they would never say face-to-face.

• Having anonymity with no actual physical contact, the cyber bully may have little feelings of empathy or remorse.

Some real life examples of cyber bullying include:

• Encouraging other students to share their "hit lists," "ugly lists," or "slut lists" online and including the bullied student on that list.

• Encouraging other students to post nasty comments about someone on a blog.

• Hacking in to a student's computer for the purpose of sending malicious codes.

- Sending threats to others or attacking others while posing as another person.
- Copying others on someone's private e-mail and instant messaging communications.
- Posting bad comments or feedback regarding another student without cause.
- Registering someone else's name and setting up a bash website or profile.
- Posting rude comments while posing as another student.
- Sending spam to others while posing as another student.
- Breaking the rules of a website or service while posing as another person.
- Setting up a vote-for site (like "hot or not?") designed to embarrass or humiliate another student.
- Sending "jokes" about another student to others or mailing lists.

304 **Educate your school staff and employees about the warning signs and dangerous consequences of cyber bullying.** A recent school study indicated that 42% of middle school students and 52% of high school students have reported being bullied online.

305 **Students need to understand what occurs when one student targets another student online.** Targeting online includes:

- A student sends mean or threatening emails to another student.
- Forwarding a private message to a number of other students.
- Degrading text messages sent to another on a cell phone.
- Mocking another student on a website.
- Posting embarrassing photos of another on a website.
- Impersonating someone to spread rumors about another person.
- Excluding someone from an online group.
- Posting private information about another person.

306 Develop a mandatory cyber bullying training program that educates students on the dangers and prevention of cyber bullying. Your teachers can play a vital role in preventing cyber bullying by educating students to:

- Never give out personal information such as passwords or private identification numbers.
- Use extreme care when posting personal information such as: names, addresses, cell phone numbers.
- Never share 'buddy' lists.
- Always delete messages from people that you don't know.
- When it doesn't sound right — get out of the chat room.
- Assume that no communication is ever private.
- Never email someone when you are angry or upset.
- Never email with friends and target someone for your entertainment.
- Never forward an email that was sent to you as a private message.

307 Teach students how to recognize what they can do if they believe they are being victimized by a cyber bully. This includes:

- Immediately telling a trusted adult — like a teacher.
- Never opening or reading messages from cyber bullies.
- Never reacting to the bully.
- Do not erase the messages/images.
- Block the bully from future electronic messages.

308 Instruct students if they are threatened with harm, the police should be contacted immediately.

309 As is the case with many school disciplinary policies, parents/guardians of students need constant reminders of your cyber bullying prevention policy. Parent/teacher conferences, and periodic mailings are effective methods to keep your community informed.

Doors and Windows

Keeping an intruder or active shooter out of your school building (or at least slowing their movements) begins by ensuring that appropriate door and window security controls are in place. There are many things your district can do to improve the security of your building's doors and windows.

310 Your school building's exterior doors should have as little exposed hardware as possible.

311 Your building's exterior 'exit only' doors do not need handles protruding to the outside. In case of an emergency, ensure these doors can be opened by a key or proximity card.

312 Never install cheaply made exterior doors. Ensure the exterior doors are made of solid wood, aluminum alloy, or steel to prevent or least slow down an intruder who may be trying to break down the door.

313 Ensure that the classroom door hardware allows staff to quickly lockdown the classrooms from the inside without having to step into the hallway. Dual cylinder, ANSI F88 locksets allow doors to be locked from either side to prevent entry to the classroom from the corridor side, but they cannot be locked to prevent egress from the classroom.

314 Ensure that staff members have access devices such as master keys or proximity cards to allow for quick entry into any room. This is especially important in an area where a student may have entered and barricaded themselves.

315 Ensure all of your doors fit tightly within their frame to prevent them from easily being pried open.

316 Use fully framed breakage resistant tempered glass for your windows.

317 Protect your exterior doors panic bar latches with pick plates to prevent tools and plastic cards from releasing the bolt.

318 Ensure your exterior doors have armored strike plates that are securely fastened to the door frame in direct alignment to receive the latch easily.

319 Equip key controlled exterior doors with contacts so they can be monitored with a central monitoring control system.

320 Use heavy duty multiple point, long flush bolts when installing your doors.

321 **Properly size your doors to avoid congestion.** This may mean installing double doors to accommodate the movement of a large group of people.

322 **Use narrow windows, sidelights, fish-eye viewers, or cameras to allow viewing anyone on the exterior side of the door.** This may be especially important during a lockdown of a classroom.

323 Periodically inspect your windows to ensure that they lock securely.

324 Instruct teachers to never leave windows open when their room is unoccupied or when they go home after school.

325 **Windows must readily open from the inside.** This may be your only means of rapid evacuation in a crisis situation.

326 Ensure that all the school's basement windows are protected with security grills or covers.

Emergency Commands

327 **Keep your emergency commands simple and easy to understand.** Use simplified emergency commands such as:

"Clear the halls."

"Secure the school."

"Evacuate the building."

"Shelter-in-Place."

328 **Post your emergency commands on a brightly colored placard in each classroom.** Simple emergency commands may be defined as follows:

329 **"Clear the halls" means that all students and staff are to exit the hallways until directed to do otherwise by the principal.** Instruct your students to go to the nearest room where there is adult supervision. Ask the students to remain calm, quiet, and away from the windows and doors. Place the students in the safest area of the room and shut off the lights. Use the classroom intercom or phone only for emergencies. Your students and staff should not exit the building.

330 **"Secure the school" means that all students and staff are to remain in their assigned work area/ classroom or immediately move to a designated area as directed by the principal.** The "secure the school" procedure should occur when an emergency situation exists somewhere in the school or in the immediate area outside of the school, where the presence of students and staff would place them in danger.

331 **"Evacuate the building" means that all students, staff, and visitors must exit the building and move quickly (and quietly) to a designated area at least 300-400 feet away from the school building.** Make sure your evacuation areas are accessible during the winter months.

A common mistake a school district makes when developing evacuation procedures is that they do not plan to evacuate far enough away from the building. Consider a bomb detonation, a chemical spill, or a building collapse because of a fire — 50, 100 or even 200 feet may not be far enough away to prevent harm. Get the students and staff as far away from the building as possible.

332 **Develop 'Shelter-in-Place' procedures.** 'Shelter-in-Place' means that dangers such as hazardous contaminants may exist outside of your school building. Students and staff should find shelter inside the building, close all the doors and windows, and immediately turn off all air handling equipment.

Evacuation

Simply stated, evacuation means that all of your staff, students, and visitors must immediately leave the building — there is never to be an exception to this rule.

General Evacuation Concerns

333 **During staff training at the beginning of the school year, ensure all your school employees are trained about their duties as outlined in your fire safety and evacuation plans.**

334 **Develop multiple indoor evacuation sites to house students during a lengthy evacuation.** Evacuating to your school's parking lot or playground is appropriate for a fire drill that lasts only a few minutes, but it is not appropriate for an evacuation that may last for hours or during the winter months.

335 **Maintain easily accessible evacuation shelters — nearby businesses, homes, churches, or other schools.** At the beginning of every school year, you need to communicate with the owners of these buildings to ensure that an evacuation agreement is in place.

336 **Visit the evacuation sites with your school staff.** Show your school employees where evacuation sites, student reunification areas, media areas, and triage areas will be located.

337 **Be aware of the weather conditions when evacuating your school.** While most students should be able to walk to a nearby evacuation shelter, extremely cold weather, snow, or rain could hamper these efforts — especially if the students evacuated the school without their coats.

338 **Meet with your bus company to determine how long it will take to mobilize school buses if students are evacuated outside during inclement weather.**

339 **Develop a plan to evacuate your disabled or special needs students.** Ensure there are specific transportation plans in place if the student cannot walk with the other students.

340 **Always attempt to evacuate the school within three minutes from the time that the evacuation announcement was made.**

341 **Develop alternative evacuation plans for your classrooms.** The crisis may be taking place where you are to evacuate or the route may be blocked. When it comes to evacuation routes — have a plan, then develop a plan to backup that plan.

Fire Evacuation

342 **Develop a red 'fire' binder to maintain your school's evacuation procedures, fire drill reports, staff trainings, and fire alarm/sprinkler system maintenance and documentation.** Make sure it is readily available in the event of a fire emergency or during an inspection by your local fire inspector.

343 Always involve your local fire and police departments in the development of your school's fire evacuation plan. They have developed these plans before and can provide valuable information to make your job easier.

344 Make sure all school employees understand that at the first sign of a fire, they are to activate the alarm. Never attempt to extinguish a fire, determine that you cannot do it, and then activate the alarm.

345 Immediately after an evacuation, ensure all staff and students are accounted for, then notify fire and law enforcement officials of any missing staff, students, or other problems.

346 As soon as all students and staff have been safely evacuated from the school building, close the doors to the fire/explosion areas if possible.

347 Only if it is safe to do so, turn off power and gas to the affected area if instructed by emergency personnel.

348 Never allow anyone to re-enter the building until the all-clear is issued by the proper authorities.

349 Designate individuals to meet with the fire officials upon their arrival, to notify them of fire location, provide a map of the campus, master key, and list of occupants not accounted for. If possible, provide these individuals with brightly colored windbreakers or vests to ensure they can be readily identified.

350 Never allow your students or staff to stop at their desks, cabinets, or lockers to gather their personal belongings.

351 Remind your teachers that if time permits, shut the windows and doors as they exit their classroom. If you are evacuating because of a fire, leave your room door unlocked so that the fire department can easily enter to fight the fire if necessary.

352 Immediately upon arriving at the assembly area, report missing students to administration. Some schools utilize the red card/green card notification system. Green denotes that all students are present, red denotes a problem.

353 Instruct your school staff to attempt to extinguish a small fire using the available fire extinguisher only if they have received training and are comfortable doing so.

354 If the fire requires more than one extinguisher, leave it for the fire department to put out and evacuate the building.

355 Annually review and update your fire safety and evacuation plans. Updates may be needed when there are changes in staff assignments, occupancy, or physical arrangement of the building.

Facility Concerns

356 It's time to stop believing that your school is a public use facility. This means that your community members and visitors should not be allowed to freely access your school buildings. All of your schools must have strict security and supervision controls in place before, during, and after school.

357 Make sure emergency announcements can be heard throughout the entire school building. During emergency situations, announcements may not be heard in all areas of the building — especially band rooms, locker rooms, or during physical education classes.

358 Make sure emergency announcements can be heard by teachers and students who are outside of the school building. This includes on the playground, during recess or a physical education class on the athletic field.

359 If emergency announcements cannot be heard in all areas of a school building, a visual means of communication, such as a colored flashing strobe light should be installed.

360 In the event of an emergency, your administration should have the ability to make a simultaneous announcement to the entire building to warn of a perceived or known threat and to convey instructions to protect staff and students. Solutions may include modifications to the existing PA system, visual alarms, or two-way radios.

361 Secure all of your electrical panels throughout your school buildings. You never want students or an intruder to have easy access to your electrical panels and shut off all of your lights.

362 All of your building operations equipment, including boilers, HVAC systems, water shut-offs, gas shutoffs, and key boxes, should be secured behind locked doors.

363 Don't label your school's room doors regarding their contents. Labeling a room door as 'electrical room' or 'mechanical room' may provide an intruder easy access to your utilities.

364 Don't use name plates to label a teacher's classroom. An intruder may be searching for a certain teacher or student — don't make it easy to find them.

365 Instruct your teachers to never post student rosters and other personal information in public areas or outside their classroom doors. Research of recent school violence incidents indicates that intruders may have used student rosters to search for specific students or to learn student names.

366 Close and secure your kitchens when they aren't occupied by school staff. An unoccupied kitchen presents a real exposure to potential weapons, such as knives, and an easy opportunity for food tampering.

367 Secure all of your custodial closets and work rooms when they are not occupied by a school employee. Don't allow anyone to have easy access to tools, equipment, and hazardous substances which could be used to commit a violent act. Securing of hazardous substances, especially in elementary schools is critical.

368 Do not allow the hanging of objects or art work that will obstruct emergency exit signs. Exit signs must be visible from all areas in the hallway and classroom. Any objects that obstruct the exit signs should be taken down immediately.

369 Ensure your classroom doors can be locked from the inside of the classroom. Classroom safety can be improved through the use of specific types of door hardware. Traditional classroom locksets require that the door be locked from the outside while the inside lever remains operable, which means that unauthorized individuals cannot lock or unlock doors without a key. But in an emergency situation this forces teachers to open the door from the inside, insert their key in the outside cylinder, turn the key to lock the door, and then close it again, which may actually expose the teacher to the very danger they are locking the door against.

A 'security classroom function' lockset has a cylinder on the inside that locks the outside lever. Teachers can lock the classroom door without having to go into the hallway. This lock type provides a door lock on the corridor side to protect occupants, yet the lever handle inside the room retracts the latch bolt with one motion for fast egress.

370 Classroom door handles and locks must meet fire code requirements for exits. Therefore it is recommended that the proper fire authority approve classroom door locks prior to installation.

371 Always close and secure all classroom doors when the room is not occupied by a teacher or school employee. Unoccupied classrooms create an opportunity for the theft of valuables, building keys, computers, and documents. Unlocked doors to unoccupied areas could be used as a temporary hiding place for those planning to commit malicious acts.

372 Do not allow your teachers to cover or decorate the glass panels and windows on classroom doors. In an emergency situation, this door may be your only visual access with the outside world.

373 Ensure that your classroom evacuation plans indicate secondary exit paths. An emergency situation may prevent a classroom teacher from using the primary evacuation path out of the building — have a plan and a plan to backup that plan.

374 Identify a large item in the classroom that could be placed against the door during an emergency lockdown. Most intruders are looking for 'easy targets of opportunity' — blocking the door with a desk, table, or filing cabinet may prevent an intruder from easily entering the classroom. At a minimum, it may slow down their efforts — gaining more time until law enforcement arrives.

375 Close and secure all windows at the end of the school day.

376 Lock all of your school building's exterior doors after normal school hours. A checklist could be used by the custodian to confirm and document that all exterior and interior doors have been examined and are locked prior to leaving the building. This document should list all doors to be locked nightly, the day's date, and signature of the person confirming the doors are secured.

377 Any individuals or groups using your school after hours should keep the door locked at all times and allow access only to known persons. This should be clearly spelled out to anyone using your school buildings.

378 Never allow anyone to park vehicles or bicycles close to your building's exterior exits. In an emergency situation, exits could be obstructed by parked vehicles. Signage or curbing could be installed to prevent vehicles from parking too close to your exit doors.

379 Locate trash receptacles far away from your building entrances. Trash cans are where arson fires are set, bombs may be placed, or weapons hidden. Additionally, a heavy trash can could be used to block an exit door. Any dangerous device or situation that occurs at these areas will remove a building's emergency exit from use.

380 Place dumpsters in secured locations so they cannot be accessed. Rolling dumpsters have been moved against the school building to access the roof or second story windows. Additionally, dumpsters are a great place to store weapons, bombs, and contraband.

381 Trim the landscaping around the school. All bushes, shrubs, and trees should be trimmed so there is a clear viewing area outside the school building. This clear zone also allows passing pedestrians to clearly see the building and activity around it.

382 Don't allow for easy roof access. Ensure building roof access is strictly controlled with roof hatches that are locked when not in use. If trees are located close to your building, an individual could scale the tree and access upper levels of your school.

383 Whenever possible, use wall-mounted fixtures close to buildings and avoid light poles if they present access to your upper windows or roofs.

384 **Ensure your schools have adequate vandal-proof exterior lighting.** This is important for vehicle and bicycle parking areas, bus loading and pickup/drop-off zones, and walkways leading to the school building entrance.

385 **Consider installing motion-sensor lights in hidden or vulnerable areas around your school building.**

386 **Limit the number of school employees who have master keys to your school building.** This means tightening the access to master keys and may mean re-keying the entire school; a costly proposition, but critical from a building security standpoint.

387 **Secure your doors during the school day.** First thing each morning, free up a custodian's time so they can perform this important security task.

388 **Your building security plan should address the high priority items first.** Not all school security measures can or have to be implemented at one time.

Restrooms

389 **Ensure that your restrooms are brightly lit and well supervised by school staff throughout the day.**

390 **Protect the restroom light fixtures with vandal proof covers to prevent them from being damaged.**

391 **Make sure restroom entry and exit doors can only be locked from the outside and not be readily blocked from the inside.**

392 **Do not allow any free standing items (plants, trash receptacles, product storage) that could be used to block the restroom door from the inside.**

393 Discourage the installation of drop ceilings in your restrooms. These above ceiling spaces could easily be used to hide weapons and contraband.

394 Use see through paper towel, liquid soap, and toilet tissue holders to discourage someone from using them as a hiding place for weapons and contraband.

395 Install only shatterproof mirrors in your restrooms.

Locker Rooms

396 Use open mesh locker doors to discourage the concealment of weapons or contraband.

Mechanical Systems

397 Ensure your building's fresh air intakes are located on secured roofs or placed high on your building's exterior walls. Remember, roof mounted air intake locations are vulnerable to flying debris in high winds, so wall mounting may be preferable.

398 To prevent tampering or vandalism, fresh air intakes should be at least 12 feet off the ground and away from any vehicle exhaust areas. Locating your fresh air intakes at an elevated height will prevent someone from introducing contaminants into your ventilation system.

399 Know the location of your building's master ventilation system shut-off to control the spread of airborne contaminants through your school building's ventilation system.

400 Ensure each of your school building's custodians and administrators know how and when to shut off the ventilation system.

Fights on School Grounds

Sometime during the school year, your employees will face the exposure of verbal and physical confrontations between students. Here are some best practices to keep in mind when dealing with students involved in a confrontational situation:

401 **Develop a strict no fighting policy.** Your district must enforce strict penalties, including suspensions and expulsions, for fighting on school grounds. During an all school assembly, your no fighting policy should be reviewed with all students.

402 **Ensure unwanted people outside your school are kept outside your school.** Fights in schools are often started by unwanted people from the outside — delinquents, dropouts, and others who show up just to cause trouble.

403 **Focus on those students who cause fights in your school.** You know who they are; let them know that they are being watched.

404 **Teach your students how to report fighting.** A confidential means of reporting fights will allow students to more freely report any fighting activity.

405 **Develop a counseling program on fighting, for bullies as well as the victims.** Talk openly with students to discover why fighting occurs in your school. Determining why students start fights is the biggest step toward stopping them in the future.

406 **Make sure all extracurricular activities are adequately supervised.** Most fights can be avoided if students know they are being supervised. Remember, the larger the crowd, the more supervisors are needed.

407 **Talk with parents when their child is involved in a fight at school.** A child who often fights in school probably has behavior issues at home.

408 **Clearly understand the physical layout of your school.** Familiarize yourself with the layout of your school — inside and out. Every school has numerous blind corners, long hallways, segregated classrooms, and isolated areas (boiler rooms, custodial closets, theatre prop rooms, locker rooms, etc.). You never want to get caught in an area where you don't know the way out!

409 **Focus on potential weapon 'hot spots' in your school.** Look for areas where students could obtain weapons — knives in the kitchen area, sports equipment in the locker rooms, potentially dangerous chemicals in the science lab, pool chemical room, and custodial closets. Your own classroom may have numerous sharp or blunt objects that could be used as weapons against you (scissors, staplers, letter openers).

410 **Remember to always lock or secure all rooms when they are not occupied by a school staff member.** This will eliminate the possibility of a student or a group of students pulling someone into an empty classroom.

411 **If there is the potential for a fight, keep your eyes on the entire group.** When removing a student from the classroom, a fight, or any other confrontation, always be aware of the group dynamics developing around you. Watch for warning signs of other students becoming involved by 'defending' the student you are confronting. This may entail a verbal or physical confrontation with another student or a distraction plan to 'rescue' their fellow student.

412 **Stay focused — when a fight begins, you don't know who will get involved.** Students may fight students, parents may step in and fight parents and/or students, or parents may fight other parents. If you're dealing with breaking up a fight between students, stay alert for threats coming your way from any direction.

413 If you are not 100% sure that you can break up a fight, get your 'knees to the breeze' — get away and get lots of assistance. A teacher is of no use if they are caught in the middle of a fight between students or groups of students.

414 Never wait too long to get help. A small problem turns in to a large confrontation when you wait too long to get assistance. There is strength in numbers — more teachers or the assistance of other respected students may help to calm the situation before it gets out of control. Know who the key individuals are who can talk down a situation.

415 As a teacher, never allow yourself to become part of 'the action.' An audience can cause some combative students to be more brazen than usual in an effort to show off to their peers. If you see a student(s) exhibiting signs of being combative or resistive, act quickly to shut down the threat.

416 Never let your guard down. The age, sex, physical size, or status of a student should never come into play when dealing with a confrontational situation. A small female student may attack a much larger male teacher when emotions come into play. Conversely, a small female teacher may face little chance of control against a much larger male student.

417 Always try to maintain a safe distance between the student and yourself. Never get caught in a closed classroom, in a corner, or any other area with limited means of escape. As I stated earlier, if you can't handle the situation, 'get your knees to the breeze' and get out of there.

418 Never assume students do not possess weapons. Past history shows that metal detectors are not foolproof in keeping weapons out of your school. Clothing trends of today allow students to hide weapons on their body, as well in book bags, purses, and athletic bags. When dealing with students, keep your eyes constantly searching for weapons.

419 **Never expect respect.** Just because you're the principal or the teacher, don't assume that all students will respect your position of authority. Coming upon a potentially hostile situation may be all that is needed for a student to 'throw one last punch' or in a worst case scenario, attack the authority figure. Never let your guard down — even for a second.

420 **During a confrontation, don't demean, don't disrespect.** Attempt to remove the confrontational student(s) as quickly as possible. Engaging in a verbal sparring match in front of other students may add 'fuel to the fire' and escalate the situation. If your presence threatens to demean a student in front of their peers, the student may feel cornered and stand up to you. Instead, remove the student(s) from the situation as fast as you can. Aggressiveness diminishes when the individual is alone and a crowd is not involved.

421 **Evaluate your school employee dress code.** A female teach er wearing dangling earrings or necklaces may be asking for trouble if they attempt to break up a student fight. A male teacher may get choked with his own tie. If you wear glasses, take them off before getting involved in a fight.

Food Security

It's always been my belief that tampering with your school's food supply is one the easiest methods for someone with bad intentions to cause mass illness and seriously disrupt your district's educational process. Now is the time to ensure that all of your schools implement proactive food security controls.

422 **Food storage rooms should only be open when they are occupied by a trusted school employee.** Never leave a food storage room unlocked if it is unsupervised, even for a minute.

423 If any of your food deliveries appear to be tampered with or damaged, contact your school administration for further investigation. If you believe criminal activities are involved, call the police.

424 If food deliveries take place after normal school hours, ensure they are placed in a secure storage area. Try to schedule food deliveries when a school employee is present to receive and secure the delivery.

Gun Concerns

There are some alarming facts relating to school shootings that have taken place over the past 25 years:

- The majority of school shooters engaged in behavior, prior to the incident, that caused others concern or indicated a need for help.
- Two-thirds of the school shooters used a handgun in their attacks.
- Almost half of the school shooters used a rifle in their attacks.
- Most of the school shooters obtained weapons from their home or the home of a relative.
- Two-thirds of the school shooters had a history of using guns prior to their attack.

For these reasons, it is critical that your school employees learn how to recognize the warning signs of a potentially violent student and maintain a high awareness for guns and other weapons in the school.

425 Educate your students of the dangers of guns. Parents, teachers and responsible adults often will not talk to children about the improper use and danger of guns for the same reasons they hesitate to discuss premarital sex or birth control — they fear their information will be interpreted as approval by the child. Accurate information regarding guns, such as how they operate, how they are stored, and how they can kill must be taught to our children.

426 Your next parent-teacher conference is a great time to teach parents that all guns must be kept away from children, preferably equipped with trigger locks.

427 **Ask parents to use trigger locks on all guns stored at their home.** Contact your local police department for assistance — oftentimes trigger locks are provided free of charge by community groups.

428 **Educate parents to lock their home gun cabinets.** The National Rifle Association can provide great gun safety educational materials for children and adults.

429 **Stress to parents that ammunition must be secured and kept separate from the guns stored at their home.**

430 **Stress to parents that they have the right to search their child's room.** Most of the school shooters had hidden an arsenal big enough to start their own army — often unnoticed by the parents.

Large Event Security

Athletic events, theatrical performances, and graduation ceremonies are great opportunities for your students to showcase their skills and for non-students to be actively involved in your school. Unfortunately large events could easily become a nightmare if a violent incident were to occur. It is critical that your school district develop controls to ensure the safety and security of everyone at the event.

431 **Develop 'away event' activity security controls.** Your school district accepts the responsibility to control the behavior and activity of participants and spectators attending a school sponsored event at your school. However, your school district may have little control over the safety and security of events sponsored at other schools, such as "away" athletic events. I strongly encourage you to contact the administrators, program coordinators, and athletic directors at these schools to ensure proper safety and security controls are in place.

432 **Develop a set of rules relating to acceptable and unacceptable student and spectator behavior.** Students may refrain from certain behaviors if the rules are clearly spelled out to them. An appropriate time to instruct your students on behavioral rules is long before the event takes place.

433 **Instruct students at the beginning of the school year (during an all school assembly), as to what types of behavior are acceptable and unacceptable at school events.** Don't forget to mention the consequences of inappropriate behavior. Have students and parents sign a copy of your 'expected behavior contract' with your school.

434 **Provide mailings and community announcements that stress your student behavior policy. Remind parents that they are responsible and possibly liable for the behavior and actions of their children at school sponsored events.**

435 **Long before an event takes place, instruct students how they can identify supervisors and where the supervisors will be located.**

436 **Ensure the supervision is appropriate for the event taking place.** Remember, there is no magical number or ratio of supervisors to spectators and students. A high school football game should have high school level supervisors. Students are less likely to act up is there is a definite relationship between the students and the supervisors.

437 **There is no such thing as having too many supervisors.** The number of supervisors needed for an event depends on a number of factors: the age/nature of the spectators, the number of spectators at the event, the size of the facility, etc.

438 Understand the occupancy limits for your facilities, auditoriums, cafeterias, bleachers, etc. More importantly, ensure these occupancy limits are never exceeded.

439 Always maintain clear walkways, aisles, and exit doors. Your supervision must be mobile, able to move freely among the spectators.

440 Instruct your supervisors to supervise the spectators, not watch the event. This means supervisors must face the audience, not the event.

441 Pair up your supervisors if at all possible. There is always strength in numbers.

442 Make sure your supervisors have communication access to '911,' police, and emergency medical services.

443 Ensure that select supervisors are trained in first aid/CPR and the use of a defibrillator.

444 During the event, periodically announce where your supervisors are stationed.

445 Dress your supervisors in easily identifiable attire — brightly colored wind breakers, vests, or armbands.

446 Supervise your parking lots before and after events take place.

Police Supervisory Controls

Maintaining a uniformed law enforcement presence at a school event creates a new level of supervision. Uniformed officers may command more respect from participants simply because spectators realize that the consequences of their actions may be more severe.

447 **Never underestimate the importance of having full-time police officers or police reserve officials at an event.** There are certain instances where a police officer can be much more effective than a school employee. Instances such as:

• Eliminating rowdiness/fighting among spectators.

• Keeping unauthorized people away from the activity or event.

• Assisting school staff members when requested.

• Calling for additional police/fire/EMS assistance.

• Checking, clearing, and directing traffic when needed.

448 **Encourage your police officers and sheriffs deputies to stop by the athletic event on a periodic basis.** This is another good reason for your school to have a full-time police resource officer.

449 **Research the use of uniformed police officers/sheriffs deputies for large event security.** Contact your local police or sheriff's department and ask questions such as:

• Does your department allow off-duty employment?

• If off-duty employment is not allowed, will you assign an off-duty officer on overtime to the large event?

• What is the cost of an on-duty officer or an officer on overtime?

• If the use of an off-duty officer is possible, what is the cost?

• Are hired police officers allowed to wear their uniforms?

450 Determine if your school district must provide insurance coverage for off-duty officers in the event of an injury or civil law suit that may arise as the result of an off-duty officer action.

Many acts of violence occur when student's actions are unsupervised. Ensuring that effective supervisors are in place will go a long way in preventing unacceptable behavior by spectators.

Law Enforcement View

Having an unannounced law enforcement presence sends a strong message to potential trouble makers that there is a definite police presence within the school.

451 Get the cops into your schools. Ask police officers and sheriff deputies to frequently stop by your school to walk through the hallways and drive through the parking lots in their squad car. 'Rattling your sabers' shows students that the cops are constantly watching.

452 On occasion, park a marked police car outside your school or near the entrance to a large event. Bad things happen when students are unsupervised. A police car parked at your school may force some individuals to think twice before acting in a negative manner.

453 Get law enforcement involved in the development of your crisis plan. Many years ago, I was assisting a small school district in the development of their crisis plan. One of the first questions I asked was "Have you involved your police and sheriff's departments in the development of your crisis plan?" The response from the district administrator was quick and rather surprising, "No, and we don't intend to — we have our plan and they have theirs!" Really? The only way to have a complete, thorough, and well thought out crisis plan that will work is if you develop it as a team. Your school district and law enforcement agencies must be working on a two way street — and that street is called communication.

Your local law enforcement agencies can assist you by:

- Identifying the level of response needed for the situation — armed intruder, gun in locker, hostage situation, assault, etc.
- Identifying key individual responsibilities for staff.
- Practicing 'what if' scenarios.
- Developing response plans for after school hour events.
- Conducting table top exercises to practice roles.

454 **You may not like what the police official says needs to be done, but do it anyway, they are the experts and you're not.**

455 **Ask your local police/sheriff's department to assist in developing building information and plans that are up-to-date and easy to read.** One of the best methods I have seen to 'map' a school is to use a digital camera to identify travel routes and exit ways. Additionally, aerial photos are a great tool for reviewing your evacuation plans. More and more police departments are equipped with computer software that will access school building plans at the touch of a button — a great tool in a crisis situation.

456 **Provide local law enforcement and emergency personnel with up-to-date copies of your school plans.** This includes the school building floor plans, maps of the surrounding area, evacuation routes, shelter areas, procedures for how you will address medical needs, transportation means, and how you will notify parents/guardians.

457 **Hire a full time police liaison officer.** A police liaison officer who is tuned in to what is happening in your school is the best investment of all to prevent school violence.

458 **Get to know students in non-confrontational settings.** Ask your police liaison officer to teach classes in problem solving, bullying/harassment prevention, internet safety, etc. Your goal is for students to view the officer as a friend, a peace keeper, and a problem solver.

459 **Ask law enforcement to meet with parents through parent-teacher associations and other groups.** Educate parents about your school district's violence prevention strategies and help them understand the importance of their support.

460 **Periodically bring in an unannounced K-9 drug dog to check student's lockers and cars.** It will get student's attention that drugs are not allowed in your school.

461 **Offer free hot lunch to police officers who eat with the students on a periodic basis.**

Lockdown

462 **If a potentially dangerous situation is taking place in or around your school (an armed intruder, an active shooter, or any ongoing threat of injury or death), lock it down, right now.** The goal of a lockdown is to isolate the intruder, whether in the hallway or completely out of your school (lockout). Do not give the intruder the opportunity to enter your school or move freely from room to room and have easy access to students and staff. Lockdown and wait for the police.

463 **Practice 'rapid response' lockdown.** Simply discussing your lockdown procedures during a teacher in-service or 'walking' through the procedure is not enough. Lockdown practice must be full force, 'rapid response' — teachers must learn to 'act not react' when a lockdown has been initiated. Valuable time is often wasted when a teacher feels the need to confirm that the lockdown is indeed real. When the lockdown code is initiated, 'rapid response' is needed. Safely behind a locked classroom door is where a teacher can determine if the lockdown is real.

464 Have a lockdown plan and a plan to back up that plan. Not all crisis plans will go perfectly as planned. If you are a teacher, know what to do if you are nowhere near your classroom when the lockdown is initiated. What will you do and where will you go when the lockdown is initiated?

465 Make sure that all school employees receive lockdown training. Often overlooked are your office personnel, food service employees, custodians, and bus drivers. Keep in mind, if an intruder comes through the front doors of your school, your office personnel may be the ones who will have first contact with this individual.

466 Keep your lockdown announcement simple and easy to understand. It doesn't get any simpler than announcing "we are in lockdown — secure your rooms" over and over again. Don't use any crazy codes that a substitute teacher or volunteer aid may not readily understand. If there is an intruder in your school, don't you think they know that the school will be going into immediate lockdown?

467 Repeat the announcement at intervals of 15 seconds because there are some areas of your school, like the band room or locker room, where the initial announcement might not be heard.

468 Make sure everyone can hear your lockdown announcement. Can school staff members hear the lockdown announcement in a loud band room, the choir room, the gymnasium with dozens of screaming students, the noisy locker room, or the pool area? Consider using emergency flashing strobe lights in those areas where hearing announcements is a problem.

469 Have a plan to notify those students and staff who are outside the school building that a lockdown is taking place. You don't want a bus load of students and teachers to return from a field trip and walk in right in the middle of a lockdown. Ensure your communication systems can notify off-site staff members not to return to the school.

470 A teacher initiating the lockdown must be calm yet decisive with his/her actions. In a crisis situation, students may regress into childlike behaviors — in stress, children regress.

471 Teachers need to be visual and verbal in their actions to their students in the classroom once the lockdown begins. Students will follow a teacher's visual signals more readily than their verbal commands — it is human nature. If the teacher becomes frantic and begins screaming wildly, you can expect the students to do the same. If the teacher's actions portray calmness, the chances of their verbal commands being followed increase significantly.

472 Secure students in your classroom, then visually sweep the hallway and gather any students not secured in a classroom.

473 It's important for staff to understand that they may need to get physical when implementing the lockdown. A student walking down the hallway may hesitate or disregard a teacher's request to get into a classroom. Time is of the essence — grab that student by the arm and pull them in the classroom.

474 Don't close your classroom's outside window blinds or shades. There is the opinion that blinds/shades should be closed; this may be your only contact (visual) with the outside world. Your local police department needs every advantage they can get — don't cut them off from visual communication.

475 Maintain a brightly colored clipboard and a wax pencil in every classroom. When in lockdown, the teacher can use the clipboard/wax pencil to communicate messages; when held up against the window, communication can be maintained with law enforcement outside of the school building.

476 Once the lockdown procedure is initiated, the classroom door is secured *and* barricaded. During the review of your lockdown procedures, identify those objects in each classroom — a desk, a cabinet, a bookshelf, etc. — which will be used to barricade the door. Make sure these objects are sturdy enough to block the entrance of an intruder, yet are easily maneuverable.

477 If the intruder is coming into the classroom and the teacher believes an imminent danger threat is present, instruct your students to throw objects at the intruder's head and face. I realize that this is a controversial best practice, but if an intruder is coming through the classroom door, I have to believe that most teachers and students would rather go 'down fighting' and try to neutralize the intruder. Items such as soup cans, baseballs, tape dispensers, staplers, etc., could be thrown at the intruder. This practice would not be recommended for elementary school age students.

478 Place the students in the safest area of the room, away from doors and windows and out of the direct sight of the intruder.

479 Shut off the lights. Remember, the hallway lights will probably remain on — the teacher should be able to see out of the classroom door (if not barricaded), and the intruder probably cannot see in.

480 During a lockdown, no one is to leave the room, not even to use the restroom.

481 Instruct teachers to enter the nearest classroom if they and their class are in transition in the hallway.

482 Students must be instructed to go to the nearest classroom. Calmly inform students as to what is happening — they may panic if they don't know.

483 Take attendance in the classroom during a lockdown. School administration or law enforcement may call the teacher to determine if their students are accounted for.

484 Do not call the office for general information. Call the office only with vital information, such as reporting the number and severity of injuries. Never identify your room number unless asked to do so by someone you know.

485 Do not allow the use of a radio or TV within the classroom.

486 Do not allow the use cell phones when in lockdown. History shows that these calls may be aired live on TV and intruders may find where you are.

487 Be as patient as possible during a lockdown. Law enforcement should be equipped with master keys to unlock classroom doors when it is safe.

488 Staff should never make the determination it is safe and they can exit the classroom. Remember, in an intense crisis situation such as an active shooter, classrooms may be locked down for hours before the school can be cleared by law enforcement. Patience and strictly following your school's 'rapid response' lockdown procedures will save lives.

489 Develop an 'all clear' code. Do not use something as simple as having a staff member knock on your door, stating it is all clear and you can come out. You never know, this could be a dangerous trap with the intruder holding a gun to your principal's head! Rather, develop a verbal/written code with law enforcement or an 'all clear' card that can be slid under the door. For this reason, I recommend that your school consider using the red card/green card system.

490 Utilize the red card/green card system to communicate with emergency responders.

The goal of a lockdown is to isolate the intruder until law enforcement can neutralize the threat. The red card/green card system is a great method to assist law enforcement in rapidly sweeping your school. Here's how it works:

• Each classroom is provided two red cards and two green cards — I suggest 8.5" x 11" pieces of laminated construction paper.

• When the lockdown is initiated, the teacher displays a green card in the exterior window (if their room has one) and slides a second green card under the door into the hallway, or affixes the card to the classroom door window, to alert emergency responders that everything is safe within the classroom. The green card placed on the exterior window notifies emergency responders located on the outside of the building.

• If possible, the teacher should display a red card in the exterior window and slide the second red card under the door or affix the card to the classroom door to alert emergency responders that emergency assistance is needed as soon as possible.

• In the event that no card is displayed from the classroom, the emergency responders will assume that there is an intruder in that classroom. Law enforcement may make the decision to immediately enter the classroom.

• Once the lockdown situation is over, school administration and emergency responders can place a unique identifying mark on the card and slide it back under the door to instruct the school staff member that the lockdown is over. Don't rely on a simple public address announcement or knocking on classroom doors to announce the lockdown is over; the intruder could be holding a gun to the principal's head forcing them to make the release announcement.

491 All of your schools should conduct a minimum of two lockdown drills each year. All schools should keep a log in the school office of the date and time these drills have been conducted.

During an intense crisis situation involving an intruder or active shooter, classrooms may be locked down for hours before the school can be cleared by law enforcement. Being patient and strictly following your school's 'rapid response' lockdown procedures will save lives.

Mail Handling

It is important that all school staff remain alert for the tell-tale signs of potentially dangerous mail and packages. Staff members should review the basic procedures and controls for handling an item that has come under suspicion.

492 Don't wait for an incident to occur before developing mail handling procedures and controls.

493 Train all school employees who handle mail how to properly identify a suspicious letter or package.

You may be suspicious of a package or letter if:

- The package/letter arrives unexpectedly or is from someone you do not know.
- It is addressed to the title of a school employee and does not list their name.
- It is addressed to a school employee who no longer works for the district.
- It is handwritten, has no return address, or the return address is not legible and legitimate.
- Common words are misspelled.
- The package/letter is lumpy or lopsided.
- The package/letter has wires or tin foil sticking out of it.
- The package/letter is sealed with an excessive amount of string or tape.

- It has specific delivery instructions such as 'Personal or Confidential.'
- The package/letter has excessive postage.
- The package/letter has stains, discoloration, crystallization, or a unique odor.
- The package/letter is leaking a liquid or powder.

494 **Post guidelines for addressing a suspicious package or letter.** Information can be obtained by contacting the Federal Bureau of Investigation at www.fbi.gov or the U.S. Postal Inspection Service at www.usps.com.

495 **Work with your local health department to determine appropriate protocols for addressing a bio-threat at your school.**

496 **Limit opening of mail to one individual staff member, in a room separated from the open, main office area.**

497 **If a suspicious package or letter is received, take the incident seriously.** Most threats are a hoax, but don't ever disregard safety and security protocols.

498 **If the suspicious package or letter is unopened or not leaking, ensure proper safety protocols are followed including:**

- Do not open it, don't pass it around and never shake it.
- Place the package or letter in a plastic bag or container to prevent leakage.
- Move all personnel a safe distance away from the area and call for assistance.
- Don't let others come in to the area.
- Anyone who had contact with the package or letter should wash their hands with soap and water.

499 If powder spills from a suspicious package or letter, enact appropriate safety and security controls.

500 Never allow your students to open the school mail.

Main Office Protocols

In most schools, the main office is the 'command center' of the school. It is in the main office where:

• School administrators have their office.

• Entrance cameras and buzzer systems are monitored.

• Bomb threats will be received by the school district.

• Visitors should be required to check in.

• Confrontations may take place with upset parents.

• Money may be secured.

• Medications may be secured and distributed.

With all of these potential security concerns in mind, consider these best practices:

501 Never divulge any information about your school's crisis procedures to anyone without verifying their credentials.

502 Ensure your bomb threat and harassing phone call protocol checklist is readily available for your school's office personnel.

503 Ensure your video security monitors are being monitored by office personnel at all times.

504 Make sure that '911' is programmed on all office phones speed dial.

505 Ensure all office safes and student records are out of sight and secured when not in use.

506 Never count money out in the open. Ensure that any money is stored in a secure area of the office such as a wall mounted safe. Only one or two trusted school employees should know the combination to your safe. If more than a couple of people know the combination and have access to the safe, it's time to change the combination.

507 Equip your office staff with pepper spray to be used as a last resort to neutralize a violent intruder. I know of a school district that doesn't allow pepper spray, but maintains wasp spray instead.

508 Identify a safe room where school administrators will go during an emergency situation. The role of a safe room is to provide a safe place which your administrators will attempt to occupy during an emergency or crisis situation. This 'command center' should be securable, out of direct sight, have communication access (computer and cell phone), and be known by law enforcement.

509 Clearly label your main office so visitors and strangers know where to go when entering your school. I've visited too many schools where the main office was not labeled or the office signs were not easily recognizable.

510 Never cover your office windows with paper, posters, or decorations. This is especially important if your office area faces a main hallway or the commons area.

Media Concerns

If a serious accident or violent incident were to occur within your school or on school grounds, you can bet the media will be there to analyze and reanalyze your district's every move. Their goal is to investigate how and why such an accident or incident could occur.

The media wants their story — the media will get their story. They will report what happened to the best of their knowledge with the information they receive from your school district and/or law enforcement personnel.

Unfortunately, the media can negatively affect the crisis. The media's involvement in school violence can:

• Increase the chances that some individuals exposed to media reports will contemplate violent responses. 'Copycat' shootings, bomb threats, and other acts of violence sometimes follow extensive media coverage of school violence events.

• Desensitize the public to the horrors associated with school violence. There are video games available that graphically simulate mass shooting situations — points are awarded for antisocial behavior.

• Exaggerate the magnitude of a real threat. This could result in parents fearing for the safety of their children when little danger is actually present.

It is best to learn how to work with the media; in fact, they can be a great asset to your crisis management efforts.

. . . .

511 **Designate a school district spokesperson or public information officer.** Your administrator should predetermine this individual. Oftentimes, the public information officer is developed from the school district, fire department, law enforcement, and emergency medical services ranks. This individual must be comfortable in front of the media, function well under pressure, and be credible in what they say.

. . . .

512 **Your public information officer should be knowledgeable about all aspects of your emergency and crisis management plan and be able to explain the various activities occurring during an event.**

513 Designate two backup police liaison officers in case the primary liaison is off site when the incident occurs.

514 Coordinate the types of information to be released with the police beforehand, especially if the event is of a criminal nature.

515 Only a pre-designated law enforcement official should release any information on the legal aspects of a crisis. Similarly, only the district's liaison should speak about school policies and procedures.

516 Prior to a crisis, consider developing 'canned' press releases describing pertinent policies and procedures.

517 Ensure accurate facts are available regarding the facility and the number of students enrolled at your school.

518 Provide your school staff, beforehand, with the name of the designated district liaison and his/her role. Make clear to staff that they are not to interact with representatives of the media, unless authorized by the liaison.

519 Provide staff with a prepared statement to be recited, if approached by a representative of the media, that refers the media representative to the district liaison.

520 If a serious accident or crisis occurs, immediately designate a media staging area. It is here that the media will be centrally located to prevent them from going off on their own. The media staging area is where your spokesperson or public information officer will conduct their business. This location should be located at a safe distance away from the students and sectioned off from the response activities. Remember to schedule ongoing press conferences and ensure that the proper officials are in attendance.

521 Before an incident occurs, determine if the media will be allowed into your school building. Most media personnel will recognize that their presence may be disruptive. If the media is not allowed into the building or near the incident scene, accommodations may be needed to provide statements and video outside the building or where the incident occurred.

522 Determine if the situation is already public knowledge. If the incident went over the police scanner, media personnel will be on your doorstep just as fast as the police. Anticipate the worst as a result of public knowledge and be prepared to respond.

523 Consult with law enforcement, emergency medical services, and the hospital prior to releasing information so as not to affect any potential criminal investigation and family notifications.

524 Weigh the public's right to know against an individual's right to privacy.

525 It is the school district's job to develop a safe and non-disruptive environment. Other considerations are sensitivity and concern for the well-being of students and staff, as well as cooperation with law enforcement agencies who may be conducting an investigation.

526 Instruct all school employees that anything that is said may have a bearing on potential future litigation.

527 Always think before you speak. Focus on the facts and don't draw any conclusions about what happened. Never go 'off the record' with the media.

528 Don't respond to the media with "no comment." In a news story, when the media hears "no comment," they will assume you are stonewalling and may search out other means to get their story.

529 Be honest and clearly explain why you can or cannot provide certain information.

If you need to buy additional time, some reasonable responses may be:

- "We are still determining exactly what occurred. If you leave your name and phone number, I will get back to you in ___ minutes/hours." If you use this strategy, follow through with your promises.

- "School officials are still investigating what happened and will update you at ___ o'clock."

- Have a secretary indicate you are not available but that you promise to respond to media calls as soon as possible.

Not an easy task is it? Your public information officer (media spokesperson) must prepare factual information and think quickly on their feet while always having an understanding of the sensitivity of the situation.

530 If the situation warrants, ensure prompt and regular media briefings and updates.

531 The best policy is to not allow media access to students on school grounds. Attempt to have staff members present during student interviews.

532 If appropriate, develop a 'grieving area' far away from the media.

533 Request the media to limit the number of 'human interest' type of stories as a result of your incident.

534 Inform your staff members not to discuss the situation with the media unless approved by the district administrator. What they say can hurt the investigation and have potential litigation concerns for the school district.

535 Never show photos/video or describe with words any information that would divulge the location or tactics of the police or SWAT team members. Always assume that the bad guy (gunman/hostage taker) has access to media links such as television, the internet, or cell phones.

536 Keep news helicopters out of the area. Their noise could create communication problems and their actions could scare a shooter to deadly action.

Parent Involvement

537 Educate parents that they may be at legal risk and can be held liable for their children's actions, including inappropriate use of a firearm on school grounds. Parents need to be made aware of the potential liability concerns if their child is involved in a violent situation. If all parents were informed of these concerns, I would venture to say they would be more involved in the lives of their children.

538 Educate parents at evening presentations on school violence, gang issues, your school's expectations, your zero tolerance policies, and local crime issues. Greatly stress your zero tolerance policy and the consequences of violating the policy.

539 Encourage parents to bring their children to school violence prevention presentations.

540 Encourage parents to inform school officials of any domestic changes at home. This may be a serious illness, retraining orders, separation/divorce, death of a family member or friend, death of a pet, etc.

541 Teach children to understand that weapons are never to be touched without the parent's permission and supervision.

542 Ask parents to take an active role in their student's school. Parents should communicate regularly with teachers and staff.

543 Use parents as classroom and hall monitors. Studies show that parental involvement significantly decreases after the child's elementary school days are complete. In truth, parental involvement must be present during the entire K-12 years of a child's education.

544 Ask grandparents and senior citizens to take an active role in your school. Encourage them to walk your school's hallways and to sit in on classes. Most kids have respect for the elderly — their presence may have a calming effect on students who may otherwise act up.

545 Offer free hot lunch to the elderly after their hall walking — this provides more supervision in your cafeteria.

546 Ask parents to volunteer in the classroom or during after-school activities.

547 Teach that violence prevention starts at home. Parents should stress that they won't accept or tolerate violent behavior at home or at school.

548 Discourage name-calling and teasing at home and at school. These behaviors often escalate into fist fights between students. The teaser may not be violent, but the victim may see violence as the only way to stop being teased.

549 Parents need to know their children's friends and whereabouts at all times.

550 Parents must tell their children that they support the school district's rules and policies as it relates to violence prevention, bullying, harassment, etc.

Playground Security

551 Whenever possible, ensure that your playgrounds and athletic facilities are in full view of the school. This is especially important when it involves the supervision of small children. This may require removing visual obstacles such as trees, bushes, or vehicle parking areas so complete supervision can be maintained.

....

552 Set back your playgrounds and play areas a minimum of 50 feet from parking areas and public streets. The play area will be easier to supervise and will limit the exposure to strangers or child abductors.

....

553 Segregate your play areas from all vehicle traffic areas. Never allow vehicles to drive across a play area when children are present.

....

554 Whenever possible, segregate the play areas of younger students from those of older students. Don't create an atmosphere where a young child could be bullied or injured by an older child.

....

555 Ensure that school maintenance vehicles and emergency response vehicles have access to play areas and athletic fields in case of a maintenance need or an emergency.

Positive Incentives to Prevent Violence

556 Rather than just focusing on punishment of student negative behaviors, develop methods to encourage positive behaviors.

....

557 Create recognition awards for students demonstrating good behavior.

558 Periodically ask local community leaders to speak to student groups to discuss ways to achieve success.

559 Bring in motivational speakers to address anti-drug, anti-drinking, and violence prevention.

560 **Every year, present an 'internet safety' training program for students.** The Facebook phenomenon has made it easy for students to bully, harass, threaten, and spread rumors about other students. Sadly, many young people don't understand their actions are wrong and oftentimes illegal.

561 Promote media coverage for all types of students who have completed positive achievements.

Principal Involvement

562 **Establish and constantly stress the zero tolerance policies for weapons and violence in your school.** Students need to clearly understand your zero tolerance policies and penalties in advance.

563 **Stress your zero tolerance policies during student presentations, parent-teacher conferences, and through the use of emails and mailings to parents.**

564 Adopt the motto "If it's illegal outside school, it's illegal inside school."

565 **Establish a faculty-student-staff committee to develop a Safe School Plan.** Invite law enforcement officers to be part of this committee. Your Safe School Plan policies and procedures for day-to-day operations and crisis handling should cover such subjects as:

• Identifying who belongs in the building.

• Avoiding accidents and incidents in corridors and on school grounds.

• Reporting weapons or concerns about weapons.

• Working in partnership with law enforcement.

• Following up to ensure that troubled students get help.

566 **Work with juvenile justice authorities and law enforcement officers on how violence, threats, potentially violent situations, and other crimes will be handled.** Meet regularly with law enforcement to review problems and concerns.

567 **Develop a memorandum of understanding (MOU) with law enforcement on access to the school building, reporting of crimes, arrests, and other key issues.**

568 **Develop ways to make it easier for parents to be involved in the lives of their students.** Provide lists of volunteer opportunities, ask parents to organize phone trees, and hold events on weekends as well as week nights. Offering free child care for younger children may help get parents into your school.

569 **Reward good student behavior.** Acknowledging students who do the right thing, whether it's settling an argument without violence, helping another student, or apologizing for bumping into someone, helps raise the tone for the whole school.

570 **Ensure that your building principals are visible in the hallways and classrooms before, during, and after the school day.**

571 Ensure that a hierarchy of consequences is in place for inappropriate behavior. To increase the student's respect for authority, your policies must match the consequences to the severity of the infraction.

572 Always enforce your disciplinary code impartially and consistently, using due process. This means the star athlete would be treated the same as the most unpopular student.

573 Each principal should be at the forefront in the creation of crisis plans for their school. At the school level, the principal serves as the leader of their crisis prevention team.

574 Establish a crisis planning team within each school. Secure commitment to crisis planning within the school by involving staff members who work at that school.

575 Each principal should identify those individuals who need to be involved in crisis planning. It's important to include community members, emergency responders, families, and school staff members.

576 For each school, create an incident management structure. This structure should provide a comprehensive organizational structure designed to address the various types of emergencies. Every crisis and emergency has certain major elements requiring clear lines of command and control.

577 Principals must understand their available crisis resources. This includes identifying and becoming familiar with resources in the school such as staff members certified in first aid/CPR, community resources such as the availability of emergency responders to counselors, and organization resources such as the parent-teacher associations.

578 Principals must set aside time to train and practice with staff, students, and emergency responders.

Frequently make time to train your staff on issues that may save their lives or the lives of their students. Loss of life, injuries sustained, and the total chaos surrounding a school crisis can be minimized if school personnel are thoroughly and properly trained on how to perform before, during, and after a crisis situation. Your training should include drills, in-service presentations, tabletop exercises, and the review of educational materials. Periodically set aside time to review and evaluate your crisis plan.

579 During a crisis, your principals must:

• Respond within seconds and lead with a serious, calm, confident style.

• Implement your crisis plan.

• Yield authority, when appropriate, to others in the plan's designated command structure, for example, law enforcement.

• Facilitate collaboration among school staff and emergency responders.

• Remain open to suggestions and information that is important to adjust your crisis response on the fly.

Rumors

The majority of school shootings had significant warning signs — rumors that something bad was going to occur. Too often, these rumors were ignored, not taken seriously, or were not reported to the proper authorities.

580 Discuss any and all rumors with police. Your school administrators and the police should meet regularly to discuss rumors and violence related issues. It is important for your school leaders and police to send a unified, consistent message to your community.

581 Address all rumors openly and honestly with your staff.

582 Never hide or sweep rumors under the carpet. It only gets worse if the media or parents find out that they weren't investigated.

583 Review your school district's policies on reporting and disciplining those who start violence related rumors. Your school district's policies and student handbooks should clearly list the disciplinary procedures for those students who make violence threats or start rumors.

584 Publicly communicate your school district's zero tolerance for rumors. Frequently communicate to parents that your school district will be proactive in addressing any violence related rumors or threats.

585 Be repetitive in your rumor communication plan. Post your rumor/threat policy on your school district's website, send out mailings to parents, and discuss it at parent-teacher conferences.

586 Hold those who start rumors responsible for their actions. At the beginning of the school year, students need to be educated on the dangers and consequences of developing violence related rumors or threats. Students need to clearly understand the expectations to report and prevent rumors or threats from occurring.

587 Ask your teachers to increase their awareness of students who excessively use their cell phones. Reinforce to teachers the importance of their heightened awareness and supervision to monitor against student use of cell phones and text messaging in classrooms and school common areas. Heightened attention to this is particularly important during times of threats, rumors, and related security incidents.

588 Develop procedures for teachers to notify school administrators of cell phone misuse and abuse.

589 Tell your teachers that they may be wrong or embarrassed when reporting or acting on rumors, but it's OK, don't fold to outside pressure.

590 Use available technology to identify those who start rumors. If threats of violence have been written on your bathroom walls, check your security cameras to identify those going in and out of the bathroom.

591 Frequently monitor comments, pictures, and videos posted on the internet. Surprisingly, many students who threaten violence simply cannot keep their mouth shut and have a need to tell the world what they are planning to do or have done.

592 Use your local media to control rumors. Ask the media to provide frequent updates to the public, particularly providing accurate information when rumors need to be dispelled.

Shelter-in-Place

To Shelter-in-Place means that everyone in your school will take immediate shelter where they are and isolate the inside environment from the outside environment.

These controls are initiated to protect your staff and students from possible chemical, radiological or biological contaminants released into the environment. This release may be accidental, such as a chemical accident spill at a nearby manufacturing facility, or on purpose, such as a planned terrorism attack.

Keep these best practices in mind when developing your district's Shelter-in-Place plan:

593 Provide training to staff and students on Shelter-in-Place procedures. This includes annual drills at all of your schools.

594 Develop an inventory of classroom emergency equipment and supplies. This equipment should include pre-cut plastic and tape to seal rooms. Inform your principal if equipment or supplies are needed.

595 Identify those offices and classrooms that have spaces appropriate for sheltering use.

596 Prepare written and pictorial instructions for immediate shut down of the school's heating and ventilation systems. Ensure your custodians and principal know how to quickly shut down your systems.

597 Clearly determine how your school employees will receive the instructions to Shelter-in-Place. These instructions may come from the school district administrator, a first responder, law enforcement or emergency management.

598 During a Shelter-in-Place, your district administrator is responsible for closing the school, activating the emergency plan, and assuming the role of incident commander.

599 Assign relevant responsibilities to other school staff members. The administrator should stay in the designated incident command center.

600 Develop a plan to communicate your Shelter-in-Place plan to those located in remote outbuildings and outside of the school building.

601 Use simple language when enacting the Shelter-in-Place plan. Simply state: "Shelter-in-Place. This is not a drill. Staff and students please move to your shelter areas." This announcement should be repeated at intervals of 15 seconds.

602 At the beginning of the school year, discuss with students the reasons for Shelter-in-Place. Take the time to review Shelter-in-Place procedures, answer their questions and reassure students.

603 Post your Shelter-in-Place guidelines in all classrooms. These guidelines should address:

- The need to turn off the classroom heating or ventilation and cover/seal the air vents with plastic.
- Providing calm instructions to students.
- Prohibiting the use of phone and email systems to request information.

When instituting a Shelter-in-Place:

604 Maintain constant communication with the district office. This is a duty usually assigned to a secretary.

605 Immediately secure all external building doors.

606 Quickly sweep the hallways and non-classroom areas for students. If students are found, quickly move them to the nearest shelter room.

607 Instruct your custodians to immediately turn off heating and ventilation systems and seal make-up air systems.

608 At your main office, monitor radio and phone systems. Parents, the media, and others may be frantically calling the school.

609 Make verbal contact with each Shelter-in-Place room to determine if first aid or other care is needed.

510 Instruct classroom teachers to sit tight and wait for instructions or information. Emergency responders on the outside will provide the necessary information as to how to proceed.

611 If appropriate, direct your teachers to seal their rooms with plastic and tape.

512 Periodically communicate updates to staff and students as information is received.

513 Only provide the "all clear" signal when safety of the environment is determined and communicated by law enforcement and emergency management personnel.

514 Systematically direct school staff and students to quietly exit the building.

615 Once the building is clear, your custodians can re-start the HVAC systems. It is important to resume normal school operations as soon as possible.

516 Prepare a report documenting the event, the response and the result of the Shelter-in-Place plan implementation. This documentation is needed to review and revise your school's response procedures as needed.

517 As quickly and accurately as possible, provide an email to staff members to provide an overview of the situation to reduce misinformation.

618 As quickly and accurately as possible, develop a communication for parents that clearly explains the situation and actions taken by the school district.

619 Remember, during a Shelter-in-Place, staff members are not to open the doors for anyone under any circumstances.

Shooter on School Grounds

620 If a shooting occurs, call '911' immediately! There have been incidents where valuable time has been wasted when school employees called the main office to report or confirm gunshots — don't waste time, call '911.' If you are wrong, it's no big deal.

621 Be prepared to provide information on the exact location of the gunshots. Police dispatchers have been trained to extract the required information for proper emergency response.

If the shooter is outside of the building:

622 Immediately instruct your students to drop to the floor. Lay face down, as flat as possible. If possible, direct your students to a safe place or cover.

623 Try to use obstructions between yourself and the gunfire. If there isn't a safe place to take cover, move or crawl away from the gunfire. Many objects may conceal you from sight but are not bulletproof.

624 If safely possible, try to get inside or behind the building.

625 When a place of relative safety has been reached, stay down and do not move. Never raise your head or take a peek to see what might be occurring.

626 Call the office from your classroom or other safe location to report the situation.

627 Wait and listen for directions from the police.

628 Disregard all school bells until your school's "safe" code/message is delivered.

If the shooter is outside of the classroom:

629 Keep students inside the classroom, lying on the floor. If possible, move students behind large objects in the classroom.

630 If possible, close and lock the classroom door. Earlier, I mentioned the importance of identifying a large object in the classroom that can be used to block the door — only block the door if it is safe to do so.

631 Turn off the lights and stay on the floor. Don't let anyone peek out of the door or windows to see what is happening.

632 If possible, call the office/'911' as soon as possible to report the location of the shooter.

Office personnel duties:

633 If notified of a shooting from a classroom or other area of the school, all persons in the office should seek cover on the floor, behind objects, or inside secured rooms. Emergency calls to law enforcement can now be made.

634 **Make sure all phone calls are limited to emergency personnel only.** Phone calls to others such as family or friends will only confuse the situation by bringing onlookers and loved ones to the school. Don't place others in unnecessary danger.

635 **Implement your lockdown procedures.** Instruct staff and students to stay in their classrooms.

636 **If the shooter is outside the office, close and lock the doors if it is possible.**

Special Needs Students

Customized security protocols of special needs students may need to be developed by your school district. Your lockdown, evacuation, and relocation plans need to address the limitations of each special needs student in your school. For example, a student in a wheelchair may not be able to use the building steps without assistance of a school staff member.

The following special needs student security concerns should be addressed by your school:

637 **Identify alternative lockdown and evacuation areas for special needs students.** During a 'rapid response' lockdown or evacuation, time is of the essence. There may not be enough time to move physically impaired students to a designated safe area. Ensure the location of these alternative areas are communicated to law enforcement personnel.

638 **During a fire, elevators will not be available to move wheelchair bound students.** Clearly designate staging areas where multiple staff members will meet to quickly move these students.

639 **Develop a plan to address students with hearing disabilities.** These students may not be able to communicate with their teacher or hear emergency announcements and fire alarms.

640 Provide basic sign language training to designated school members.

641 Ensure that your school's doorways, hallways, stairways, and exits are always kept clear to allow for prompt evacuation of special needs students.

642 Prior to a crisis, address the required medical needs of your special needs students. This may involve medical equipment, power supplies, and medicines.

643 In the classroom, be prepared to address the physical mobility requirements of special needs students. During a tornado or lockdown, a special needs student may not be able to bend over or sit on the floor.

Suspicious People and Vehicles Around Your School

Suspicious people and vehicles on or around your school grounds can create very real fear and concern among your staff and students. Unusual or suspicious activity does not necessarily mean that a violent act is about to occur but it is important to be aware of the following suspicious behaviors:

• Unknown individuals acting secretively and suspiciously.

• Individuals who avoid eye contact when confronted.

• Individuals who depart quickly when seen or approached.

• Individuals in places they don't belong.

• A strong odor coming from a building or vehicle.

• An overloaded vehicle.

• Fluid leaking from a vehicle, other than the engine or gas tank.

• An individual who is overdressed for the type of weather.

Consider these school security ideas when addressing suspicious people or vehicles:

644 **Contact your local police department to provide information and training on how to address suspicious vehicles and people around your school.** They will tell you that your best and safest option is to notify police of all suspicious activity that takes place on or around school grounds — before, during, or after school.

645 **Ask your police department to increase patrols and drive-bys of school facilities.** Request that police patrols are conducted at random times in marked police vehicles.

646 **Ensure your bus, playground, and any other supervisors outside with students are highly visible by their dress — orange vests or arm bands for example.** Bad guys strike when there is little or no supervision. They certainly don't want confrontation with a supervisor.

647 **Ensure your supervisors always carry cell phones to immediately call for assistance.** If their cell phone has a camera, take a picture to report a suspicious vehicle or person.

648 **Watch for suspicious or unknown people who are taking pictures or videotaping school activities or buildings.** Go with your gut feeling, if it doesn't appear right, call the police.

649 **Recognize the activities that should cause a heightened sense of suspicion:**

- Someone who displays suspicious or unusual interest in school activities.

- Someone involved in surveillance which is suspicious in nature.

- Someone taking inappropriate photographs or videos, note-taking, drawing of diagrams, annotating maps, or using binoculars or night vision devices.

Suspicious People

650 If you observe suspicious behavior, do not confront the individuals involved. Instead remember the acronym **S-A-L-U-T-E.**

S stands for Size — note the number of people involved, their gender, their ages, and physical descriptions. Compare your height and weight to theirs. Look for some unique characteristic that will help to identify the person(s) later.

A stands for Activity — describe exactly what they are doing.

L stands for Location — be able to provide the exact location of the suspicious activity.

U stands for Uniform — be able to describe what they are wearing, including their footwear. An obvious indicator such as a piece of clothing allows for quick identification by police.

T stands for Time — be able to provide the date, time, and duration of the suspicious activity.

E stands for Equipment — be able to describe the vehicle (make, color, license plate number), the use of cameras, guns, or any other equipment.

Suspicious Vehicles

651 If suspicious vehicles are noticed around one of your schools, administration needs to have a plan in place to address this concern.

652 Get the message out to your staff as well as surrounding neighbors to be aware of suspicious activity or vehicles around the schools.

653 Watch for any vehicles driving slowly and without lights. A vehicle that is following a course that appears aimless or repetitive is suspicious in any location.

654 Watch for parked, occupied, vehicles containing one or more persons, especially if observed at an unusual hour around one of your schools.

655 Watch for vehicles being loaded with valuables on school grounds.

656 If an incident occurs, be prepared to provide the police with accurate information. What happened? When and where did it occur? What is the vehicle's license plate number? What is the vehicle's direction of travel?

657 Be prepared to present an accurate description of the number of persons or vehicles involved.

Acts of school violence, abduction, or terrorism are very difficult to predict but oftentimes there are warning signs that something is to occur. It is important to ensure that all school employees are on the lookout for things that are out of the ordinary and arouse suspicions. You never know, your suspicion may just prevent a violent act from occurring at your school.

Student Behavior

Three of the most significant factors that lead to school violence are bullying, harassment, and intimidation — verbal confrontations that have never been fully resolved. Oftentimes these factors are overlooked and never addressed by school staff.

658 Your district's zero tolerance policy must address all violent acts including threats, fighting, pushing/shoving, bullying, harassment, name calling, and intimidation.

659 It's OK to regulate your students' dress. A school official should never be afraid to tell a student what constitutes acceptable (and unacceptable) dress.

660 **During the school day, ban long full-length coats and the carrying of large purses and book/gym bags.** How do you think school shooters are getting large guns and hundreds of rounds of ammunition in to the school undetected? Oftentimes they were hidden beneath their clothing or concealed in a gym bag.

661 **Ban gang member clothing, insignias, and actions.** Talk to your local police department about gang member trends in your community.

662 **Talk with your school's 'negative leaders.'** They are tuned in to what is going on in your school and may provide valuable information regarding any problems or violent situations.

663 **Teach your students that weapons, drugs, and other contraband are never allowed in school.**

664 **Encourage students to report any crime immediately through the school's tip hotline.**

665 **Encourage students to report bullies.**

666 **Instruct students to report suspicious talk or behavior by other students.**

667 **Encourage students to become peer counselors to work with classmates who need support.**

Student Release Concerns

The development of timely student release procedures is a crucial component of your crisis planning. As is the case with all school crisis planning, the safety and security of your students is your main priority. During a crisis, your 'traditional' student release procedures may be unsafe or otherwise inoperable. Your school's comprehensive crisis plan needs to include certain procedures such as:

668 **Update your student rosters.** Your rosters should be updated at a minimum of twice a year; some districts update their rosters on a weekly basis.

669 **Distribute updated student rosters to your teachers.** All of your teachers need updated student rosters for all their classes. This information should be stored in the classroom so a substitute teacher can easily find it.

670 **Maintain a copy of all student rosters in your school's crisis response box, as well as with the principal.** It is critical to know which students are present on school grounds during a crisis.

671 **Create student emergency cards.** At the beginning of the school year, make sure the school develops an emergency card for each student containing:

- Information on parents/guardians, as well as several other adults who can be contacted if the parent or guardian is not available.

- Information as to whether the student is permitted to leave school grounds with any of the adults listed on the card if necessary.

- All pertinent medical information, such as allergies, medications, and doctor contact information.

672 **Ask parents/guardians of your students to authorize one or more parents/guardians of other children at your school to pick up their child.**

573 Store your student emergency cards in your main office, both in hard copy and in electronic format.

574 Create student release forms to be used in times of crisis and store them with your crisis response materials. Create a back-up plan if forms are not available.

575 Designate student release areas as well as back-up options. These areas should be predetermined and communicated to student's families. If necessary, changes should be communicated through email, the media, and postings on your school website.

576 Assign specific student release roles for your staff. Understand that several staff members will be needed to meet families and sign out students. Make sure you assign these roles long before a crisis occurs.

577 Create simple, easy to follow, student release procedures. Family members will be panicked, wanting immediate access to their children after a crisis at one of your schools.

578 Never release custody of students to anyone who is not listed on your student emergency card. It may take time, it may upset people, but proof of identity must be required to pick up one of your students.

579 If custody is a family issue, never release a student to a noncustodial guardian. A well-intentioned friend may offer to take a child home; however, school staff must be certain that students are only released to the appropriate people as listed on the student emergency card so families will know where their students are located.

580 Be prepared to transport students who are not taken home by a parent or guardian. It may also be necessary to arrange for temporary shelter and provisions.

681 Use all of your available communication outlets to keep families, the media, and your community informed during and after the crisis. Use communication outlets such as email, your district's website, television, and radio to signal the end of the crisis as well.

Supervision

Your school has the duty to protect students in your custody from reasonably foreseeable harm. Your school also has the duty to anticipate reasonably foreseeable dangers and to take appropriate precautions to protect the students in your custody from such dangers.

Remember, students under a school's care, custody, and control may be unable to protect themselves due to mental or physical limitations or inexperience — meaning they may not be knowledgeable enough to understand potential dangers.

682 Teach the '3 C's of supervision' to your staff — care, control, and custody. Students under your school's 'care' and 'control' may not be able to protect themselves due to physical or mental limitations. Your school has a duty to supervise when students are in your 'custody' — during the school day and at school sponsored events.

683 Adequate supervision is required on your school grounds when students are present during school hours. Bad things tend to occur when and where no supervision is present.

684 Ensure that your school staff is mobile and moving. Continually monitor your hallways, bathrooms, locker rooms, and anywhere else that students may assemble.

685 Encourage students to not come to school early and to leave school promptly. Continually remind your students and parents of the hours when your school is 'open for business.'

686 When your school buildings are unlocked for students to enter, ensure that adequate supervision is present. This may mean that adult supervision is needed 10-30 minutes before the school day begins and 10-30 minutes after students are released at the end of the school day. Supervision in the morning is key — the majority of school shootings occurred first thing in the morning.

687 If you have school sponsored events before or after school, your district has the duty to supervise the students involved in those events.

688 Monitor the secluded areas of your school such as restrooms, storage rooms, boiler rooms, etc. With the exception of restrooms, these areas should be kept locked when not in use by a staff member.

689 Develop bathroom supervision procedures. This includes:

690 Be aware of the student's age; younger children may require more supervision.

691 Be aware of the location of your school's bathrooms; bathrooms that are segregated from other areas of the school may require more supervision.

692 Bathrooms accessible by non-school employees or visitors may require more frequent supervision.

693 Bathroom supervisors should be of the same gender. Do not allow male staff to supervise the girl's bathroom.

694 Ask your teachers to conduct random checks of the bathrooms throughout the school day.

695 Consider the use of a pass system where only one child is allowed to leave the classroom at any one time to use the bathroom.

696 Take appropriate precautions when screening and selecting parents, volunteers, or substitutes who are to be used as supervisors.

697 Inform parents/guardians of the school district's supervision policies. Evening presentations, emails, and parent-teacher conferences are good times to review your district's supervision policies.

698 Let parents know of those areas or activities where additional supervision may be needed. Ask for their assistance with supervision.

Things Teachers Can Do To Prevent Violence

699 Ask your teachers to always report any rumors, violence threats, signs of or discussions of weapons, signs of gang activity, or any other conditions that may lead to violence in your school.

700 Develop student behavior norms for the classroom. Ask your students to assist with the development of penalties and the enforcement of the rules. As a teacher, your goal should be to refuse to permit violence in the classroom.

701 Talk frequently with parents about their children's grades, progress, and any concerns they may have. Many school districts use the district's internet site to post up-to-date grades and progress reports.

702 Learn how to recognize the warning signs that a child might be headed for violence and know how to access school resources to get appropriate help.

703 Encourage and sponsor student-led anti-violence activities and programs ranging from peer education to teen courts to mediation to mentoring to training.

704 Offer to serve on a team or committee to develop and implement a safe school plan which includes how teachers should respond during emergency situations.

705 Enforce classroom and all-school violence policies consistently with all your students.

706 **Insist that students refrain from name-calling, teasing, bullying, and harassment of others.** Encourage students to demonstrate the respect they expect by involving them in the development of acceptable behavior standards.

707 **Teach with enthusiasm.** Students engaged in work that is challenging, informative, and rewarding are less likely to get into trouble.

708 **Teach conflict resolution and anger management skills.** Assist your students in applying these skills in their everyday life.

709 Incorporate discussions on violence and its prevention into the subject matter you teach, whenever possible.

710 Encourage students to report crimes or activities that look suspicious to them.

711 Train your school employees on how to verbally defuse a potentially violent situation or break up a fight. Your police department or school resource officer can provide the verbal tools needed to deal with or defuse conflict situations.

712 Consider an in-service program of self-defense training for all school employees. Self-defense training can be fun and will allow a school employee to develop the skills to physically handle and remove themselves from a violent situation.

713 If you are alone and a confrontation turns violent, get out of there. Get your 'knees to the breeze' and get plenty of assistance.

714 Encourage teachers to be highly visible and interactive. Teachers should periodically walk hallways, parking lots, and school grounds before and after classes, and be present in the cafeteria, the playground, and bus pick up areas. Frequent interaction and under-standing between your teachers and students is what stops violence from boiling over.

715 Offer free hot lunch to teachers who will sit and eat with their students.

716 Instruct your teachers to dress for respect. Teachers need every advantage they can find and dressing appropriately is one of these advantages.

717 Whenever possible, decrease the number of students assigned to each teacher to reduce the chance of classroom violence.

718 If your school district requires staff to wear identification badges, make sure they are being worn and are secured. Staff identification badges must be kept on their person or secured so that no other staff member, student, or visitor can use them.

719 Identification badges should always be worn above the waist and located where they are visible at all times.

720 Instruct all staff members that keys and fobs should be kept on their person or secured so that no other staff member, student, or visitor can use them. Oftentimes I observe teacher keys/fobs lying out in the open on a teacher's desk and no one is in the room.

Terrorism Concerns

We've learned that unpredictable acts of terror are intended to create universal fear and weaken our belief in our government's ability to protect us.

Rightfully, our government has chosen to focus anti-terrorism resources on securing governmental infrastructures. Less secured targets, such as one of your schools, may become a more attractive terrorism target in the future.

The risk of your school being affected by a terrorist attack is much lower than the risk of many other crises or emergencies; however, it is important to be prepared for the worst. As with other crisis incidents, a terrorist attack may result in the following:

• Damage beyond your school boundaries (as with a tornado).

• Victims who are contaminated (as with a hazardous materials spill).

• A crime scene to protect (as with arson), or

• Wide-spread fear and panic (as with a large scale school shooting).

The following best practices are designed to increase your school district's awareness of potential terrorism risk factors:

721 **Make sure your school maintains an appropriate number of supplied emergency kits.**

722 **Consider maintaining at least a two day supply of medications for those students required to have medications at school.**

723 **Offer first aid and first responder training, including defibrillator training, for your staff members throughout the year.** Your school can never have enough trained responders, especially during a medical emergency.

724 **Make sure your walkie-talkies and cell phones are fully functional and back up batteries are available.**

725 **Properly screen all educational staff members as well as all food service employees, bus drivers, custodians, substitute teachers, and volunteers.** Your local police department can assist in developing effective screening protocols. Do not limit your searches to the use of internet databases, typically they are not accurate. Your school district's employee screening process should include a trace of the individual's social security number to determine if there are any out of state issues that warrant further attention.

726 **Ensure that your district's outside contractors, suppliers, and vendors have conducted thorough background reviews of their employees.** For security purposes, these individuals should always be treated as 'strangers in your school.'

727 **Be especially vigilant of anyone seeking access to your school's alarm and communication systems, utilities, chemical storage areas, maintenance rooms, etc.** Even if an approved subcontractor is used, don't allow them to access these areas by themselves. And don't ever issue master keys to them.

728 Ensure that your district's outside contractors, suppliers, and vendors are required to follow your visitor control procedures. These may include:

- Checking in and out at each school facility.

- Wearing a proper identification badge that has a photo and lists the person's name and company.

- Allowing these people to enter the school through designated entrances only. Vendors and suppliers often simply walk in through the unlocked food service door or the unlocked garage door of the technology education area.

729 If the identity of outside contractors or service personnel cannot be verified, don't allow them in your schools. If your increased security awareness causes a delay in someone's day, it's not a big deal, it's better to be safe than sorry.

730 Never leave school building doors unlocked or wedged open for an anticipated contractor, service, or delivery personnel visit. I have noticed that this has become a common practice in many food service and maintenance areas.

731 Unrestricted access to your school's entrances, maintenance areas, food storage areas, or utility areas should never be provided to outside contractors. A bad practice seen at a number of schools — master keys are provided to contractors to access your school at any time.

732 Maintain vehicular traffic in one direction only around your school buildings. Signage can instruct contractors, vendors, and suppliers that they are not to drive in certain areas.

733 Educate your students about where they should and should not walk when entering or exiting these pre-designated areas.

734 Whenever possible, do not allow buses, cars, trucks, or any other vehicles to park close to your school buildings. Minimize the chance of someone parking a vehicle full of explosives next to one of your school buildings.

735 Ensure that objects around the perimeter of your school do not provide easy access to your school's roof. Telephone poles, trees, dumpsters, small storage sheds, and other objects should be maintained at least 15-30 feet away from your building to prevent easy access to your school's upper floors or roof.

736 Trim tree branches and bushes to ensure good visibility in and out of your school buildings and to eliminate building access.

737 Construct securable, protective enclosures around mechanical, electrical, and utility equipment outside your schools. Padlock key access to these enclosures must be strictly controlled.

738 Always secure and control the access to your school's mechanical and utility rooms to prevent an intruder from placing hazardous materials in your building's ventilation system.

739 All crawl spaces, tunnels, and other means to access your school buildings must be secured with strict access controls in place. I have visited many schools where tunnels and other hidden spaces were left unsecured, presenting an inviting area for an intruder to hide, plant explosives, and stash weapons.

740 High traffic areas such as playgrounds and parking lots should be under constant visual surveillance. Try to locate your playgrounds so they always can be seen from someone inside your school.

741 Ask your police department to use their marked squad cars to patrol your parking lots and around your school during normal school hours. The frequency of these patrols should increase during the first few hours of the school day when the majority of violent incidents occur.

742 Position your video cameras to provide coverage of as much of your school's parking lots as possible.

743 Use central alarm stations to monitor your school building's alarm and fire systems. It is important to be able to notify authorities of an emergency when the school building is unoccupied, such as on weekends and during the summer months.

744 Develop an understanding of the emergency crisis concerns of nearby factories and businesses. Some of your district's schools may be located near companies that could put your students and staff in danger during an emergency, such as an explosion or chemical spill. Meet with these companies to review these exposures. It is important to be on the emergency call list of these businesses in case of an emergency.

745 Ensure your school district is on the emergency call list of nearby businesses.

746 Evaluate your district's exposure to any potential terrorism targets near one of your schools. These could include municipal facilities, chemical manufacturing or storage facilities, petroleum refineries, airports, buildings where large numbers of people frequently congregate, etc.

747 Determine if any railroad lines are in close proximity to your schools. If a railroad line is nearby, meet with the proper authorities to determine if hazardous substances are transported on this line which may present an exposure to your school if there was a railroad accident.

748 Educate all school staff members so they know how to respond to suspicious packages, items, or other objects that might be found in the classroom or anywhere on school grounds. In most cases, the appropriate response is to not touch the object and immediately report it to the police.

749 Secure the dumpsters around your schools to prevent the hiding of hazardous materials, contraband, or weapons. Additionally, you do not want anyone to climb into your dumpsters or to push the dumpsters against your building to access the roof.

750 Erect a securable enclosure around your dumpsters which can only be opened by the waste hauler or a school maintenance employee.

751 Ensure your emergency back-up power system is fully operational. Your school's critical systems such as exit signs, fire alarm systems, means of egress illumination, and emergency voice/alarm communication systems must be supplied with an emergency backup power source. Backup power should be provided for smoke management systems, fire pumps, elevators, and emergency power loads.

752 Place smoke detectors in each school's ventilation duct-work. If the smoke detection system is part of your fire alarm system, it can immediately shut down the air handling units.

753 A 'heightened awareness' for suspicious activity, people, or vehicles should be maintained by all staff members. Anything that is out of the ordinary should be reported immediately to the police. Refer to the chapter on recognizing suspicious people and vehicles for further information.

754 Check to ensure that all roof hatches and access points are secured when not being accessed by a school employee.

755 At the end of every school day, close and secure your classroom windows, especially those on the first floor.

756 Maintain heightened security awareness during any activity taking place outside of the school. Supervisors must be extra vigilant during playground recess, physical education classes, field trips, etc., that take place outside or off school grounds.

757 Even for after school events, maintain strong visitor control procedures. This may include:

- Restricting the number of building doors that are accessible from the outside to one designated entrance only.

- Stressing the importance of your staff greeting and challenging strangers, recognizing and reporting suspicious individuals, vehicles, and activities.

- Allowing visitors access only to pre-designated areas of your school building.

758 Maintain strict security access to your boiler rooms, utility areas, and all other facility operations areas. Often, these areas are left wide open for anyone to access at all times of the day.

759 Maintain strict security access to your outdoor heating, ventilation and air conditioning systems and utility controls.

760 When not occupied by a school staff member, all maintenance closets and cleaning product storage rooms must be secured.

761 If your students and staff are detained for an extended period of time, ensure an adequate supply of food and water is available.

762 Lock up your food and beverage products before, during, and after school hours. Don't invite an intruder to tamper with your food.

763 Purchase school food products, beverages, and supplies only from reputable suppliers who have the appropriate permits or licenses. Require your food suppliers to follow strict food security plans and measures.

764 A reputable food supplier should be properly licensed and inspected by the appropriate state or federal health authorities. It's OK to request a copy of the Certificate of Inspection and their license or permit.

765 Request proper references and contact information from your food suppliers. Ask for references from other local school districts they have supplied in the past.

766 Work with your district's food supplier to ensure a recall procedure is in place for tainted or questionable food product.

767 Obtain a signed agreement from all suppliers and contractors that states they will comply with your school district's visitor control, security plan, and food safety plan requirements.

768 Allow food product to be delivered in tamper proof packaging only. If food product is delivered and the tamper proof seal is broken, reject it and send it back to your food distributor.

769 Know when and where the food suppliers, contractors, and delivery personnel will be arriving at your school. It is important for the district to know the names of the company providing the service, the names of their employees, their expected time of arrival, and what/how much will be delivered. These controls are especially important for deliveries that occur after normal school hours.

770 Allow deliveries to take place only if someone from the school district is present. Never allow unsupervised deliveries to be dropped off before, during or after school hours.

771 Unless a school employee is present, all loading dock areas, food storage areas, and kitchens must be secured to prevent product tampering or theft. It's not acceptable to leave the loading dock door open because a delivery person is coming 'sometime this morning.'

772 Remove the keys and lock the doors of all delivery trucks when they are not being loaded or unloaded.

773 Don't allow your kitchens or food preparation areas to be used for special events or outside groups unless your food service staff is present. Allowing outsiders to use school kitchen facilities increases the chance of food tampering and/or theft of equipment.

774 Test your water and ice on a regular basis to make sure it is safe to drink. Your local municipal water company can provide valuable water testing assistance.

775 Require your cashiers to always wash their hands after handling money and prior to preparing, serving, or handling any food or equipment.

Theft and Fraud Prevention

Although it's not common, employee internal theft is a threat that your school district faces every day. If an internal theft of money or valuable equipment occurs, your school district may easily lose taxpayer trust — possibly affecting future budgets or building referendums.

Keep these internal theft controls in mind to safeguard your school district's assets:

Check Handling Procedures

776 Develop a policy where two signatures are required on checks, with one of the signatures being that of an administrator outside your accounting department. It is common for a school district to require additional signatures on 'high dollar' checks — keep in mind that most school related check fraud occurs with smaller dollar amounts. The dishonest employee often thinks that smaller dollar amounts will go unnoticed.

777 Require your board of education to establish dollar amount limits for disbursements that may be made with a single signature versus those that require additional signatures.

778 Always match the original invoice to the check before it is signed.

779 Require that checks be signed by an employee other than the person who is preparing, authorizing, or recording the check. Each check signer should compare the amount of the check to the supporting documentation to ensure it is appropriate.

780 Do not allow employees to post-date checks, sign blank checks, or use checks made payable to the 'bearer.'

781 Your bank statements and cancelled checks should be mailed to a school administrator instead of the accounting department. This administrator can ensure that all signatures are accurate and can verify check amounts. The administrator should also oversee any money transfers from one account to another. Not every check needs to be reviewed — just having a periodic 'spot check' policy in place may be enough to prevent fraud from occurring.

782 At all times, maintain blank checks and check stock in a secure location.

Bank Account Procedures

783 **Keep your district's federal ID number in a secure location that is not available to school employees or the public.** A stolen federal tax ID number can be used to open a bank account.

784 **Keep the district's bank statements and check images in a secure location to prevent forgery.**

785 **Immediately shred all banking correspondence that is not required to be archived, to** prevent duplication and to limit access to account information.

Deposit Procedures

786 **Secure all undeposited cash and prepared deposits in a safe until they are deposited in the bank.** Ensure that access to your safe is limited to a few select employees.

787 **Deposit cash on a timely basis.** Do not allow deposits to remain in someone's possession or in the safe for an extended period of time.

788 **Vary the times when deposits are made to the bank.** Ensure the employee carrying the deposit remains in areas that are frequented by other people, preferably during daylight hours.

789 **If your school has a police liaison officer, ask them to assist with escorting bank deposits.**

790 **Don't carry an easily identifiable bank bag in plain view.** Conceal the bank bag in a purse, computer bag, or on the employee's body when leaving the school. Don't make yourself an easy mark for theft.

Collection Procedures

791 **Assign a separate cash drawer for each employee who is responsible for collecting cash.** Maintaining a separate cash drawer will provide individual accountability over the cash that is received. If an employee or volunteer (such as at a concession stand) is stealing money, the individual cash drawer system may make it easier to trace the theft.

792 **Endorse all checks as soon as they are received.** This will ensure that the check can only be deposited into the school district's bank account.

793 **Only accept checks for the amount that is due.** Don't allow your school district to become a check cashing operation.

Wire Transfer Controls

794 **If your wire transfer software is maintained on a local hard drive, ensure that the computer on which the software resides is in a locked area with strict password protection.**

795 **Before in-house wire transfers take place, require two passwords (executed by two different individuals) to be provided.** This will require the person who is preparing the wire transfer to obtain the approval of a supervisor.

796 **Ensure that firewalls and intrusion detection controls are in place to prevent intrusions from hackers.**

797 **If a wire transfer is conducted by fax or phone, require the bank to confirm the destination and amount of the transfer by calling a school district representative before the wire transfer takes place.**

Vendor Controls

798 Maintain a complete list of approved vendors which can be compared to the invoice before the check is issued.

799 Require vendors to provide complete street addresses and social security numbers/federal tax ID numbers. Post office boxes are often used to create phony vending operations.

800 Your competitive bidding process should be periodically reviewed to ensure all bids are fairly awarded. It is important to avoid bids from employee's relatives or to vendors who are not among the lower bidders.

Computer Controls

801 Secure your district's computer servers and wiring closets. Limiting the access to these areas can prevent unauthorized access to information or theft of equipment.

802 The school district's computer use policy should educate employees on how to secure their laptops. Oftentimes, school computers are left unattended in a vehicle or in the classroom.

803 Require all employees who use school computers to sign a computer use policy. The policy should specify that the computer is not to be used for personal use and should outline the consequences of misuse of the computer.

804 Monitor employee access to the district's network. If employees are logging in at unusual times, such as the middle of the night or on weekends, it could indicate a problem with a hacker.

805 School computer users should store sensitive information on the network and not on the computer hard drive. If the computer is stolen, sensitive school related information could be obtained if it is stored on the computer hard drive.

806 Never allow school sensitive information to be stored or shared on portable devices such as data sticks.

807 Ensure that all schools sensitive data is removed from devices if they are being serviced by repair/warranty vendors. Even your copiers and printers have hard drives that could store sensitive information.

808 Completely erase data or physically destroy the computer's hard drive before disposing of the computer.

Equipment Controls

809 Develop a formal policy that outlines the school district's guidelines for maintaining control over equipment. This policy should address:

- The equipment that is covered under the policy and the persons responsible for the equipment.
- The minimal cost below which equipment will not be inventoried.
- The types of inventory records that should be maintained.
- The physical controls that are in place (or should be in place) to protect the equipment.
- The timeframe for conducting periodic inventories.

810 Engrave the name of the school district (or some other type of unique marking) on valuable school equipment. The marking should be in a location where it cannot be easily seen or removed.

811 Assign responsibility of small, high dollar equipment (laptops, phones, projectors, power tools, etc.) to a specific employee. These employees should be responsible for the equipment's use and secured storage.

812 Conduct an inventory of school equipment on a yearly basis.

813 Commonly used items such as gasoline, paper, or food should be maintained in a locked, controlled setting.

814 Use magnetic strips in high value books to prevent theft.

815 Use door readers and alarmed exits in your library to prevent theft of books and equipment.

Additional Controls

816 Whenever possible, limit the use of cash since it is difficult to track its use.

817 Limit the use of credit cards to a few select school employees. Upon completion of use, the credit card should be turned in, along with all original receipts.

818 Ensure that all proper documentation and/or invoices are attached to all employee expense reports before they are approved.

819 Control payroll fraud by periodically looking for names of unknown employees or employees who are no longer employed by the school district.

The controls listed here are far from being complete. To be successful in preventing fraud and internal theft, training, periodic reviews, and a check and balance system must be implemented on a frequent basis.

Traffic Control Before, During, and After a Crisis

Simply due to the configuration of the roadways and pick up/drop off areas around a school, traffic congestion concerns, and the perceived traffic danger during student arrival and dismissal times, some parents may be reluctant to allow their student to bike or walk to and from their school.

This often results in more parents driving their children to school, thereby increasing the safety and security problems associated with traffic congestion.

Can you imagine how your safety and security concerns would be elevated to another level during and after a crisis? For this reason, there are a number of traffic security concerns that should be addressed before a crisis occurs. By addressing your school's drop-off and pick-up process, traffic conditions become safer for all, including pedestrians, bicyclists and vehicles.

Before a Crisis Occurs

820 Consult with your local police department to develop controls to avoid drivers' blind spots, speeding, and traffic conflicts around each of your schools.

....

821 Don't hesitate to control traffic flow and speed around your school buildings by utilizing speed bumps, traffic circles, and one way traffic patterns.

....

822 Ensure that landscaping, signs, and fencing around your school do not block a driver's vision.

....

823 Locate your bus drop off and pick up areas in a designated, marked, loading and unloading zone near a designated and supervised entrance.

824 Design your bus drop off and parking areas so a bus does not have to back up or turn around to park.

825 Repeatedly instruct students to never walk in front of a bus. This is especially important for your younger students.

826 Mark the curb lanes around your school as prohibited parking.

827 Ensure your student drop off and pick up areas are clearly marked and kept separate from bus traffic.

Traffic Control During and After a Crisis

A critical crisis planning consideration that is often overlooked involves the control of both incoming and outgoing traffic at your school during and after a crisis.

828 Develop a plan to address the spontaneous arrival of family members, onlookers, volunteers, the media, and staff members from other schools.

Understand that the immediate control of traffic on your school grounds may not be an important law enforcement matter, especially if they are busy dealing with the crisis.

829 Consider utilizing school staff members, wearing reflective orange vests, to direct traffic away from the school once the crisis has been addressed. As mentioned earlier, if law enforcement is dealing with a crisis, traffic control is not one of their priorities.

830 Meet with your local law enforcement and emergency responders to coordinate your district's roles and responsibilities for traffic control (both vehicular and pedestrian) on school property. This must be done long before a crisis occurs.

831 Each of your schools should have a plan to allow emergency vehicles access to all areas of your school facilities and grounds. Walk around your school and look for areas that are cluttered by vehicles or objects that would prevent emergency vehicles from providing a clear and 'rapid response' to one of your schools.

832 Inform your emergency service volunteers (fire fighters, EMS personnel) where they should park if they respond with their private vehicles.

833 Strictly enforce the parking regulations around your school buildings. This means maintaining clear access for fire lanes, handicap parking areas, etc.

834 Develop plans for walk-away evacuations that clearly indicate the routes to assembly locations and methods to ensure accountability of your students. If an immediate evacuation is ordered, students can be instructed to rapidly walk away from the school building. This is often the case if there is not enough time to assemble your buses.

835 Develop bus staging or loading areas that are away from the school building or areas of risk. If a crisis is taking place in the school, your bus pick up area cannot be located right outside the school.

836 If at all possible, do not allow parents to pick up their students at the school if an evacuation is underway. The release of students in evacuation situations should be done at prearranged locations away from the crisis area.

837 When it is safe to do so, use your local television and radio stations to provide parent-student reunification information to the general public.

838 **Students who drive to school should not be allowed to utilize their own vehicles for evacuations.** Think about it, a large number of student vehicles leaving your school grounds could easily hinder evacuation and block access of responding emergency vehicles. Additionally, if students are leaving in their own cars, it will be impossible to account for the whereabouts of all students.

Visitors in Your School

Your visitor control program must clearly define your school district's position on authorized and unauthorized visitor access as well as the responsibilities and interaction of your staff with these visitors. Keep these ideas in mind when developing your visitor control best practices:

Door Controls

839 **Place signage on all of your exterior doors identifying your school's visitor control procedures.** All visitors should be directed to one main entrance door.

840 **Exterior door visitor signs should be highly visible (blaze orange) and readable (large font).** Locate the signs at eye level.

841 **Whenever possible, maintain only one main entrance near the school office for visitors to enter your school building.**

842 **Consider the use of a camera, intercom, and buzzer system at the school main entrance to screen visitors who attempt to enter your school.**

Access controls for these doors should be located at the desk of each main office secretary. Make sure your office personnel understand the protocols for allowing (or not allowing) visitor access to your school.

843 Immediately after the majority of your students have entered your building, secure all of your exterior doors, including the main entrance doors. I have consulted with a number of schools that allow 45 minutes to one hour to pass before the doors are secured. Keep in mind, most school shootings occur in the morning.

844 Doors used by students to go outside for recess or other activities should be locked behind students and only opened when the class is returning to the building. A school employee could be present to admit students who are re-entering the building or the instructor/supervisor should use a key or fob to re-enter the building. A staff member should never wedge open a door for later entry.

845 Use school staff proximity cards with card readers at the most frequently used doors. This may include teachers' parking lot entrances, the main entrance, doors used for recess and playground activities, doors used for physical education classes, etc.

846 Never chain or block a door to keep it closed; it must always be available as an emergency exit.

847 Consider using magnetic locks on doors so they close more easily.

848 Minimize the number of exterior doors which may be opened from the outside.

Visitor Controls

849 Use a brightly colored visitor sign-in/sign-out book in your main office.

850 Ask all visitors to provide photo identification to verify their identity.

851 Require visitors to leave their driver's license or car keys at the office when signing in. This will ensure the visitor returns to main office when leaving the school.

852 Require your visitors to wear brightly colored, easily identifiable badges. A 5"x7" brightly colored (orange/lime green) badge worn around the visitor's neck will allow school staff to identify approved visitors from a distance.

853 Don't be afraid to say 'no' to a visitor's request. If the visitor is dropping off an item for a student, the visitor doesn't have to take it to the classroom; that's a duty for the hall monitor.

854 Call a student to the office to see a visitor — don't send the visitor to the student.

Main Office Controls

855 Never provide detailed information regarding your school's emergency response plans to unknown individuals. If an unknown individual makes such a request, simply state that the school has emergency response procedures but we cannot discuss them. Better yet, refer them to your district administrator.

856 Provide a duress alarm or panic button for the school receptionists. A duress alarm could be added to your existing alarm system to provide a signal to several locations, such as the principal's office, the police department or the school resource officer.

857 Keep an eye on your video security monitors. Oftentimes the security monitor is located in another room and cannot be observed by office staff. The security monitors should be centrally located to ensure that multiple office staff members are able to view the monitors at all times.

Building Controls

🔑 **858** **Consider placing a highly visible large-screen monitor in the hallway to provide a constant reminder to students and visitors that their actions are being monitored and recorded.** I've heard the argument from schools that they don't want to tip their hand and let students know where the cameras are located. I would bet that most students know where your cameras are located throughout your school — you're just letting them know they are being supervised.

859 **Secure your delivery doors, technology education garage doors, and custodial entrances when not in use.**

860 **Maintain a delivery log.** This includes the name of the vendor company, name of the delivery employee, the license plate number of their vehicle, the date and time of their arrival and departure, and any other pertinent information.

861 **Develop an emergency announcement regarding the entrance of an unauthorized visitor or intruder into the school building.** Your lockdown procedures may need to be used if the visitor or intruder cannot be found and identified quickly.

Staff and Student Controls

862 **Develop a procedure for your students to report strange or suspicious visitors on school grounds.** This procedure should allow students to report suspicious activities using email, text messaging, voice mail, your school's website, etc.

🔑 **863** **Ensure all school doors are closed and secured when your custodians are working inside the building during after school hours.** This is especially important to protect school employees working late at night. It's also important to require night custodians to carry a cell phone for emergency purposes.

864 Employees working in the school after-hours should never open doors to allow strangers to enter the building.

865 Educate all school staff on how to confront potential strangers. At a minimum, your staff should be trained how to report strangers to the office if they do not feel safe in approaching someone. Consider these visitor approach strategies:

866 Simply ask "Can I help you?" Those four words may be the most effective when approaching a visitor or stranger in your school. Simply asking "Can I help you?" places the visitor in a 'defensive' approach — they must now answer why they are in your school. Once the visitor provides an answer to "Can I help you?" assist them if possible.

Go with your gut feeling; if it doesn't feel right, it probably isn't right and further action is required.

867 If it is safe to do so, escort visitors to the office to sign the visitor log book. Tell them to wait in the office and the student in question will be brought to the office to see them.

868 State to the visitor "I forgot your name... " A visitor with good intentions will have no qualms about providing their name and showing appropriate identification. A visitor with bad intentions does not want to give his or her name; they don't want to be noticed, supervised, or identified. Here's a little trick that is quick and effective, forcing a visitor to provide their name:

Let's say the visitor answers "Tom." Your reply: "No, I know your first name is Tom, I just can't remember your last name."

This may place the visitor on the hot seat. Will they provide their full name as well as identification that will reveal their identity? If they do provide their full name and their identification appears to be legit, escort them to the main office. Remember to go with your gut feelings — if it doesn't feel right, they probably shouldn't be there.

869 **Ask a stranger, "How is your mother doing?"** The only thing a visitor with bad intentions dislikes more than physical contact is someone getting too personal with them. By asking "How is your mother doing?" you can get a stranger to think you know his or her family. This is a great method to force a visitor's hand — get personal.

870 **Understand how and when to get physically close to strangers.** Visitors who are in your school for the wrong reasons do not want confrontation or to be touched. By simply placing a hand on the visitor's arm or shoulder, you have violated their personal space — potential panic time. Asking "Can I help you?" with a physical touch is often very threatening to a stranger and may tip you off to their intentions.

871 **Instruct your students to never open school doors to strangers or even adults they may know.**

872 **If you are not comfortable in approaching a visitor — don't hesitate, call the police.** This is the easiest, safest, but least used method to deal with an unknown visitor. Police are paid for the risks they take; this is one of those risks. A visitor with good intentions has nothing to worry about — it's just a few minutes out of their day to explain their actions.

873 **Throughout the school year educate parents about your school's visitor control procedures and the importance of everyone following the rules.** Mailings, emails, and parent-teacher conferences are great tools to get this message out to your students' parents.

Parents may become confrontational when asked to follow your visitor control plan every time they visit your school. These security controls are in place to protect your students and staff; they must be followed by all.

Warning Signs of a Potentially Violent Student

Would you believe me if I said that the majority of school shooters provided 'signals or warning signs' — both direct and indirect — to others regarding their problems? Nearly all of the school shooters engaged in behavior that concerned others — usually adults. Unfortunately, these behavioral concerns often go unnoticed or unreported.

874 **Educate school employees on the early warning signs of a potentially violent student.** These early warning signs may include:

- Depression.
- The individual telling others 'I'm depressed.'
- Drug and alcohol use.
- Threats of suicide.
- Stops hanging around with his/her usual friends.
- Change in eating habits.
- Noticeable change in dress.
- Grades begin to drop — low school interest.
- Low self esteem.
- Individual is a loner.
- Does not fit into any peer group.
- An affiliation with gangs.
- An obsession with a particular person.
- An obsession with violent acts, weapons, and bombs.
- Irresponsibility — they won't take responsibility for their actions; it's always someone else's fault.
- Individual is cruel to animals — they brag about it.
- Behavior changes — major mood swings.
- Threats of violence: always take them seriously — act on rumors.
- Inappropriate access to, possession of, and use of guns.

- Has brought a gun or other weapon to school in the past.

- Has a background of serious disciplinary action.

- Has little or no supervision/support from parents or responsible adults.

- Has been a victim of or witness to continual abuse — both physical and mental.

- Has been a victim of bullying and harassment.

- Expression of violence in writings and drawings.

875 Learn to recognize the 'imminent' warning signs of a potentially violent student. When a student displays imminent warning signs, immediate action must be taken to maintain school security. It is paramount that you quickly mobilize law enforcement and appropriate school personnel.

These imminent warning signs include:

- Possesses and/or uses a firearm or other weapon.

- Repeated suicide threats and statements.

- Detailed threats of lethal violence stating the time, place, and method.

- Development of a 'hit list.'

- Severe rage for minor reasons.

- Severe destruction of property.

- Serious physical confrontations with family members and other students.

- Seeks information on how to obtain a weapon such as a handgun.

876 Seek out your school's negative leaders and the less popular when asking for student input or when organizing committees within the school. Schools in particular have huge issues with student problem solving, tending to cater to the popular — the athletes or the best students. This type of naïve focus will only compound your problems.

877 Consider developing peer mediation groups involving all types of children, from the straight 'A' student to the most troubled. During these peer mediation groups, provide equal responsibility to the most influential kids of the 'positive' and 'negative' groups to force them to interact with each other.

878 Establish peer mediation groups that provide an opportunity for children to have a platform, establish membership, and a place for them to talk with a neutral person who will be honest with them. Each child deserves their turn to talk. No profanity or disrespect is allowed. Draw straws to see who talks first. You may not agree with what a child is saying or how they express themselves but it is important that you hear what they have to say.

879 Develop a uniform disciplinary code. For example, if a child from a 'negative' group is disciplined, the star athlete better receive the same punishment for the same offense. Problem students have a strong idea of justice — listen to them. If your school disciplinary policy is unfair, your school will pay every day until justice is served.

880 Don't lecture students, talk with them. Kids are not looking for another lecture when they screw up — they get enough of that at home. All students want to feel 'membership' in their school. Students are crying out for opportunities to make better choices with their lives — give it to them.

881 Reach out to a troubled student every day. Challenge every school administrator, teacher, coach, and custodian to reach out to one troubled student every day — a pat on the head, saying hello, or just asking "How is your day going?" Interceding when a student hits a bump in the road by showing them you truly care will reap great dividends. Become a hero to a troubled student. Affect our children's lives by listening and by truly caring — not just teaching them math or science.

"Proper preparation prevents poor performance."

– Charlie Batch, NFL quarterback

SCHOOL **SAFETY** BEST PRACTICES

Your school district's safety program should focus on five main concerns:

- Ensuring all of your school buildings and grounds are free of unsafe physical hazards and unsafe conditions.
- Ensuring your students and staff are not involved in unsafe behaviors or unsafe acts that may lead to accidents and injuries.
- Protecting your students and staff from threats outside of the school environment — weather related, traffic concerns, contaminants in the air, etc.
- Protecting all students and staff from unwanted physical contact or confrontation with one another (also a school security concern).
- Protecting students and staff from unwanted physical contact or confrontation from others outside of your school (also a school security concern).

When effective school safety plans have been developed and implemented, your students, their parents, and your staff members can focus their attention on the 'business of learning,' rather than worrying if their school is safe.

Throughout the school year, your various school safety plans should be thoroughly reviewed with all staff members — it is then your administrators' and teachers' responsibility to enforce the applicable safety rules with the students under their supervision and care.

Aerial Lifts

Sometime during the year, your school district will use an aerial lift, whether it is owned or rented, to allow employees to work at heights unreachable with a ladder.

In many schools, untrained parents, students, and staff members use the aerial lifts to decorate for a dance or theater production. The chance of an aerial lift accident resulting in serious injury or even death is just too great to allow this unsafe practice to continue.

A recent safety study concluded:

- Three-quarters of fatalities in tip-overs of aerial lifts result from falls.
- Nearly two-fifths of the tip-overs occurred when the scissor lift was extended over 15 feet, mostly while driving the lift.
- In one-fifth of the falls the operator was ejected from the scissor lift, mostly when an object struck the lift.
- Further fall deaths occurred after removal of chains or guardrails, or while standing on or leaning over railings.

The majority of these accidents and deaths can be prevented if your school implements and enforces stringent aerial lift safety practices.

882 **Never allow your students to operate an aerial lift.** Many school districts allow their students to use aerial lifts when decorating for dances, prom, or a theater production. Even with proper training and their parent's permission, students should never be allowed to operate the aerial lift.

883 **If your school district decides to make the unwise decision to allow students to operate aerial lift devices, ensure they are trained in the safe operation of the specific device they will operate.** This training should be provided by your district's safety coordinator, an authorized and qualified in-house staff member, or an outside qualified trainer.

This training should include, but not be limited to:

- Classroom training on the specific aerial lift device.
- A hands-on test to prove competency.
- Instructions on pre-use inspection.
- Recordkeeping requirements.
- Training must conform to all OSHA requirements.

884 **Ensure all lift operators understand, sign and return an 'Operating Manual Acknowledgement Form and Training Record.'** Many examples of these forms can be found on the internet.

885 Ensure that all lift operators are trained and certified in the safe operation of aerial lifts in accordance with your district policy, the manufacturer's recommendations, and OSHA regulations CFR 1926.453 and 29 CFR 1926.67 and that these devices are maintained in accordance with the manufacturer's recommendations and sound safety practices.

886 Don't loan your aerial lifts to outside contractors. If they are borrowed, the contractors who operate or use the school owned aerial lift devices must comply with the following:

- Only employees of contractors who are approved to perform work on school property may be permitted to borrow your aerial lift devices.

- The employee of the contractor must review and sign the 'School District Aerial Device Use Waiver and Indemnification Agreement.'

- The supervisor responsible for the contracted work shall return the signed form to you buildings and grounds supervisor prior to beginning the job.

887 Remove the key of the aerial lift when the operator is not present. The key should be returned to the head custodian or immediate supervisor (if the head custodian is not present) when the operator no longer needs the aerial lift for the elevated task.

888 Never allow anyone to use your aerial lift without a trained school staff member present.

889 Never make a change or modification to the original equipment manufacturer (OEM) aerial lift design without the written permission of the manufacturer. This written permission from the manufacturer should be kept on file in the equipment records of the school's buildings and grounds department.

890 Lift operators should always wear hard hats if an overhead hazard exists. Your district's safety coordinator should be consulted if additional personal protective equipment or other safety equipment is required when operating the aerial lift.

891 **Inspect your aerial lift as the manufacturer requires.** This is usually every 3 months or after 150 hours of use, whichever comes first.

892 **The operator(s) must perform pre-use inspections on the aerial lift device.** Report any lift deficiencies, damage, repair needs, or unsafe conditions to your supervisor immediately. Check operating and emergency controls, safety devices (such as, outriggers and guardrails), personal fall-protection gear, wheels and tires, and other machine components specified by the manufacturer. Also look for possible leaks (air, hydraulic fluid, and fuel-system) and loose or missing parts. These inspection forms can be obtained from the lift manufacturer.

893 **The operator(s) should conduct an inspection of the work area to ensure that the area in which the device will be operated is free of unsafe conditions.**

- Check the area where the lift will be used, looking for a level surface that won't shift.
- Check the slope of the ground or floor — a lift may not work properly on steep slopes that exceed slope limits set by the manufacturer.
- Look for hazards such as holes, drop-offs, bumps, debris, overhead power lines, and other obstructions.
- Don't ever forget to set outriggers, brakes, and wheel chocks — even if you're working on a level slope.

894 **Remove from service any aerial lift or platform that does not operate properly or is in need of repair.** A qualified mechanic must make all repairs using equivalent replacement parts. Substitution of parts is not wise; they have been known to cause accidents. De-energize and lockout/tagout aerial lifts before attempting any maintenance or repairs.

895 **When the aerial lift is in use, make sure the lift platform chains or doors are closed.** Many operators have fallen from an elevated lift simply because they failed to secure the chains or doors on the lift platform.

896 **Remind lift operators to always stand on the floor of the lift platform.** Operators should never climb on or lean over the guardrails or ride on the bumpers.

897 **Never exceed the manufacturer's load-capacity limits.**

898 **Be sure proper personal fall protection is provided and used.**

899 **Never exceed vertical or horizontal reach limits or the specified load-capacity of the lift.**

900 **When using an aerial lift near pedestrian traffic, always use work-zone warnings, such as caution tape, cones, and signs.** The last thing you want is a custodian working in an elevated lift in front of a door when students are exiting the area.

901 **When students are in the hallway between classes, lower the lift and wait for everyone to disperse.**

902 **Never drive an elevated lift platform.** When elevated and moving, you may not be able to see what is directly below you.

903 **When the aerial lift is not in use, store it in a secured area away from students.** If the lift cannot be stored in a segregated area away from your students, ensure the key is removed and a sign is placed on the lift stating 'Keep Off.'

A fall from an elevated aerial lift will almost always be serious. Proper safety controls must be followed each and every time a lift is used in your school.

Animals and Plants in the Classroom

Service Animals

The Americans with Disabilities Act defines a 'service animal' as a dog that is individually trained to work or perform tasks for the benefit of a person with a disability. This definition does not include animals whose function is to provide comfort, companionship, or emotional support.

904 **Determine if the service animal is required because of a disability, if it has been properly trained, and how it will assist the individual.**

905 **Ask your school district legal counsel to develop service animal policies and procedures.** As a starting point, many good examples of animal policies and procedures can be found on the internet.

906 **Require a written request that details the specific need for the animal and the service it will perform.** This information needs to be submitted before the animal is allowed in your school.

907 **Require documentation from the requesting individual's health care provider outlining their specific needs.**

908 **Require documentation that the service animal has received proper training and all appropriate vaccinations have been provided.**

909 **Require a signed waiver indemnification agreement that provides proof of insurance that would address any damage or injury caused by the service animal.**

910 Develop a policy that restricts service animal use if it cannot be properly controlled by its handler, interferes with school activities, or poses a threat to the safety and health of others within the school.

911 Develop animal interaction training programs for students and staff. These training programs may include:

- Asking a student who uses a service animal to demonstrate how the animal assists in their daily activities.

- Asking the trainers to present a demonstration for everyone in the school.

- Showing videos that provide information on the use of service animals.

Non-Service Animals

912 Allow non-service animals in the school only when they are part of an educational program.

913 Ensure these animals are controlled by a qualified handler, to reduce the accident and injury exposures if the animal were to come in to contact with students or staff members.

914 Obtain written certification that the animal is in good health and is not a carrier of any disease.

915 Develop a list of animals that will not be allowed in your school at any time. Creatures such as black widow spiders, hamsters, snakes, and birds should not be allowed in your school.

Plants in School

916 Teachers should thoroughly familiarize themselves with any plants they plan to have in their classroom.

917 Ask parents and students beforehand if there are any student allergies associated with the handling of plants.

918 Never allow poisonous or allergy-causing plants in the class-room.

919 Never allow the burning of plants which might contain allergy causing oils, such as poison ivy.

920 Clearly understand which plants are edible and non-edible before they are brought into the classroom. This is especially important when young children are involved.

921 Never allow students to taste plants without clear direction from the teacher.

922 Require students to wear gloves while handling plants and wash their hands afterward.

Appliances in School

Every year, I am contacted by schools to determine if it is acceptable to allow teachers and other staff members to use personal home appliances in their classroom. When determining if school employees can bring appliances into the school, there are a number of general safety and fire safety concerns that you should consider:

923 The best (and safest) recommendation is to ban all outside appliances from your school or classroom setting. Some schools allow appliances to be used in the classroom but only after they have been inspected and approved by the maintenance department — a monumental task for any school. Cold weather and winter holidays can attract even more electrical items such as decorative holiday lights, coffee warmers and portable heaters.

924 Check the school district's insurance coverage which may have specific requirements concerning electrical appliances.

925 Use a request form requiring prior approval from the principal or other administrator before allowing employees to bring microwaves, coffee makers, space heaters, or other appliances to school for personal use. The application should emphasize that adult supervision is required, as personal appliances such as coffee makers and microwave ovens can cause serious injuries to students when hot liquids are spilled.

926 Understand the cost to operate personal appliances in your school. Over the course of a school year, a small appliance may cost $20 — $30 in electricity to operate; larger appliances such as refrigerators and window air conditioners may cost between $50 — $75. Multiply these costs by the number of classroom appliances in your school and you will see that these costs can add up quickly.

927 If your district has been trying to reduce energy costs, mention appliance energy savings in your policy. Some school districts charge a fee, between $20–$75, for an appliance in the classroom, to help defer utility costs.

928 Be aware of the fire safety concerns with personal appliances. Small appliances such as heaters and fans could be knocked over presenting a serious fire exposure if the motor were to overheat.

929 If you allow various appliances in your school, they must be Underwriters Laboratories (UL) approved. This still won't prevent the appliance or its electrical components from being damaged and starting a fire somewhere down the road — a potentially dangerous proposition if appliances are left plugged in (and unsupervised) during weekends or vacation times.

930 Recognize that appliance electrical cords may present trip and fall concerns. I'm sure you've seen it before — electrical cords are often strung in walking areas presenting a significant trip and fall exposure.

931 Never allow light-duty household decorative lights in the school. When lights are strung from ceiling tile grids or thumb-tacked to walls, the insulation can become damaged and cause electric fires.

932 Portable heaters are typically designed for occasional use in small residential spaces and are not appropriate for constant operation in large settings such as classrooms. Schools contain literally tons of paper which can pose a serious fire safety hazard if located too close to heaters.

933 Require the use of classroom microwave ovens or appliances be related to the curriculum and that they be used only under strict teacher supervision.

934 Limit appliances to your teacher lounge where student access can be restricted. If you allow such appliances in the teacher lounge, be clear that the school district is not responsible for loss or damage to personal property.

935 Always maintain at least 36" of clearance between the appliance and any combustible products such as wood or paper.

936 Ensure that the appliances will only be used where students will not have access to or contact with the appliance. This is especially important around small children.

937 Unplug all appliances when not in use. This is important during the weekends and vacation times when no one is present in the school.

As you can see, the potential serious life safety concerns associated with allowing the use of outside appliances by staff members is great; the required safety components are monumental. The best and safest option is to develop a policy that bans the use of personal appliances in your school.

Art Class

With the ever present exposure to combustible materials, kiln fumes, and potentially hazardous substances, art class teachers must ensure that adequate safety controls are in place and followed at all times.

938 **Make sure your kiln is located in a separate, secured, fire rated room.**

939 **Ensure your kiln is covered with a hood or ventilation system that exhausts fumes to the outside of the building.** Over the years, I have come across a number of school kilns where there is no ventilation system in place. I have also seen ventilation systems that exhaust the fumes in to another part of the building — poor planning when the kiln was installed.

940 **Ensure your kiln is equipped with an automatic shutoff control.** This is especially important since the majority of kiln firing takes place after normal school hours.

941 **Develop procedures where the after school custodian checks on after-hours firing of the kiln.** The art teacher must inform the custodian when the kiln is to be fired and when it is set to shut off. These checks by the custodian should be documented to ensure they are taking place.

942 **In reality, an in-use or hot kiln should not be left on overnight unless it is supervised.**

943 **Flammables, combustibles and aerosols should never be stored in your kiln room.** Only clay products should be stored in this area.

944 Periodically inspect the refractory fire brick inside the kiln unit to ensure that it is not cracked and is in good condition.

945 Make sure heat and smoke detectors are installed in the kiln room to provide emergency notification, especially during after-hours firing.

946 **Kilns must not be started or unloaded by students.** Only qualified school staff should fire and unload the kiln.

947 **Limit student entry and exit to the kiln room.** Ideally this room should be locked and have a window so activities can be viewed at all times.

948 Ensure glazes used in the art room are labeled 'non-toxic' or 'safe for use on eating utensils.'

949 Require all paint spraying to be performed outside of the building unless there is a functioning exhaust system that is away from all ignition sources.

950 Use extra care when students are using electrical appliances or tools to heat, mix, spray, burn, or etch. Good supervision is needed to ensure students maintain a safe distance from one another to prevent an accident from occurring.

951 **Ensure that sharp tools are secured when not in use.** Knives and scissors should be accounted for at the end of each class period. Paper cutters should be equipped with a finger barrier especially when used around small children.

952 Provide ground fault circuit interrupter (GFCI) protection for electrical outlets near water sources such as clean up sinks, pottery wheels, etc.

Automated External Defibrillators

Even though the incidence rate of cardiac arrest is greater in adults than in children, research indicates that cardiac arrest in children is increasing — just one incident of this nature can have a devastating impact on your school district.

You can no longer consider your schools are just for children. Schools are frequented morning, afternoon, and evening by all ages — faculty members, parents, grandparents, school visitors, and sports spectators. When people of all ages use your school facilities, the chance that your school will use an automated external defibrillator (AED) increases.

953 **Utilize your school nurse to oversee the school district's AED program.** Just as school nurses oversee school district screening programs for vision, hearing, and other health related issues, they are well suited to take the lead in developing your district's AED programs.

954 **Ascertain how many AED units are needed in your school to ensure 'rapid response' in an emergency situation.** Review the size and layout of your building to determine the best location for and the number of defibrillators needed.

955 **Maintain readily available AED units throughout the school within a 1-1.5 minute walk from anywhere in your school.**

956 **Set a goal of no more that 4-5 minutes from the time the victim collapses to defibrillation with the AED unit.**

957 **Review the types and locations of athletic events and extracurricular events relevant to the location of the defibrillators.**

958 Ensure the critical components of an AED program are part of your school district's emergency response plan.

959 Ensure your emergency response plan shows how to activate your AED team.

960 Make sure an adequate number of AED response team members are available whenever school is in session or school sponsored activities are taking place.

961 Ensure an effective communication system is in place that will provide emergency AED response to activities held outside of the school building.

962 Schedule maintenance of the AED units according to the original equipment manufacturer's guidelines.

963 Consider having a physician review your school district's AED program and assist with employee training regarding appropriate use and misuse of the AED.

Bleacher Safety

According to a current study by the Consumer Product Safety Commission, more than 19,000 people are treated annually in hospital emergency rooms for bleacher related injuries.

Falls from bleachers occur when guardrails are missing from the backs or open sides of the bleachers. Falls also occur when there are openings between components in the seating and guardrails that are big enough for a person to pass through them.

Regular inspection and maintenance of your bleachers can significantly reduce this accident exposure.

964 Never allow children to climb on the bleacher guardrails. Your event supervisors should be instructed to keep an eye on children who are climbing on the guardrails.

965 Allow adequate time for your custodial staff to set up bleachers prior to an event. Accident and injury exposure increases when custodians are hurried to set up the bleachers. Oftentimes this occurs when an athletic coach does not relinquish the gymnasium and allow adequate time to properly set up the bleachers.

The following twelve best practices are from the Consumer Product Safety Commission's Guidelines for Retrofitting Bleachers. This document can be obtained by visiting their website at: www.cpsc.gov.

966 Guardrails should be present on the backs and portions of the open ends of bleachers where the footboard, seat board, or aisle is 30 inches or more above the floor or ground below. Bleachers with the top row nominally 30 inches above the ground may be exempt from this recommendation.

967 The top surface of the guardrail should be at least 42 inches above the leading edge of the footboard, seat board, or aisle, whichever is adjacent.

968 When bleachers are used adjacent to a wall that is at least as high as the recommended guardrail height, the guardrail is not needed if a 4-inch diameter sphere fails to pass between the bleachers and the wall.

969 Any opening between components of the guardrail or under the guardrail should prevent passage of a 4-inch sphere.

970 Any opening between the components in the seating, such as between the footboard, seat board, and riser, should prevent passage of a 4-inch diameter sphere where the footboard is 30 inches or more above the ground and where the opening would permit a fall of 30 inches or more.

971 The preferable guardrail design uses only vertical members as in-fill between the top and bottom rails. If there are openings in the in-fill that could provide a foothold for climbing, the widest measurement of the opening where the foot could rest should be limited to a maximum of 1.75 inches. Opening patterns that provide a ladder effect should be avoided. If chain link fencing is used on guardrails, it should have a mesh size of 1.25 inch square or less.

972 Aisles, handrails, non-skid surfaces, and other items that assist in access and egress on bleachers should be incorporated into any retrofit project where feasible.

973 The option of replacing bleachers as opposed to retrofitting should always be considered.

974 Materials and methods used for retrofitting should prevent the introduction of new hazards, such as bleacher tip-over, bleacher collapse, guardrail collapse, and contact or tripping hazards.

975 Bleachers should be thoroughly inspected at least quarterly by trained personnel and problems corrected immediately. Records of these actions should be retained.

976 A licensed professional engineer, registered architect, or company that is qualified to provide bleacher products and services, should inspect the bleachers at least every two years and provide a written certification at such time that the bleachers are fit for use.

977 Records of all bleacher incidents and injuries should be retained.

Canoeing and Kayaking

Many school districts incorporate canoeing and kayaking activities in their physical education and outdoors club programs. It is important that proper risk management controls are in place to ensure your students always demonstrate safe and responsible behaviors to manage risks and prevent injuries during these water activities.

Instruction

The amount and level of instruction and direction required by the student may vary based on circumstances such as the student's personal experience, skill level, and physical condition.

978 **Instruction should be provided by a trained and certified national coaching certification program/instructor or from an experienced paddler/rower.** This individual should be capable of demonstrating competencies of a certified instructor, as appropriate, depending on various factors such as level of risk, intensity, accessibility, experience, and skill.

979 **All training sessions should be conducted in a safe environment where students can be made aware of the potential risks involved in canoeing and kayaking.**

980 **Student safety rules are to be reviewed and learned prior to any water participation.** Students must know and follow the rules prior to entering the water for the first time.

981 **Make emergency rescue strategies a critical component of the student training program.**

982 **Each session should start with a proper warm-up, cool-down, and appropriate fitness work.** Drinking water should be made available and consumed by your students as needed.

983 The instructor/supervisor must be familiar with waters the group is paddling in, being aware of hazardous conditions such as rocks and strong currents.

984 Ensure the weather and water conditions are appropriate for the students' capabilities. Don't take your students canoeing in freezing cold water.

Supervision

There are two types of recommended supervision: on-site supervision during instruction and in-the-area supervision during the outings.

985 Ensure your instructor/supervisor or a designated person has lifeguard certification or current first aid qualifications.

986 Ensure all safety rules and procedures are enforced when on the water — no exceptions.

987 Have an emergency action plan in place to deal with accidents and injuries that includes knowing what to do in a person-overboard emergency.

988 Always maintain an accurate up-to-date list of students on the water.

Equipment

989 Make sure all canoeing and kayaking equipment is appropriate and in good condition. Prior to use, all equipment should be inspected regularly by a qualified person.

990 All paddles and oars must be the correct size for the student.

991 All students must wear a properly fitted approved lifejacket or Personal Flotation Device (PFD) with a whistle attached. Require one PFD for each person.

992 A boat safety kit should be carried for each canoe, including a bailing device, a waterproof flashlight, a signaling device (whistle) and 50-foot floating nylon rope.

993 Consider carrying an extra paddle in each canoe.

994 The instructor/supervisor must have a first aid kit and cell phone available at all times.

Facility/Environment Concerns

995 Your instructor/supervisor should check the local weather conditions, forecast, and temperature prior to each outdoor session.

996 Provide a map of the route or the course that is clearly marked, making sure to brief students prior to entering the water.

997 Ensure that an emergency rescue boat is available.

998 Make sure the water course is free of hazards or the hazards are clearly marked.

Clothing/Footwear

999 All students must wear appropriate footwear. This includes footwear that will not easily slide off their feet and has a non-slip sole.

1000 All jewelry should be removed prior to entering the water.

1001 Appropriate protection from weather conditions should be stressed to students. This may include hats, jackets, sunglasses, sun screen, etc.

Other Considerations

1002 Your students should have a medical checkup and a medical history review prior to starting the program.

1003 Ensure your students have submitted a signed 'parent declaration and consent' and 'student declaration form' (student under 18) or 'student declaration form' (student 18 and over) prior to beginning the program.

1004 Encourage parents to register their student in an accident insurance plan.

1005 Any students who suffers an injury during the water activity must be referred to appropriate medical personnel for treatment and rehabilitation and should not return to training until cleared by a qualified medical professional.

1006 Ensure the water activity is suitable to the student's age, ability, mental condition, and physical condition.

1007 Never allow horseplay or students canoeing/kayaking off on their own without the instructor's knowledge.

Canoeing and kayaking activities can be an exciting aspect of your school district's outdoor educational program. Ensure that appropriate safety controls are in place before the activity takes place to avoid accidents and injuries.

Celebration Concerns

Homecoming, athletic championships, and community celebrations often mean a celebratory parade. Oftentimes students, coaches, and other school personnel ride on floats, fire trucks, or other types of vehicles and equipment. Participants must clearly understand their safety responsibilities to minimize the possibility of accidents.

1008 **All school related participants riding on a float or any type of moving equipment should sign a release and waiver form.** This form must clearly explain the activity to take place and the risks involved.

1009 **No one should be allowed to participate if a signed release and waiver is not turned in to your school administration prior to the event.**

1010 **Ensure that your school district's legal counsel approves any release and waiver form before it is implemented.** The waiver form should specifically address the nature of the activity.

1011 **Develop parade safety rules and regulations to be reviewed with all school related participants.** Parade participants must clearly understand they must adhere to the school district's safety rules and regulations.

1012 **Do not allow the use of water guns, bubble machines, silly string, etc. by the parade participants.**

1013 **Closely monitor the dispensing of candy or any other items that may entice observers (especially small children) on to the parade route.** You don't want small children running out close to or in front of a moving vehicle or float.

1014 **Never allow participants to sit on the hoods or trunks of moving vehicles.**

1015 Participants must not sit on vehicles or equipment that is not intended for that purpose — on top of the fire truck hoses, for example. We've all seen the sports championship team riding on top of the fire truck; a tragic accident waiting to occur if someone were to fall off of the truck and be run over by a vehicle.

1016 Your school administration should closely monitor parade activities and immediately correct any risk activity that may lead to an accident. If you determine that an entry or participant is posing a risk to anyone by activities occurring on, or affiliated with the float/vehicle, they must be asked to immediately discontinue such activities.

1017 Your school administration should reserve the right to remove any float, vehicle, or participant at any time. Removal should be based on the administration's assessment relating to safety and security concerns, interference with the progress of the parade, or any other reason that is deemed appropriate.

1018 Protective equipment, especially helmets, must be worn for activities such as rollerblading, biking, skateboarding, and horseback riding.

1019 No alcohol is to be allowed on any float or vehicle at any time.

1020 Never allow smoking on or near floats or motorized vehicles.

1021 No small children should ever be allowed to ride on school sponsored floats.

1022 All drivers must possess a valid driver's license.

1023 All moving floats and vehicles must allow drivers to maintain a 180-degree view of the route at all times.

1024 Emergency exit accessibility must be available on all floats and vehicles.

1025 All parade entries, detached or otherwise, should have direct communication with the driver.

1026 If the blowing of horns, sirens, and playing of loud music is allowed on the parade route, keep it to a reasonable level. Acceptable noise levels should be determined by school administration and any requests to adjust sound levels must be enforced.

1027 Limit the height of all parade floats or activities. Always be careful to prevent floats from striking low hanging branches or coming too close to overhead power lines.

1028 All units carrying people must be equipped with adequate restraining devices (body harness, protective railings) capable of stopping anyone falling from the unit. Anyone riding on the unit must be properly braced and seated.

1029 Instruct all float or vehicle riders that they shall not extend their arms outside of the entry.

1030 Instruct parade participants that in the case of an emergency, they must move to the right of the parade route to allow clear, unobstructed access for the emergency vehicles.

Bonfire Concerns

Every year, I receive phone calls from school administrators asking about the liability and safety controls associated with their time honored tradition of a school sponsored bonfire.

Of course, the risk manager in me believes the best course of action is to not allow a bonfire due to the potential serious injury and property damage concerns.

Understandably, many school districts still allow a school sponsored bonfire. If your district sponsors a bonfire, there are a number of concerns that must be addressed.

1031 **Maintain a minimum of 100 feet (or more) from any type of building or vehicle.** The location of the bonfire is critical.

1032 **Avoid building your bonfire near any low hanging branches, tall grass, or brush piles.** Stay clear of any items that could easily ignite and cause the fire to spread.

1033 **Build a fire pit for the bonfire.** This is one of the best precautions your school can implement. Instead of building the fire on the surface of the ground, dig a hole at least 12-18 inches deep.

1034 **The diameter of your fire pit should be at least two feet wider than the fire itself.** Consider placing small rocks or gravel in the bottom of the pit for proper drainage with a circle of larger stones around the perimeter of the pit.

1035 **Constant adult supervision is required at all bonfires.** Only a responsible adult should tend the fire. Adult supervisors should be placed around the entire perimeter of the bonfire when others are present.

1036 **Small children should never be allowed too close to the bonfire.**

1037 **Never pile firewood too high on the bonfire.** A small amount of wood, combined with kindling materials is enough to start a good fire.

1038 **When possible, don't let flames exceed 3-5 feet in height or width.**

1039 Don't allow your bonfire to take place on a windy day.

1040 Ensure spectators are instructed to stand upwind of the bonfire.

1041 Ask your local fire department to provide a fire truck and fire fighters. If they cannot, maintain fire extinguishers nearby.

1042 Make sure that an adult who knows how to operate the fire extinguisher is present.

1043 Keep a number of five-gallon buckets of water nearby.

1044 Never allow your students to throw flammable materials on the bonfire. Only a responsible adult should tend the fire.

1045 Don't allow the stacking of flammable materials near the fire pit.

1046 Allow only dry, seasoned wood to be used in the bonfire. No railroad ties, no items that are coated or treated, and no old furniture should be allowed on your bonfire.

1047 Never, never, never allow anyone to add gasoline or lighter fluid to the bonfire.

1048 Ensure that a first aid kit is available — just in case of an injury.

1049 Once the bonfire burns out, use a shovel to turn the materials in the fire pit so blowing embers won't sweep out of the pit and start a fire elsewhere. Then douse the area with water.

1050 Adult supervision must be present until the bonfire is completely extinguished and there is no chance of the fire restarting.

Child Care/After School Programs

Your school district may offer child care or after school programs that involve the supervision and care of students beyond normal school day hours. There may be liability in these activities if they take place on your school grounds, in your school facilities, and if the participant must pay for the service.

Your school district may want to consider the following controls to reduce your liability exposure:

1051 Clearly define your after school program's 'hours of operation.' Is this a program that takes place for 1-2 hours after school? Is it available for half an hour at the conclusion of a school sponsored event such as a choir concert or athletic event?

1052 Ensure that adequate adult supervision is provided and a background check has been conducted on all adult supervisors.

1053 Ensure that background checks have been conducted on all of your student age supervisors.

1054 Understand that there is no magic ratio number of students to supervisors. Younger children and special needs children may require more supervision.

1055 At no time should an adult supervisor leave the area or room. Bad things occur when children are unsupervised — never leave the area, even for a minute.

1056 **Keep the children in an area that can be clearly supervised.** Do not have the children in separate rooms with one adult attempting to bounce back and forth between rooms. It is important to avoid segregated areas such as a classroom far away from the activity.

1057 **Parents and guardians must show proper identification when picking up their child.** There should be no exceptions to this rule.

1058 **Require parents and guardians to sign in and sign out their child, including exact times and dates.**

1059 **Do not allow a 'friend of the parent or guardian' to pick up another child.** Children can only be released to the parent or guardian who dropped them off. An exception may be the case of a grandparent (or relative) who comes to pick up the child with prior written notification from the parent or guardian.

1060 **Ensure the care area is secured and supervised to limit intruders from entering or a child from sneaking out without the knowledge of a supervisor.**

1061 **Supervisors or students should never dispense medications even if approved by the parents or guardians.**

1062 **Establish rules of conduct for the children and review them with the parents or guardians.** If a child does not follow the rules of conduct, you may want to consider discontinuing their care.

1063 **Ensure that life safety plans are in place.** This includes fire protocols, evacuation, lockdown, first aid training, etc.

1064 **Ensure that contact phone numbers of the parents and guardians are kept on file in case of emergency.** It is important to maintain an updated listing of the parent's and guardian's home and cell phone numbers.

1065 **Never make the unwise decision to take a child home by vehicle, even with permission.** There have been instances where parents did not come on time to pick up their child and the supervisor made the decision to drive the child home — not an acceptable practice. Immediately contact your school administration if this occurs.

1066 **With respect to the concern of sexual assault activities, ensure that supervisors and students are of the same gender.** Use female supervisors if there are female children in the activity.

1067 **Instruct supervisors to never be segregated in an isolated area or room with a child — especially opposite gender — such as an adult male supervisor and a female child.**

1068 **Never physically harm or strike a child for any reason.**

Classrooms

Your students spend the vast majority of their time in the classroom. For this reason, it is imperative that appropriate safety controls are in place to reduce or eliminate the chance of an accident or injury.

1069 **First aid kits should be readily accessible in the classroom.**

1070 **Post your emergency phone numbers by each classroom phone.** If classroom phones are not present, the teacher should maintain emergency phone numbers on speed dial of their personal cell phone.

1071 Make sure each teacher's classroom keys and emergency crisis plan are readily available in case of an emergency.

1072 Keep your classrooms free of tripping hazards. Teachers should be constantly on the lookout for hazards such as loose floor tiles, frayed carpet corners, protruding nails, holes, loose boards, and objects on the floor.

1073 Classroom aisle widths should be maintained at a safe distance. Keep all exits free of trip hazards. This is especially important during fire or crisis evacuation drills.

1074 Don't place a mirror on or near a classroom exit door. During an emergency, students may mistake the mirror as the exit door.

1075 Ensure that all of classroom mirrors are shatter-proof. This is especially important in elementary schools where small children are present.

1076 Items should be stored at a minimum height to prevent them from falling on to students. Too often, especially in elementary schools, I see items stored on top of cabinets or high on multi-tiered shelving units. A serious injury could occur if these items were to fall on students below.

1077 On a regular basis, require your teachers to remove combustible stored material. Trash and debris should be regularly removed from the classroom to reduce the fire potential.

1078 Ensure that all televisions are secured to their carts. This usually involves strapping or bolting the television to the cart.

1079 **Limit the height of the television carts in the classroom.** Short two tiered carts are preferred to reduce the chance of a child pulling the cart on top of them.

1080 **Pull down projection screens and maps must be secured.** This is to prevent the screen/map from accidentally 'jumping' off its hooks if it is rolled up quickly.

1081 **Periodically inspect all desks and chairs to ensure they are in good condition.**

1082 **Make sure your classroom furniture has no sharp edges.** The chance of a small child cutting themselves on the edge of a sharp desk corner is real. Get down to the child's eye level when inspecting the furniture.

1083 **Ensure storytelling areas or niches are all on one level.** If they are recessed or elevated, they need to be designed to prevent hidden activities or fall injuries.

1084 **Make sure that all classroom shelves, shelving units, and free standing walls are sturdy and secured to prevent them from toppling over or collapsing.**

1085 **Discourage the use of wooden loft areas in the classroom. If you have a loft area, ensure it:**

- Conforms with state building code requirements regarding acceptable indoor wood grade materials.

- Has steps, ladders, and handrails that are in accordance with proper dimensions and load requirements.

- Has guardrails and safety gates that are in accordance with proper dimensions and load requirements.

- Has a fire retardant coating (UL/FM approved fire retardant paint or stain) that reduces the spread of flames and smoke generation.

It's my professional opinion that the use of loft areas (especially in elementary schools) is not a good idea due to the potential fire and student injury exposure and should be removed from your classroom.

1086
Though not recommended in the classroom, play tents should be strictly controlled. Ensure your play tents have:

- The manufacturer's label certifying its construction and flame retardant treatment.
- No heat producing devices such as a computer or monitor, battery, or electric lamps, radios, etc.
- No cords inside or within 36" of the tent.
- No more than two students in the tent at one time.
- No snaps, ties or zippers on the entry flaps or doors.
- A manufacturer recommended flame retardant treatment that is applied after the tent is washed or cleaned.

1087
Prevent second hand or upholstered furniture from being brought to the school. Sanitation and flammability are the major concerns. Educate your teachers that:

- Upholstered furniture can harbor a variety of molds, mildews, and other contaminants which can be transferred from student to student.
- Residential upholstered furniture is not intended for the educational environment.
- At a minimum, the furniture must be treated with a UL/FM approved fire retardant.

1088
Always store sharp edged objects (knives, scissors and paper cutters) out of reach of children. Besides the obvious injury exposure when using these objects, a scissors or knife could be used as a weapon during a combative situation in the classroom.

1089
Store all potentially dangerous materials in a secure locked location out of the reach of children. This includes flammable liquids and cleaning supplies such as bleach, soap concentrate, ammonia products, and disinfectants.

1090
Use ground fault circuit interrupter protection (GFCI) for electrical receptacles near sinks or water sources.

1091 Keep areas around the sinks kept clean and dry. This is important to reduce the exposure to slip and fall incidents.

1092 Ensure teachers never use extension cords as a substitute for permanent electrical wiring. Extension cords are forbidden from running through holes in walls, ceilings, floors, doorways, windows, or attached building surfaces. Extension cords cannot be concealed behind walls, ceilings, or floors.

1093 Electrical outlets should be covered all at all times unless they are in use.

1094 Make sure your hallway student hall monitoring or tutoring stations do not block exit accesses, exits, or exit discharges. Take a common sense approach to ensure tables, desks, benches, and chairs do not create obstructions in the exit corridors.

Climbing Activities

The majority of school districts incorporate climbing activities in their physical education and extracurricular programs. The chance of student injuries from falls is significant but can be reduced by implementing proper fall protection procedures that address the climbing equipment, fall protection requirements, protective surfacing, and student/staff training.

1095 All climbing walls, ropes, nets, and other equipment must be designed for the intended use. Never try to save a few dollars and allow the use of homemade or donated climbing equipment.

1096 All climbing equipment must be installed, used, and stored according to the instructions of the manufacturer. If the climbing equipment is installed improperly, modified, or misused, the liability exposure of the manufacturer is often minimized.

1097 At a minimum, the design and installation of your climbing equipment should conform to the American Society for Testing and Materials (ASTM) standards.

1098 Wall system installations, climbing equipment (including harnesses and ropes), points of attachment, and hardware must be designed and certified by a qualified engineer prior to use and every year thereafter.

1099 Inspect your climbing equipment — every day if it is used frequently or before each use if it is not used on a regular basis. All hardware — including the harnesses, ropes, fixtures, fittings, quickdraws, belay points, and bolt hangers must be inspected. These inspections must be documented and reports retained. No piece of equipment should ever be used if it does not pass the inspection.

1100 Don't develop your own inspection forms if it can be avoided. Contact the equipment manufacturer for appropriate inspection forms.

1101 Ensure that all supervisors know how to properly inspect the equipment per the manufacturer's guidelines.

1102 Always ensure that good supervision controls are in place. Problems arise when a number of students are climbing the wall and only one supervisor is present. If this occurs, limit the number of climbers or increase the number of supervisors.

1103 Train your supervisors on safe use of the climbing equipment as well as first aid and CPR procedures.

1104 Check and double check that students are always secured in their climbing harness.

1105 Provide students with a qualified attendant (the belayer) if they have problems during the climb. The belayer can support the student, prevent them from falling and safely lower them down the climbing wall.

1106
All climbing participants should be wearing approved head protection.

Protective Surfacing

1107
A fall cushioning surface beneath and around the fall zone should be in place that will absorb the impact of a fall. The ANSI Standard F-1292 "Standard Specification for Impact Attenuation of Surface Systems Under and Around Playground Equipment" is a valuable resource to use to develop proper surfacing protocols. Twelve inches of padding (minimum) should be placed at the base of the climbing wall and extend outward to at least eight feet or more.

1108
Always contact the equipment manufacturer to determine the fall height requirements of their equipment.

Student/Staff Training

1109
All students and staff using climbing equipment must receive training on the proper use of the equipment and safety devices.

1110
Student training should include testing whereby students are required to obtain a 100% completion before being allowed to use the climbing equipment.

Minimal training should address:

• Harness/rope inspection procedures.

• How to properly wear body harnesses.

• Techniques for belaying another climber.

• Necessary emergency response procedures.

• Rules and regulations for climbing the walls.

Additional Safety Concerns

1111 Before a child is allowed to participate in a climbing activity, the parent or guardian must be contacted to review rules and concerns of the climbing activity.

1112 Never leave climbing ropes or equipment unattended. Students should never be given the opportunity to use the climbing equipment when a qualified supervisor is not present.

Equipment

1113 Ropes, nets, walls, or other equipment must be specifically designed for the intended use.

1114 Equipment, especially ropes, must be stored according to the manufacturer's instructions.

1115 Climbing safety equipment, including harnesses and ropes, should conform to American Society for Testing and Materials (ASTM) and/or International Association of Alpine Associations (UIAA) standards.

1116 Wall system installation, equipment attachment points, and hardware must be designed and certified by a qualified engineer prior to use, and at least annually thereafter. The design and installation should conform to Climbing Wall Industry Group or ASTM standards as a minimum.

1117 Structural inspections should be carried out at the manufacturer's specified interval.

1118 All hardware including ropes, harnesses, fixtures, fittings, maillons, quickdraws, belay points, and bolt hangers must be inspected daily or prior to use if the climbing wall is used infrequently. All inspections and conditions found must be documented, preferably using a checklist developed specifically for each installed system.

1119 Safety cables should be used where there is any chance of failure of ceiling hardware.

1120 Cargo nets should be raised out of reach when not in use.

1121 The climbing wall installer should provide certificates of insurance, including completed operations, with the school named as an additional insured.

Fall Protection

1122 **Supervise all climbing activities.** In most cases, the supervisor will be a physical education teacher or someone who has been trained not only in the proper and safe use of equipment but also first aid and CPR.

1123 The climbing system should be secured as it is likely that students will want to play on the wall when no one is around to supervise.

1124 **Students using the equipment should be secured in a climbing harness.** The harness should be supported by an overhead rope and the students should be constantly attended by a qualified person (a belayer) so that if the student gets into trouble the belayer can support them, keep them from falling, and lower them safely to the ground.

1125 **The belaying rope must have a controlled-descent device so that if the belayer is unable to support a falling student the device will automatically control the fall.** This technology is used in fall protection for construction workers as well.

1126 **Provide adequate fall protection under and around climbing equipment.** This protection should conform to ANSI Standard F-1292 Standard Specification for Impact Attenuation of Surface Systems Under and Around Playground Equipment.

1127 The fall area under and around the equipment must be protected with a fall cushioning surface that will absorb the impact of a falling student to the point where a head injury would not be sustained. Although there are no standards published specifically for gym ropes, cargo nets, or walls, ANSI Standard F-1292 provides valuable guidance outlining that:

- A minimum of 12" of padding should be at the base of the wall extending out to 8 feet or more.

- Equipment suppliers should be contacted for recommendations specific to the equipment and critical fall height of their products.

Training

1128 Students and teachers using the equipment must have special training in the use of climbing equipment and safety devices. Training should include testing and records of such training and testing should be retained. At a minimum, training should include:

- Harness and rope inspection procedures.
- Proper belaying techniques.
- Emergency response procedures.
- Response to belay device failure or entrapment.
- Rules for climbing walls.
- Set up and take down procedures.
- Reporting problems.

Releases and Waivers

1129 Students must provide a medical certificate stating that a physician has examined them and that they are physically able to safely climb and descend a rope or net of the length required.

1130 An 'Informed Consent' agreement signed by the Parent, Guardian, or Child Custodian must be completed and retained on file prior to any climbing activity.

Compliance Programs

Compliance training is an important (and required) element of every school district's risk management plan for protecting employees and students from injuries and illnesses.

Your district's maintenance employees, custodians, cafeteria employees, science teachers, art teachers, technology education teachers, agriculture science teachers and other select teachers and school personnel will need training that is specialized as well as training that is common to all groups. *Additionally, your compliance training must be presented by a knowledgeable presenter who understands your district's exposures and can interact with your employees to answer any questions they may have.*

The table at the end of this chapter lists some of the requirements for and frequency of training regarding compliance standards for school personnel. The standards that require written plans are also listed.

1131 **Your school district must maintain an OSHA 300 log.** The deadline is March 1st of each year for public sector employers. Additionally, you are required to complete form SBD-10710 annually, which asks for the same information that is on the OSHA 300A form. Unlike OSHA, which requires completion of the log by companies with 10 or more employees, the Wisconsin Department of Commerce makes no distinction; whether your school district has 1, 100, or 1,000 employees, the log must be completed.

It is also your school district's responsibility to:

1132 **Develop Injury and Illness Recordkeeping — Employee Involvement (OSHA 1904.35) procedures.** When hired, your school district must tell each employee how to report an injury or illness. No specific training documentation is required.

1133 **Develop and implement Emergency Action Plans (OSHA 1910.38).** All school employees who may need to evacuate the facility in an emergency must be trained when initially hired. A written emergency action plan should be maintained at each of your school's facilities.

1134 Evaluate your Occupational Noise Exposure (OSHA 1910.95). Any school employees who are exposed to noise at or above an 8-hour time-weighted average of 85 decibels must receive training and be provided appropriate hearing protection. Initial training should precede exposure to the noise level and be repeated annually thereafter.

1135 Determine the appropriate Personal Protective Equipment (OSHA 1910.132) that must be worn by your school employees. Each employee required to use personal protective equipment must be trained in its proper use. This training must take place before the employee is allowed to do work requiring the use of personal protective equipment. Certify the training with the employee's name, date, and subject of training.

1136 Evaluate your district's need for a Respiratory Protection program (OSHA 1910.134). All school employees who use or have the potential to use a respirator must be trained in the proper use and limitations of respirators. The training must precede the use of a respirator. Retraining must be conducted annually and whenever necessary to ensure safe use. If your school provides respirators for voluntary use or if the school district allows employees to use their own respirator, certain precautions need to be in place to ensure that the respirator itself does not present a hazard. The school district is required to maintain records of employee medical evaluations and fit testing results.

1137 Determine if your schools have Permit-required Confined Spaces (OSHA 1910.146). Training must be provided for any employees who have active roles in confined space entry operations. Your school district must train those employees before the initial confined space entry assignment, before a change in duties, whenever there is a change in permit space operations that presents a hazard about which an employee has not previously been trained, or whenever the employer has reason to believe either that there are deviations from the permit space entry procedures required or that the employee's knowledge of these procedures is inadequate.

Employee rescue service personnel must make practice rescues at least once every 12 months.

Affected supervisors must fill out and sign the permit required for permit space operations, verifying that all appropriate precautions have been taken. Canceled entry permits must be retained for at least one year. Training certifications must include each employee's name, the signatures or initials of the trainers, and the dates of training.

1138 **Your district's best option may be to subcontract any required confined space work.** If your district is not able to subcontract the work to be performed, your maintenance director should be required to be on site during entry to ensure all requirements for personal safety are being followed.

Some examples of confined space entry work in schools include: any entry into manholes, tunnels, incinerators, tanks, pits, or heating/ventilation systems.

1139 **Determine your school district's need for a Lockout/Tagout program (OSHA 1910.147).** Training must be provided for all employees whose job duties include performing servicing or maintenance on equipment that must be locked or tagged out for protection.

Lockout/tagout training must precede the exposure to locked out equipment or the use of a lockout system. Retraining shall be conducted whenever necessary to re-establish employee proficiency or to introduce new or revised procedures.

Your school district must certify that employee training has been accomplished and is being kept up to date. The certification shall contain each employee's name and dates of training.

Some examples of school exposures that would require lockout/tagout include: HVAC equipment, replacement of any electrical gear, replacement of ballast, replacement of electrical outlets/switches, or when making additions to electrical circuits.

1140 **Evaluate each school's needs for Medical Services and First Aid (OSHA 1910.151).** Train designated emergency first aid providers when a medical clinic or hospital that is used for the treatment of injured employees is not in near proximity to the school. Employees must be trained prior to responding to any first aid emergency situations.

1141 Implement a Portable Fire Extinguishers program (OSHA 1910.157). If portable fire extinguishers are provided for employee use in the workplace, employees are to be trained in the general principles of fire extinguisher use and associated hazards. All employees who have been designated to use fire fighting equipment as part of an emergency action plan are to be trained to use the appropriate equipment. Training should take place upon initial assignment and at least annually thereafter.

1142 Determine if your school district uses Powered Industrial Trucks (OSHA 1910.178). Anyone operating a powered industrial truck (tow motor, fork lift, etc.) must be trained and evaluated. This training and evaluation must occur before the employee operates the vehicle without direct supervision. Refresher training in relevant topics is needed when the vehicle is operated in an unsafe manner, after any accident or near miss, after an evaluation shows retraining is needed, upon assignment to a different type of truck, and upon changes in the workplace that affect safe truck operation. An evaluation is required at least every three years.

The school district must certify that the operator has been trained and evaluated. The certification must include the operator's name, the dates of the training and evaluation, and the name of the trainer.

1143 Evaluate your district's need for Electrical Training (OSHA 1910.332). All employees who face a risk of electric shock, and/or who work on or near exposed energized parts must be trained. This training must precede exposure and can be of the classroom or on-the-job type.

1144 Address your employee's exposure to Bloodborne Pathogens (OSHA 1910.1030). All school employees who may have occupational exposure to bloodborne pathogens must be trained. This includes your first aid responders. Employees must be trained prior to initial exposure to bloodborne pathogens. Annual retraining is required.

Very specific bloodborne pathogen training records must be maintained. This information must include dates of training, contents of the training sessions, names and qualifications of the trainers, names, and job titles of those trained. These records must be retained for three years.

Bloodborne pathogen exposures in your schools include but are not limited to:

• The school nurse who provides first-aid to sick and injured students and staff members.

• The school building secretary who provides first-aid when the nurse is not in the building.

• Custodians who clean up blood and body fluid spills on the school premises.

• Special education personnel who care for the high-risk students, i.e. those students who drool, bite or are incontinent of stool or urine. This may include the occupational therapist, the speech therapist and the aides to the high-risk students.

• Athletic coaches and trainers who administer first-aid to an injured athlete.

....

1145 Determine which hazardous substances fall under the Hazard Communication Standard (OSHA 1910.1200) —

also known as Right to Know. Train all school employees who have an exposure or a potential for exposure to hazardous chemicals. Employees must be trained prior to initial exposure and when a new chemical hazard is introduced.

The following table provides a comprehensive listing of the compliance programs your school district should address:

Safety Topic	OSHA Standard	School Employees Most Likely Affected	Written Plans and Training Requirements
Asbestos	**1910.1001**	Maintenance and custodial personnel exposed to asbestos (usually during removal or maintenance)	Initial assignment and annually thereafter

Safety Topic	OSHA Standard	School Employees Most Likely Affected	Written Plans and Training Requirements
Access to Employee Exposure and Medical Records, Employee Information	1910.1020	All school personnel	Initial assignment and annually thereafter
Benzene	1910.1028	Science, Art, and Maintenance personnel	Initial assignment and when there are changes in the workplace
Bloodborne Pathogens	1910.1030	Recommended for all school employees	Initial assignment and annually thereafter **Written Compliance Plan is required**
Control of Hazardous Energy (Lockout/Tagout)	1910.147	**Maintenance, Custodial, and Science personnel**	Initial assignment and when there are changes in the workplace **Written Compliance Plan is required**
Electrical	1910.332	Maintenance, custodial, and science personnel	Initial assignment and when there are changes in the workplace
Eye and Face Protection	1910.133	All school personnel	Initial assignment and changes in workplace
Exit Routes, Emergency Action Plans, Fire Prevention Plans	1910.33-39 and 1910.38	All school personnel	Initial assignment and changes in workplace **Written Compliance Plan is required**

Safety Topic	OSHA Standard	School Employees Most Likely Affected	Written Plans and Training Requirements
Fire Alarm Systems	**1910.165**	Maintenance and custodial personnel	Initial assignment and when there are changes in the workplace
Fire — Portable Fire Extinguishers	**1910.157**	**Anyone expected to use a fire extinguisher**	Initial assignment and when there are changes in the workplace
Fire Detection Systems	**1910.164**	Maintenance and custodial personnel	Initial assignment and when there are changes in the workplace
Fire Protection	**1910.155**	Anyone expected to use a fire extinguisher	Initial assignment and when there are changes in the workplace **Written Compliance Plan is required**
Fixed Extinguishing Systems	**1910.158 and 1910.160**	Maintenance and custodians if they inspect extinguishers	Initial assignment and when there are changes in the workplace
Flammable and Combustible Liquids	**1910.106**	Should be reviewed with all school employees — especially maintenance, custodial, and science personnel	Initial assignment and when there are changes in the workplace
Formaldehyde	**1910.1048**	Usually science personnel	If data indicates exposure at or > 0.1 ppm must train at initial assignment and changes in workplace

Safety Topic	OSHA Standard	School Employees Most Likely Affected	Written Plans and Training Requirements
Hazard Communication	**1910.1200**	All school personnel	Initial assignment and when there are changes in the workplace **Written Compliance Plan is required**
HAZWOPER and Emergency Response	**1910.120**	Maintenance and Emergency Responders at the school district level	Initial and annually training thereafter Special training requirements based on job level assignment. Trainers require special certification **Written Compliance Plan is required**
Ionizing Radiation	**1910.1096**	Anyone exposed	Initial assignment and when there are changes in the workplace
Machinery and Machine Guarding	**1910.211**	Maintenance, custodial, tech ed., and food service workers	Initial assignment and when there are changes in the workplace
Mechanical Power Presses	**1910.217**	Maintenance, custodial, and tech ed. employees	Initial assignment and when there are changes in the workplace
Medical Services and First Aid	**1910.151**	First Responders and Emergency Rescue personnel	Initial assignment and when there are changes in the workplace

Safety Topic	OSHA Standard	School Employees Most Likely Affected	Written Plans and Training Requirements
Occupational Exposure to Hazardous Chemicals in Laboratories	**1910.1450**	Science personnel and school district administrators	Initial assignment and when there are changes in the workplace **Written Compliance Plan is required**
Occupational Health and Environmental Control	**1910.94**	Maintenance and custodial personnel	Initial assignment and when there are changes in the workplace
Permit-required Confined Spaces	**1910.146**	Maintenance Personnel	Initial assignment and when there are changes in the workplace **Written Compliance Plan is required**
Occupational Noise Exposure	**1910.95**	All school personnel	Initial assignment and when there are changes in the workplace **Written Compliance Plan is required** (if action level 85 decibels exceeded)
Personal Protective Equipment	**1910.132**	All school personnel	Initial assignment and when there are changes in the workplace **Written Compliance Plan is required**
Powered Industrial Trucks	**1910.178**	Maintenance and custodial personnel	Initial assignment and when there are changes in the workplace

Safety Topic	OSHA Standard	School Employees Most Likely Affected	Written Plans and Training Requirements
Powered Platforms, Manlifts, and Vehicle Mounted Platforms, Personal Fall Arrest Systems	**1910.66-67**	Technology Education and maintenance personnel	Initial assignment and when there are changes in the workplace
Respiratory Protection	**1910.134**	Maintenance and custodial personnel	Initial assignment and when there are changes in the workplace
Safety Instruction for Accident Prevention and Tags	**1910.145**	All school personnel	Initial assignment and when there are changes in the workplace
Servicing multi piece and single-piece rim wheels	**1910.177**	Maintenance and select tech ed. teachers	Initial assignment and when there are changes in the workplace
Welding, Cutting and Brazing	**1910.252**	Maintenance, custodial, and tech ed. personnel	Initial assignment and when there are changes in the workplace
Welding — Oxygen-Fuel Gas Welding and Cutting	**1910.255**	Maintenance, custodial, and tech ed. personnel	Initial assignment and when there are changes in the workplace
Welding — Arc Welding and Cutting	**1910.254**	Maintenance, custodial, and tech ed. personnel	Subpart Q 1910.252 Initial assignment and when there are changes in the workplace
Welding — Resistance Welding	**Subpart Q 1910.255 (a)(3)**	Maintenance, custodial, and tech ed. personnel	Initial assignment and when there are changes in the workplace

Ergonomics

Ask any custodial supervisor regarding the greatest injury exposure to their staff, inevitably the answer will be injuries from manual material handling and slips/trips/falls. A number of ergonomic products are available to significantly reduce or eliminate these exposures.

1146 **Purchase a desk mover.** Desk movers are a 'back saver' when moving desks between classrooms or when moving a large number of desks during the summer cleaning months.

1147 **Use chair movers.** Chair movers operate on the same principle as the desk mover. It is possible to stack a number of chairs on the mover for easier handling.

1148 **Purchase or build your own bleacher puller.** A variety of pullers are available ranging from full-power systems to manual bleacher pullers. Manual bleacher pullers can be built by your school for minimal cost.

1149 **Powered truck tailgates can make it easier to load and unload items transported by truck between your school facilities.** The initial cost of a powered truck tailgate may be significant, but the back injuries that it prevents will justify the cost.

1150 **Use powered and manual pallet jacks.** Pallet jacks are used to safely move pallets of materials and supplies.

1151 **Use hydraulic and electric hoists.** These devices can be used in areas where heavy equipment and materials are handled on a frequent basis.

1152 **Purchase lightweight wrestling mats.** Lightweight wrestling mats are available weighing 30-40% less than conventional mats.

1153 Consider using bottom drain mop buckets. A mop bucket full of water can exceed 50 lbs. in weight. Bottom drain mop buckets can prevent an employee from having to lift the bucket to the sink to empty it. The buckets are drained at floor level by opening the bottom bucket drain when over a floor drain.

1154 Use existing wall space for storage shelves and racks. Shelves and racks keep supplies off the floor at a height that facilitates easier loading and unloading.

1155 Install larger wheels on all school carts. Larger diameter wheels make carts easier to push and maneuver. Placing wheels on carts is a good project for your technology education classes.

1156 Determine where roller conveyors can be used to move material from one area to another with minimal material handling. Roller conveyor systems are often used in food storage areas.

1157 Purchase slip resistant overshoes for your custodians. These are overshoes equipped with non-skid grip type soles and are intended to be worn when working on slippery, wet, or icy surfaces. Purchase brightly colored overshoes so you can easily determine if they are being worn.

1158 Use a salt spreader for your icy sidewalks. Push type lawn spreaders are great for spreading salt evenly on sidewalks. Besides providing a consistent application of salt, the use of a spreader can reduce your employees' slip and fall exposures.

1159 Use a power brush or sweeper to remove snow from your sidewalks. Mounted to a riding lawn mower, a power brush can clean a sidewalk better than a conventional snow plow. Cleaning down to the bare pavement, the power brush can remove the thin layer of snow left behind when using a plow.

1160 Purchase lightweight building entrance mats. These mats reduce the weight handled by custodians. Efficient entrance mats will reduce the amount of snow and water brought in to the school, thereby reducing the slip and fall hazard.

This is just a short list of the many available ergonomic products that will make your custodial staff's job easier. Talk with your custodians to determine which tasks provide the greatest potential injury exposure. Investing a few dollars each year in the purchase of ergonomic equipment will make your custodian's duties easier and safer.

Extension Cords

Extension cords are used frequently in schools often in an unsafe manner. Extension cords also present serious trip and fall exposures and fire concerns.

1161 Your maintenance department should inspect all electrical cords on a quarterly basis. I recommend that you follow the OSHA Assured Grounding Program where different colored tape is placed on the cord on a scheduled basis after it has been inspected.

1162 Use only commercial grade extension cords that have been provided and approved by your maintenance department. All extension cords must have a grounding prong plug. The two wire light duty cords that are often used at home are not appropriate for school use.

1163 Instruct your teachers to inspect extension cords prior to each use.

1164 Limit the use of classroom extension cords to activities such as operating a projector. Extension cords should never be used as permanent wiring — after each use, the extension cord should be removed and stored.

1165 **Never run your extension cords over ceiling grids or under a rug or hang them from nails.** This will damage the cord insulation and may result in a fire.

1166 **Avoid the use of multi-tap outlets and numerous power strips.** These products can easily overload the electrical circuit, causing a fire.

Field Trips

Off-site field trips are an important and interactive component of your school curriculum. Whether you are spending a day at the zoo, taking a trip across the country, or flying overseas, field trips present a number of safety and security controls that must be addressed.

1167 **Long before an activity occurs, your school administration should approve a detailed description of the activity, the group, travel arrangements, and supervision controls.**

1168 **Use permission slips and waivers for all your field trips.** The permission slips and waivers should be kept on file for the duration of the student's attendance at your school.

1169 **Students under the age of 18 must have their parent/ guardian sign a permission slip stating that they accept the child's participation in the field trip.** Many good examples of permission slips can be obtained on the internet.

1170 **Students age 18 and older must sign a waiver stating they accept full responsibility for their actions and the legal implications of their participation in the field trip.**

1171 **Keep and use an ongoing attendance list.** Develop an attendance list that includes the name of each student and that is checked periodically during the field trip. Pay special attention when getting your students on and off the bus. You never want to forget a child at the museum and realize your mistake when you get back to the school.

1172 Use only school district approved transportation.

1173 If at all possible, avoid using volunteers or personal vehicles to transport students for a field trip activity.

1174 Self transportation by your students (students driving fellow students) should never be allowed by your school district.

1175 Require all field trip participants to wear proper attire. This may include rain gear, appropriate cold/warm weather clothing, or sun screen. Don't allow students to wear open toed shoes such as flip-flops or sandals.

1176 Ensure that adequate supervision is provided for all of your field trips. Pre-approved adult supervision (chaperones) must be present on all field trip events.

1177 If your event includes an overnight stay, ensure that references and background checks have been conducted on all chaperones.

1178 The number of chaperones will be dictated by the age and number of students present. A good rule to follow is to have one adult chaperone for every three to five students.

1179 The number of chaperones may increase depending on the complexity of your field trip. A group of students walking through a museum may require only 1 or 2 chaperones while the same number of students at an amusement park may require many more chaperones.

1180 Dress your chaperones in easily identifiable clothing. Wear brightly colored windbreakers, orange vests, or arm bands so students can easily identify the chaperones of their group. Additionally, easily identifiable supervisors may deter strangers from interacting with your students.

1181 **Ensure that your chaperones are prepared to handle emergencies.** Always carry walkie-talkies or cell phones and make sure your chaperones know the phone numbers of the other chaperones, the school's main office, and the phone numbers of other important contacts.

1182 **Take a basic first aid kit on all field trips.** You may not be able to prevent every injury on a field trip but having a first aid kit available may minimize the injury.

1183 **Know the location of and how to access the medical facility closest to your field trip location.**

1184 **Be able to quickly assemble your group and take a head count if necessary.**

1185 **Develop controls to keep your group together.** This is especially important with small children. A colored rope which all children must hold on to or large easily identifiable signs should be considered.

1186 **Review your field trip rules prior to the activity.** Each student should read and sign a 'rules contract' prior to the activity. Basic rules such as staying with the group, always listening to the chaperone, don't talk or leave with strangers, and what to do in case of an emergency should be reviewed.

1187 **Teach children the basic 'stranger danger' controls.** The chance of child abduction increases in large public areas where there are a lot of people present and the chaperone could lose sight of a student. Before and during the field trip, educate your students on the potential dangers of talking to and interacting with strangers.

1188 **Students should understand that they are only to talk with their field trip chaperones or a police officer in uniform.**

1189 Develop and implement strict controls for overnight stays.

1190 If male and female students are present, male and female chaperones must be present.

1191 If both male and female participants are involved, they must be placed in separate rooms at segregated locations within the hotel.

1192 Always request non-adjoining hotel rooms that do not have a shared doorway.

1193 A 'lights out' time should be determined and enforced during any overnight stays.

1194 Your chaperones should conduct nightly documented bed checks of all participants.

1195 Field trip pick up and drop off controls should be developed and implemented. Parents/guardians should be required to pick up and drop off their children in a timely manner.

1196 Do not allow other parents or friends to transport children unless prior permission has been provided in writing to your school office.

1197 Pick up and drop off areas should always be in a well lit, public area. Ideally, pick up and drop off areas should be at a school location.

1198 During student pick up after a field trip, ensure there are only as many students as there are seatbelts available in the transporting vehicle.

1199 A chaperone or activity coordinator must remain onsite until all students have been safely picked up by their parent/guardian.

1200 Maintain a list of parent/guardian home and cell phone numbers and call them if they are late in picking up their children. Never make the poor decision to drive a child home.

Charter Bus Trip Concerns

1201 Review the safety record of the charter bus company and ensure that they maintain appropriate levels of liability insurance.

1202 Verify the assigned driver's credentials when using charter transportation for trips.

1203 The school district must verify that the driver assigned to the trip is the same driver that reports for duty on the day of trip departure. Don't hesitate to ask the driver for their verification credentials.

1204 Prior to any chartered trip, chaperones should review the safety controls with all participating students. Your supervision requirement is the key safety control that must be discussed.

1205 Chaperones and group leaders should spread out throughout the bus to provide maximum supervision.

Overseas Travel Concerns

1206 **Before departing for an overseas trip, research the people and their culture along with any problems the country may be experiencing that could affect your travel plans.** Examples of this would be civil unrest or anti-American protests. Encourage your students to learn as much as possible about the countries in which they plan to travel.

1207 **It is important to avoid demonstrations, civil disturbances, and other situations that may become unruly or where anti-American sentiments may be expressed.**

1208 **Clearly instruct students about the practices that are and are not allowed in the countries you are visiting.** Keep in mind, when you are in a foreign country you are subject to their laws. Become familiar with the basic laws and customs of the country you plan to visit before you travel.

1209 **All chaperones and group leaders must be aware of emergency procedures and communications.** It is important to maintain a list of emergency phone numbers and to know where the closest medical facilities are and how to contact them.

1210 **Know the location of the nearest United States embassy and consulate where you are traveling or staying.**

1211 **Make sure all of your school travelers have a signed, valid passport and visas if required.**

1212 **Students, trip chaperones, and group leaders should always fill in the emergency information page of their passport.**

1213 **All school travelers should make copies of their passport's data page and any visas.** A copy should be kept on file with the school and with a chaperone during the trip. Students should keep a copy at home with their parents in the event that their passport is lost or stolen.

1214 Before the trip takes place, hold a mandatory attendance meeting of parents to answer questions, review trip concerns, and sign release forms.

1215 Appropriate release forms should be obtained from all students. These should be obtained long before the trip takes place.

1216 Instruct everyone in your group to never leave luggage unattended in any public area.

1217 Instruct everyone in your group to never accept or transport packages from strangers.

1218 Do not become an easy target for thieves by wearing conspicuous clothing and expensive jewelry when traveling overseas.

1219 Instruct your group not to carry large amounts of cash or unnecessary credit cards.

1220 Instruct students that cash and other valuables should be carried in the front pockets of their pants.

1221 Female students should refrain from carrying purses that can be easily ripped away.

1222 Make sure insurance coverage is in place that will cover emergency medical needs while traveling overseas. Every year, many students become ill or suffer injuries overseas. It is essential that students have medical insurance and medical evacuation insurance that would cover a medical emergency abroad.

1223 Visit the Centers for Disease Control and Prevention's website at www.cdc.gov. Educate yourself regarding any illness or outbreaks of concern for the countries you are visiting.

Fire Safety

Fire Alarm Systems in Schools

The protection of an effective fire alarm system allows your students to learn and teachers to teach with peace of mind. In the event that a fire does occur, students and staff will be quickly and safely evacuated from the building resulting in lives being saved.

Not only does a fire alarm protect lives, it also protects school property. By detecting a fire in its early stages, a fire alarm system automatically notifies the fire department enabling them to extinguish the fire before it causes catastrophic damage to property. This is even more critical during those times when your school building is unoccupied and no staff are present to react to a fire.

Although a fire alarm system does provide automatic protection for people and property, there are additional steps your school district should take when developing your districtwide fire safety plan. These include:

1224 **Conduct a fire hazard analysis of each school and the surrounding areas.** Identify those hazards that are most likely to affect your school. Your local emergency management personnel can assist with this assessment, with some of the common fire and life safety hazards being:

- Missing or broken fire safety equipment.

- Burnt out exit lights.

- Accumulated trash — pay special attention to theater work rooms and technology education areas.

- Open fire doors — often propped open by students and staff.

- Blocked stairways.

- Missing or lacking emergency kits.

- Fire extinguishers — make sure they are operational and current on inspections.

- Emergency contact lists need to be accurate and up to date.

1225 Develop proactive procedures to respond to identified fire hazards. Develop written procedures to respond to hazards that are identified but cannot be eliminated. This involves consideration of the unique features of each school building and its occupants. The plan should be made available to all employees, including those who work weekends and night shifts.

1226 Train your students and staff in fire safety. Students and staff must be trained on how to use the plan and what their responsibilities will be in a given response. There are some basic steps that should always be performed:

1227 If an alarm sounds or fire is suspected, call the fire department immediately.

1228 Never wait to investigate the situation before notifying the fire department. Any delay will allow a fire to grow and further endanger the building and property.

1229 Do not silence the alarm until given permission to do so by the Fire Department personnel or emergency operator.

1230 Close all doors when exiting the building and areas of the building. By closing doors, you can help limit the spread of smoke and fire throughout the building.

1231 Never use elevators during a fire emergency. Elevators often fail during a fire, potentially trapping occupants. In addition, elevators need to be available for the use of the arriving fire fighters.

1232 A meeting place should be established for students, staff, and teachers. This allows for everyone to be accounted for. The meeting place should be away from the building, out of harm's way.

1233 **If you are unable to leave the building, create an area of refuge.** This can be done by sealing the room you are in using wet cloth or similar objects around doors and vents.

1234 **Windows should not be broken, as flames and smoke can come back in from the outside.** If air is needed, open the window a crack. The freshest air is near the floor, so stay as low as possible. Lastly, signal for help. Use a cell phone or hang something from the window.

1235 **Conduct fire evacuation drills.** Drills should be conducted on a monthly basis, per state statutes, to test the plan and to get students and staff comfortable with the process. All participants should be debriefed at the conclusion of each drill. The feedback by the participants is used to identify strengths and weaknesses of your fire plan. The plan can then be modified to improve upon any weaknesses.

As you can see, there are many components to an effective fire safety plan. It is a process that must be tested on a regular basis to ensure that when an emergency does occur, your plan will be executed quickly, efficiently, and without issue. Making this a priority for your school district will ensure peace of mind for students and staff, but more importantly will potentially save lives.

I would like to thank H&H Fire and Security, a leader in fire alarm, security, and life safety systems for the development of these fire alarm system best practices. You may contact H&H Fire and Security at 608.273.4464 or info@hhfireandsecurity.com.

The very real threat of fire exists in all of your schools. Even a small fire with large amounts of smoke could be devastating causing significant loss of life. Schools have instituted basic fire safety controls and conducted evacuation drills forever. However, I believe many school districts could do more to prevent the chance of a fire.

Consider addressing these proactive controls of fire safety:

1236 **At all times, keep room doors and hallway doors closed to prevent air movement and the spread of smoke and flames.**

Fire Drills

1237 Conduct fire drills on a regularly scheduled basis with the initial fire drill for the school year beginning in early September.

....

1238 Instruct students to always take your school fire drills seriously and evacuate when the alarm sounds.

....

1239 Ensure that all school employees (including volunteers and substitute teachers) know how to evacuate their work areas and perform their fire drill duties during an emergency.

....

🔑 **1240** Instruct your staff to always sound the alarm at the first sign of smoke or fire. Human nature directs us to seek out the origin of the smoke — time wasted if a fire is actually in its beginning stage. Hundreds of young lives may depend on your staff's prompt response. At the first sign of smoke or fire, act swiftly and sound the fire alarm.

....

1241 Not everyone needs to know how to operate a fire extinguisher — select a few key individuals throughout your school. Your first response should be to evacuate the area and only fight the fire if you are trained in how to operate the fire fighting equipment and have an exit nearby.

....

1242 Teach your staff how to operate fire extinguishers, fire blankets, and fire hoses. Ask your local fire department to provide instructions and demonstrations on how to operate fire extinguishers, fire blankets, and fire hoses.

Laboratories

1243 **Properly store flammable liquids and always dispense them from an approved safety container.** You might be surprised by the number of teachers who maintain flammable liquids in their classroom, often stored in a potentially dangerous manner.

1244 **Ensure that flammable and combustible waste materials are controlled so they do not contribute to a fire emergency.**

1245 **Use only approved flammable cabinets to store flammable or combustible liquids.** Ensure the cabinet is labeled properly, is constructed of double wall metal construction, and has a two inch door sill.

1246 **Always make sure the flammable cabinet doors are closed securely and are kept locked when not in use.**

1247 **Avoid storing incompatible chemicals next to each other as interaction may occur and cause a fire or explosion.**

1248 **Survey chemicals annually and discard those that are obsolete or show signs of decomposition.** Your insurance carrier may be a great resource to assist with a chemical inventory in your science/chemistry areas.

1249 **Order and store only the minimum supply of flammables, chemicals, and hazardous substances needed.**

1250 **Repair all electrical hazards and avoid overloading outlets.**

1251 **Keep Material Safety Data Sheets (MSDS) readily available.** It's a good idea to provide copies of your data sheets to your fire department so they know the type of hazardous substances that are in your science/chemistry areas, in case of a fire.

Gymnasium/Auditorium

1252 **Test your emergency lighting on a monthly basis.** Maintain written records of these tests.

1253 **Ensure your exit lights are always working.** During low light conditions, the illuminated exit lights may be the only way to identify exits in a gymnasium or auditorium — critical when a large number of people must be quickly evacuated.

1254 **Always keep all doorways clear.** Your worst nightmare is to have hundreds of people unable to exit a gymnasium or auditorium because an object is blocking the doorway. I mention this because many schools use the hallways leading to the gymnasium as a storage area for equipment.

Extension Cords

1255 **Extension cords should only be used for temporary wiring purposes and should never be used for permanent wiring.** This applies everywhere in your school, especially in the classroom.

1256 **Extension cords should never be allowed for portable appliances, hand tools, or fixtures.** This is an unsafe practice that is often allowed in classrooms.

1257 **Never allow extension cords and relocatable power taps to be attached to structures or placed under doors or floor coverings.**

Facility Concerns

1258 Never allow open flame candles or open flame fixtures in the classroom.

1259 Do not use the area beneath staircases or in stairwells for storage. This means no placement of vending machines, desks, or other equipment in these areas.

1260 Maintain at least 18" of clearance beneath all sprinkler heads and at least 36" around all sprinkler control valves.

1261 Ensure that all fire extinguishers have a label that indicates the month and year the extinguisher maintenance was performed. Fire extinguishers should be inspected monthly with the inspection documented on the backside of the inspection tag.

Kitchen and Home Economics

1262 Regularly clean the lint traps on dryers and the filters on vents, fans, and air conditioners.

1263 Ensure that all cooking equipment, hoods, filters, and ducts are free of grease accumulation. At a minimum, a monthly inspection procedure should be established.

1264 Never leave hand irons plugged in. Any electrical outlets used for plugging in irons should be equipped with a pilot light.

Technology Education

1265 **Avoid overloading outlets and use approved extension cords only on a temporary basis.** Too often, I see extension cords used as permanent wiring for machinery and equipment. Electrical outlets and frayed cords can cause burns and shock injuries.

1266 **Secure all compressed gas cylinders in an upright position.** It's important that students avoid dropping, rolling, or knocking cylinders together.

1267 **Never allow welding in areas where combustible material is stored.**

1268 **Provide suitable waste cans for disposal of oil soaked rags and paint rags.**

1269 **Instruct your staff and students to keep their work area clean and check daily for fire hazards.**

1270 **Use safety cans for storing and dispensing small amounts of flammable liquids.**

1271 **Ensure good ventilation controls are in place for painting operations, including scheduled clean up of paint overspray.**

Office and Storage Areas

1272 **Avoid overloading electrical outlets and keep wiring away from doorways, windows, or under carpeting.**

1273 **Carefully store and handle cleaning compounds and polishes.** These substances often give off flammable vapors.

1274 **Maintain good housekeeping and cleanliness conditions in all storage rooms.** As mentioned earlier, all storage rooms should be locked when not occupied by a staff member.

1275 **Store your gas powered equipment, such as lawn mowers and snow blowers, in a shed outside of the main school building or in a fire-rated room with a one-hour fire separation.**

Classrooms, Doorways and Hallways

1276 **Identify exits with lighted exit signs and keep them unobstructed.** This means that artwork and decorations cannot be hung from your hallway ceilings — no exceptions.

1277 **Avoid wedging open hallway doors.** Closed hallway doors will limit the spread of fire and smoke throughout the school.

1278 **Check your emergency lighting every month to ensure it is in proper working order.**

1279 **Test your fire doors regularly to make certain that the doors do not jam and that the hardware is not detached.**

1280 **Ensure that no more than 20% of your classroom walls are covered with combustible materials such as paper or decorations.** This is one of the most common serious fire hazards that I observe in elementary schools.

1281 **Install safety plugs on all unused electrical outlets especially in elementary school classrooms.**

1282 **Clearly mark the evacuation route on the school floor plan, placing it at eye level, adjacent to the classroom door.** Additionally ensure secondary evacuation routes are identified in case the primary evacuation route is blocked.

1283 Never allow the storage of combustibles in boiler rooms, electrical rooms, or furnace rooms. Oftentimes, teachers believe moving these materials out of their classroom and in to other rooms is an acceptable practice.

1284 Keep all combustible materials away from heaters. This is a good reason to not allow teachers to bring portable heaters in to the classroom.

1285 Instruct your teachers to unplug all appliances during weekends and school breaks.

1286 Dispose of trash daily. Don't allow paper and other flammable products to accumulate in your school.

Food Service

A recent insurance company workers' compensation claim study of school food service injuries shows that manual material handling, slips/trips/falls, and knife cuts, account for over 60% of the total number of injuries and almost 80% of the total workers' compensation costs in our schools.

With this in mind, consider these best practices to prevent these types of accidents:

1287 Have your food supplies delivered directly to the food storage room (including being placed on shelving units) rather than being handled by your food service personnel. Food supplies are often unloaded in a haphazard manner in the kitchen area. Food service employees are then required to 'double handle' the product when lifting and carrying it to the storage areas. Eliminating this need to 'double handle' objects may also prevent a number of trip and fall accidents from occurring.

1288 **Mount trash containers on wheels to allow for easier movement.** Wheels on trash containers will significantly reduce the need to lift or carry the trash containers. Also remember, the bigger the wheel, the easier it is to push the container.

1289 **Instruct your employees to never overload trash containers or trash bags.** Better yet, use smaller trash bags to reduce the weight that needs to be lifted. Overloaded carts are often difficult to handle and can easily tip over.

1290 **Instruct your food service employees to push carts and trash containers rather than pulling them.** Pushing a cart is always safer than pulling it.

1291 **Clean up all spills immediately!** Always try to eliminate the slip and fall hazard. Oftentimes a warning cone is placed in the slippery area and the hazard never gets cleaned up.

1292 **Ensure your food service employees always wear proper non-slip footwear.** Not all tennis shoes are the best choice of footwear when working in slippery conditions.

1293 **On shelving units, store the heavier food supplies at waist level or below.**

1294 **Instruct food service employees to never climb on shelving units.** When reaching for a box on an upper shelving unit, employees sometimes climb on the shelves rather than get a ladder. This results in many serious fall injuries in a school kitchen.

1295 **Provide small three-step ladders to reach items on kitchen shelving units.** Make sure the ladder is located in an easily accessible area. Employees won't use ladders when they are buried behind product in the food storage room.

1296 **Instruct your food service employees to never stand on chairs, tables, or overturned pails.**

1297 Ensure that all drain covers are in place to prevent trips from occurring.

1298 Make sure all changes in floor elevation are clearly marked.

1299 Ensure all floor mats are in good condition and are small enough to be picked up easily.

1300 Prevent slips and falls in walk-in refrigerators and freezers by keeping the floor free of water or ice.

1301 Instruct food service employees if they drop a knife — let it fall. Never attempt to catch a sharp knife.

1302 Knives should be in use or in storage; never leave a knife out on the counter.

1303 Always lock the knife drawer when the kitchen is unoccupied.

1304 Never leave knives in soapy water with other kitchen utensils. Many hand lacerations have occurred when a food service employee reached into soapy water and grabbed a sharp knife.

1305 Ensure that all of the large mixers have guards over the bowls. Guards may be opened but they must have an electrical interlock to shut down the mixer when opened.

1306 Ensure that all food processing equipment such as meat slicers, choppers, grinders, and shredders have guards that are never removed when the equipment is operating.

1307 **Develop written safety procedures for cleaning the food processing equipment that are followed each and every time the equipment is cleaned.** This includes having a procedure for unplugging the equipment before removing any guards. This is the most important control — unplug all equipment before cleaning.

1308 **Ensure 'On/Off' switches on electrical equipment are shielded or guarded to prevent accidental starting.**

1309 **Never distract or talk to another employee when they are operating equipment such as mixers or slicers.** A distracted employee could easily have their hair, fingers, or clothing pulled in to the moving components of the equipment.

1310 **Protect all kitchen electrical outlets with a ground fault circuit interrupter (GFCI) to prevent accidental shock.**

Lab/Science Rooms

1311 **Periodically check fume hoods for ventilation efficiency.** Ensure the fume hood is properly ventilated through the roof.

1312 **Never allow the fume hoods to be used as a storage area.** When product is stored in the fume hood area, the efficiency of the ventilation system is compromised.

1313 **Maintain separate disposal containers for broken glassware and flammables.**

1314 **Make sure all students understand the emergency and escape plans for each room.**

1315 **Fire exits must be clearly marked and all exits must be unobstructed.**

1316 Make sure secured master cut-off switches/valves are available in each laboratory.

1317 Keep the water, gas, and electricity turned off when not in use.

1318 Remove any unlabeled, expired, or contaminated chemicals from the school. Your insurance company's loss control consultant may be able to conduct a chemical inventory review to determine which chemicals should be removed.

1319 Prohibit eating and drinking in your lab and science areas. Additionally, lab and science refrigerators are not to be used for the storage of food items and drinks.

1320 Make sure your spill control kit is readily accessible.

1321 Post the National Fire Protection Association (NFPA) 'diamond' at all chemical storeroom entrances. This posting is needed to denote the most hazardous chemical in each category. Make sure that your school district provides an updated copy of your inventory to your local fire department.

1322 Allow only chemicals to be stored in your chemical storage room.

1323 Ensure your chemical storage cabinets and rooms are kept locked and controlled by the instructor at all times. Never allow easy access to chemical storage areas. These substances could be used to start a fire or build an explosive device.

1324 Store all flammable materials in a storage cabinet that meets the National Fire Protection Association (NFPA) criteria. The cabinet must be properly labeled and kept locked when not in use.

1325 Store chemicals in appropriate places such as:

- Below eye level.
- In large containers no higher than two feet above the floor.
- Acids stored in corrosive cabinets.
- Acids physically separated from bases and oxidizers physically separated from organics within secure, limited access, adequately ventilated storerooms.
- Solvents in OSHA/NFPA approved flammable cabinets.

1326 Ensure adequate shelving units are provided to prevent chemicals from becoming overcrowded and inaccessible.

1327 Ensure that all chemical shelving units have protective safety lips.

1328 Ensure all poisons are marked with the skull and crossbones and the word 'poison.'

1329 Order chemicals only in quantities that your school needs. Expired chemicals can pose hazards, such as becoming volatile and explosive.

1330 Never allow portable LP gas containers in the classrooms.

1331 Ensure all appropriate personal protective equipment is provided and is worn by students and teachers.

1332 Ensure proper ventilation is provided for all laboratory activities.

1333 Ensure the area is equipped with fire extinguishers, fire blankets, emergency showers, eyewash stations, and hand washing areas.

1334 Ensure your chemical lab/science rooms are equipped with emergency eyewash stations that are capable of 15 minutes of continuous water flow.

1335 Ensure all electrical equipment is properly grounded.

Library and Computer Labs

1336 Arrange bookshelves to provide clear paths for exit in case of an emergency or crisis.

1337 If your library has free standing bookshelves, they should be double-wide and limited to shoulder height for stability.

1338 Ensure all wall mounted shelves are securely fastened to the wall.

1339 Secure computer cabling and power bars to prevent students and staff tripping over them.

1340 Ensure all workstations chairs are ergonomically designed with a 5-point base to prevent a computer user from falling over.

1341 Secure your computer equipment to discourage theft. This includes locking the classroom door whenever the instructor is not present.

Lightning Concerns

Your school district lightning response plan should be developed in advance of any outside activities, taking into consideration the weather conditions and available shelter.

1342 **Monitor the weather conditions at least 24 hours prior to your outdoor practice or event.** Be especially aware of potential thunderstorms that may form during scheduled practices or athletic events.

1343 **When you first see lightning or hear thunder, activate your emergency plan and seek shelter immediately.** Lightning often precedes rain, so don't wait for the rain to begin before suspending activities.

1344 **'If You See It, Flee It; If You Hear It, Clear It.'** This is a great safety slogan to teach your school staff and coaches.

1345 **Make sure your staff has identified the 'safe structure or location' closest to the field or playing area.** A safe structure or location is any building normally occupied or frequently used by people, such as a building with plumbing and/or electrical wiring that acts to electrically ground the structure. Know just how long it will take to get to that safe structure or location.

1346 **If a safe structure or alternative location is not available, a vehicle with a hard metal roof (not a convertible or a golf cart) and rolled-up windows can provide a measure of safety.** It is not the rubber tires that make a vehicle a safe shelter, but the hard metal roof which dissipates the lightning strike around the vehicle. Additionally, instruct students to not touch the sides of the vehicle.

1347 **If a safe structure or alternate location is not available and students are outside, instruct them to:**

- Find the low ground. Seek cover in clumps of bushes or in a dry ditch.

- Remove all metal objects from the body.

- Minimize the body's surface area in contact with the ground. Instruct students not to lie flat on the ground. Lightning current often enters a victim's body through the ground rather than by a direct overhead strike.

- "Place your feet together, lower your head, crouch down with only the balls of your feet touching the ground, and wrap your arms around your knees."

1348 **If you are in a group outside in an open area, spread out, keeping people several yards apart from each other.**

1349 **Know what constitutes an unsafe shelter.** Unsafe shelter includes: all outdoor metal objects (for example, under the metal bleachers), near or around flag poles and light poles, near fences and gates, near machinery, etc. Avoid trees, water (ponds, creeks, and rivers), open fields, and high ground.

1350 **Wait a minimum of 30 minutes from the last observed lightning or thunder before resuming outdoor activities.**

Pool Lightning Safety

Recently, a school district business manager asked if a policy should be developed that addresses the use of an indoor swimming pool if a thunderstorm that involves lightning is taking place. Even though hundreds of indoor pools are open every day during thunderstorms and there's never been a documented case of a death in an indoor pool attributed to lightning, a policy and procedure addressing this potential exposure should be considered.

According to the National Lightning Safety Institute (NLSI), few reports of deaths or injuries in indoor pools are related to lightning causes. However, a July 10, 2010, incident at the Kingsport (TN) Legion Pool is one reported event. The pool's policy was to evacuate the pool at the first sign of thunder or lightning. The pool's staff did this, but a lifeguard went into the pool's mechanical room and was touching a metal pipe at the moment lightning struck. He was sent to the hospital and then released.

The physics of the event are well understood: when a body is free-floating in water, it is not a part of any circuit path (this does not include 'direct lightning strikes') and cannot receive shocks. When a body in water is in contact with a circuit path, it will conduct current.

'In contact' can mean:

• Feet on the pool floor.

• Touching sides of the pool.

• In contact with ladders, underwater lights, railings, etc.

Persons not in the water but inside a pool building, who are a part of the circuit path, can become victims, just as they may be at risk in any dwelling. Wet floors at pool facilities are very good conductors.

With this being said, the important points for your school to consider include:

1351 Develop a pool lightning policy that will suspend activities during approaching storms.

....

1352 Do not be in contact with metallic objects which may become energized by lightning.

....

1353 Designate a responsible person as the weather safety lookout. That person should keep an eye on the approaching weather. Use a 'weather radio,' the Weather Channel or other TV program to obtain good local, advance weather information.

....

1354 When thunder and/or lightning are first noticed, use the Flash-To-Bang (F-B) method to determine its approximate distance and speed. This technique measures the time from seeing lightning to hearing associated thunder. For each five seconds from F-B, lightning is one mile away. Thus, an F-B of 10 = 2 miles; 15 = 3 miles; 20 = 4 miles; etc. At an F-B count of 30, the pool should be evacuated. People should be directed to a safe shelter nearby.

1355 At the first signs of thunder or lightning, all pool activities should be suspended (including taking showers) until 30 minutes after the last observed thunder or lightning. If you hear thunder after 27 minutes of activity suspension, start your 30-minute clock all over again.

1356 Pool activities should remain suspended until 30 minutes after the last thunder is heard.

1357 Pool managers and other school staff members should be trained to recognize and report potential electrical issues as part of their daily facility check.

1358 During thunderstorms, all exterior doors and windows in the pool area should be kept closed.

1359 School employees and students must not be allowed to use landline phones or take showers during this time; employees and students must be encouraged to stay in the building. It is possible for lightning to strike from distances greater than 10 miles (about the distance thunder can be heard), so the safest option is to clear the water whenever you can hear thunder. A school's best practices should be the safest possible option, not necessarily the easiest or most popular to implement.

1360 A qualified electrician should conduct a comprehensive inspection of the pool and facility on a regular basis.

Physical Education

1361 At the beginning of the school year, physical education teachers need to be aware of the medical background and physical limitations of their students. This includes knowledge of students with medical conditions such as heart disorders, asthma, diabetes, severe allergies, anaphylaxis, etc.

For students with medical conditions such as asthma, life threatening allergies, diabetes, etc. ensure an emergency action plan for that medical condition is in place, in case of an emergency, and medical support is readily available when needed.

1362 Prior to any off site activity (canoeing for example), a signed parent/guardian acknowledgement or permission form must be received for each participant. It is important that parents are aware of the mode of transportation and student expectations. The form must contain details of the activity and its inherent risks, including the transportation risks.

1363 Inform parents/guardians of activities which take students off the immediate school property but where transportation is not required, such as cross-country running.

1364 Parents/guardians must be made aware of safety precautions related to environmental factors (effects of sun, hypothermia, frostbite, dehydration, viruses transmitted by insects, etc.) if activities take place outdoors.

1365 A fully-stocked first aid kit must be readily accessible for all physical education activities. When activities are offered off school property, a portable first aid kit must be readily accessible.

1366 When physical education activities take place off school property, your instructor must carry a cell phone for emergency communication.

1367 Ensure your emergency crisis plan addresses physical education activities. For example, if your class is playing soccer outside and a lockdown is initiated, you probably don't want these students coming back into the school.

Equipment

1368 To provide a safe environment, your physical education teacher should make a pre-activity check of the equipment to be used. This could be done visually or recorded on a checklist. If broken equipment is found, it should be removed from use.

1369 Encourage your students to report any equipment problems to the teacher.

1370 Never allow home-made athletic equipment to be used during school sponsored activities.

1371 Ensure protective mats are placed on all designated landing areas. This includes climbing activities, chin-up bars, etc.

1372 Running shoes/tennis shoes should be a minimum requirement, regardless of the physical activity taking place.

1373 Running shoes with higher heels, wheels, open toes, open heels, or cleats and sandals are not appropriate. Remind students to tie their shoelaces securely — especially your younger students.

1374 During physical activity, students should not be allowed to wear hanging or dangling jewelry. Any hanging jewelry that cannot be removed and that presents a safety concern, such as a medical alert identification, must be taped and covered.

1375 Don't allow students to wear hats if they pose a risk of impairing vision.

Facilities

1376 Visually check the activity area prior to any activity to ensure that hazards are identified and addressed. Look for obstacles that could cause injuries to your students.

1377 If any classrooms are used for physical activities, they must provide enough space that is unobstructed by furniture and other equipment to allow for free movement by students.

1378 Remove excess equipment and furniture if it is stored in the gymnasium, hallways, concourse areas, stage areas, etc. The hallways leading from the gymnasium should never be used for equipment storage. Imagine the chaos that would occur during a mass evacuation of your gymnasium.

1379 Bring any potentially dangerous and immovable objects to the attention of your students. Where there are immovable objects, (trophy cases, goalposts, protruding stage), create a 'safety zone' of at least three feet around the perimeter of these objects. Another good practice is to mark these areas with pylons or protective mats.

1380 Use restraints in your physical education storage rooms to prevent equipment (volleyball net posts, nets, etc.) from falling or tipping over.

1381 Ensure protective guards cover the physical educa-tion storage room lights to prevent them from being damaged. Lights are often damaged when struck by large objects being moved in and out of the room.

1382 Ensure the lights in your gymnasium have protective guards over the lighting to ensure they cannot be damaged. Normal gym activities such as a flying ball can easily damage overhead gym lights.

1383 Periodically inspect gymnasium fixtures, such as bleachers and basketball backstops, to ensure they are securely fastened to the wall.

1384 If a power drill is used to raise or lower basketball backstops, it should be operated only by a trained school employee. Don't ever allow students to use a power drill to raise/lower basketball backstops; they could easily get their hair or clothing caught in the rotating drill head.

1385 Periodically inspect all gymnasium floor sockets to ensure they are flush with the floor.

Special Rules and Instructions

1386 Ensure all physical education activities are appropriate for the age and ability levels of the students and the facility where the activity is taking place.

1387 The number of students participating in an activity in any location must never present a safety concern. If you think too many students are involved in an activity, consider splitting the class into two groups.

1388 Early in the school year, establish routines, rules of acceptable behavior, and appropriate duties for students. Reinforce these throughout the year and require that students adhere to them.

1389 All games and activities must be based on skills that are appropriate for the student's age and physical abilities.

1390 Instruct students regarding the proper use of physical education equipment before allowing them to use it.

1391 Constantly remind students to keep a safe distance from one another and from furniture, equipment, and structures such as walls, doors, and windows.

1392 Inform students that body-on-body contact and equipment-on-body contact are never allowed.

1393 Instruct teachers to be vigilant to prevent one student from pressuring another student into trying activities for which he or she is not ready. When a student displays hesitation, verbally or non-verbally, the teacher must determine the reason(s) for it. If the teacher believes that a potential hesitancy during the activity could put the student at risk, direct that student to a more basic activity.

Playgrounds

Every school district faces potentially serious liability exposures through its playgrounds. Your playgrounds are used by students throughout the entire year and in all kinds of weather. Developing playground rules and supervising children at play isn't enough to ensure your students' safety on the playground. Your school district must ensure that the playground equipment and the surrounding area are also 'child safe.'

Your playgrounds must be properly designed, maintained, and supervised to be as safe as possible for your students.

Studies show that falls from equipment is the number one cause of injuries on school playgrounds. Your school must also address the injury exposures associated with student entrapment, often caused when students are caught between components of equipment or protective railings.

To reduce your school district's playground liability exposure, keep the following best practices in mind:

1394 **Conduct regularly scheduled inspections of all playground equipment.** Sample playground inspection forms can be found at a variety of internet sites including the Consumer Product Safety Commission (CPSC) (www.cpsc.gov) and the National Recreational and Park Association (www.nrpa.org).

1395 **Maintain accurate records of your playground inspections.** In a liability situation, it will be important to show that your school district has a history of inspecting and maintaining the school district's playground equipment.

1396 **Any missing or broken components should be addressed immediately or the equipment should be taken out of service.**

1397 **Don't forget to inspect your playground equipment during the summer months.** Typically, during the summer months the playground is not supervised and inspections are put on hold until school begins after summer break. In reality, during the summer older children may be playing on the equipment or others may use the equipment in unintended ways — the slide becomes a climbing board or guard rails become walking beams. Summertime is not the time to place your playground safety program on hold.

1398 **Install proper protective surfacing.** Playground surfacing beneath and around the equipment should be soft enough to cushion a fall. Refer to the Consumer Product Safety Commission Playground Guidelines to review the variety of surfacing materials and recommended depths.

1399 **Focus on your fall zone exposures.** The area around and beneath a piece of playground equipment where a child may fall is known as the fall zone. Surfacing depths must be adequate to absorb a fall. Remember, the fall zone may not always be directly under a piece of playground equipment. A swing set may have a fall zone that extends 10-15 feet from the swing set.

1400 Address all protrusion hazards. Any piece of hardware that might impale or cut a child must be immediately addressed. Refer to the Consumer Product Safety Commission Playground Guidelines for specific information on protrusion hazards.

1401 Watch for pinch, crush, shearing, and sharp edge hazards. Constantly be watchful for sharp edges or pinch points that could crush a child's hand or finger.

1402 Correct all possible entrapment openings. All openings in railings, between steps, etc., must be checked to ensure that an entrapment hazard is not present. Again, refer to the Consumer Product Safety Commission Playground Guidelines for specific information on this hazard.

1403 Ensure sufficient spacing exists between equipment. If a child could fall from one piece of equipment and strike another, the equipment is spaced improperly. Ensure that your spacing of equipment takes into account the radius of swings and merry-go-rounds.

1404 Recognize the trip hazards on and around your playground. Exposed trip hazards such as old tree stumps, tree roots, wooden borders, and footings should be addressed.

1405 Use age appropriate playground equipment. For example, high elevation climbing bars would not be acceptable for very small children due to the fall exposure.

1406 Be concerned about playground platforms with no guardrails. Accidental falls are more likely to occur when proper guardrails are not in place.

1407 The use of pressure treated wood should not be allowed for playground equipment. While it may last longer than untreated wood, it can release hazardous contaminants such as arsenic, which may make the area dangerous for students and adults.

1408 When pressure treated wood is removed from the playground, the wood and the soil/sand in which it rested may also need to be removed. The hazardous substances in the pressure treated wood could leach in to the ground resulting in contamination.

1409 Know the equipment that is not recommended for your playgrounds. The Consumer Product Safety Commission Playground Guidelines list the types of equipment that are not recommended due to their inherent dangers and high frequency of accidents.

1410 Don't allow the use of homemade playground equipment. Parent and community groups may mean well when they donate homemade playground equipment; however, in most cases, this equipment does not meet the safety requirements of the Consumer Product Safety Commission Playground Guidelines.

1411 If a local community group donates equipment to your school, ensure that it adheres to the CPSC guidelines. Before accepting any donated equipment, contact your insurance company's loss control representative and request a review of the equipment's safety controls.

1412 Never allow a child to use the playground equipment while wearing a helmet. Helmets provide good protection while skating, boarding, or riding a bicycle but can easily lead to strangulation or entrapment on playground equipment.

1413 Do not allow children to take toys such as canteens, hula-hoops, backpacks, etc. onto play equipment. These items can easily get caught on a piece of equipment and lead to a child getting hurt. If they are left on the equipment they could cause someone else to trip over them.

1414 Never allow a lack of playground supervision. Your school's playground equipment should be located so supervisors can easily observe all children at play.

1415
Require your playground supervisors to wear reflective vests. Easily identifiable supervisors should become a supervision standard.

Pool Concerns

According to the National Safety Council, over 600 children and adults annually drown in swimming pools. Swimming alone or without adult supervision is a significant factor in many of these drownings.

Additionally, many severe injuries result from falling on slippery walkways and decks and falling from diving boards and ladders. Diving and jumping into shallow water are also major causes of serious injuries.

Although many pool accidents are related to running and roughhousing, numerous injuries are also attributed to the pool, its accessories, and general environment.

The use of water slides in school pools is on the increase. The severity of injuries associated with swimming pool water slides — permanent disabilities for some adults and children who went head first down the slide and struck the bottom of the pool — has led to a greater focus on developing mandatory water slide safety standards.

Your school district should be aware of the various pool hazards that may be present: sharp edges and protruding bolts, slippery ladders, decks, and diving boards, lack of depth indicators, shock hazards from electrical wiring, and problems of exploding filter tanks.

Keep these pool safety best practices in mind:

1416
Even adults should never swim alone. Some school districts allow community members or staff members to use their pool before and after school. An accident to a lone swimmer could result in serious injury or even death. Make sure all adults always have another adult present when using your pool.

1417
Ensure competent adult supervision is always present when the pool is in use. A pool supervisor is there to supervise, never to participate in swimming activities.

1418 Keep rescue devices and first aid supplies near the pool. These items should not be stored in an office or require someone to travel a great distance to obtain.

1419 Keep all electrical appliances such as televisions and radios out of the pool area because of the significant electrical shock hazard.

1420 Ensure that all electrical equipment is installed by a licensed electrician in accordance with local safety codes. Faulty electrical installations could cause serious or fatal electric shock — your school electrician should probably refrain from performing this type of work.

1421 Place non-slip surfacing on your pool deck, diving board, and ladder rungs.

1422 Make sure the pool ladder has handrails on both sides, small enough for a child to grasp. Additionally, there should be a ladder at each end of the pool.

1423 If your pool has a diving board or slide, confer with a reputable pool contractor to be sure the water depth is sufficient. Always put a slide in a deep area of the pool — never in shallow water.

1424 Instruct your students to always go feet first when using water slides.

1425 Constantly remind students that before they dive or use a slide, they must ensure that other swimmers are out of the way.

1426 Conspicuously mark water depths. Use a safety float line where the bottom slope deepens.

1427 Regularly inspect the pool and equipment for cleanliness and good maintenance. This includes covering all sharp edges and protruding bolts, repairing rickety or broken ladders/railings, and replacing non-slip materials when they wear out.

1428 When children are involved in pool activities, caution them against showing off, running, and rough play.

1429 Clearly explain the dangers of running and diving recklessly. Students must also be instructed to never push others into the pool.

1430 Teach students what they must do in case of an emergency. An alarm bell that could summon emergency assistance would be a good idea. Students should know how to get the immediate attention of the instructor and know where the phone is located to call for assistance.

I have consulted with some school districts that have constructed outdoor pools — oftentimes small wading pools. If an outdoor pool is present in your district, consider these best practices:

1431 There should be a fence at least six feet high around all sides of the pool with a locked gate to keep children out when there is no supervision and the fence should be constructed so it is difficult to climb.

1432 Lawn furniture, trees, and shrubs should not be close enough to provide an easy boost over the fence.

1433 Avoid using a side of the school building as part of the fence. Small children have wandered out through an open door or window and drowned.

Safety Committee Development

A commonality among proactive school safety programs is the effective use of a districtwide safety committee. If developed and implemented appropriately, your safety committee can focus on a number of safety and security functions:

1434 **Address safety and security concerns throughout your entire school district.**

1435 **Perform safety compliance audits of your various school operations.** The committee can review the many required compliance programs to ensure all employees have been adequately trained (refer to the Compliance Programs chapter).

1436 **Coordinate employee loss driver safety training programs.** Focus your safety training on those issues that provide the greatest accident exposure to your school district. By reviewing past accident history and working with your insurance carrier, you can determine where and what types of accidents are taking place. Focus your efforts on those schools or operations that historically have the greatest frequency and severity of claims.

1437 **Conduct safety surveys of various schools, departments, and grounds to review workers' compensation, general liability, and auto liability exposures.** Recommendations or suggestions of improvement can be reviewed by the safety committee. The risk assessment process discussed later in this chapter is a great tool to review and rank these potential risks and exposures.

1438 **Conduct hazard assessments of those school-related tasks that present unique exposures.** There may be many tasks, primarily in custodial and food service operations, which present unique or serious accident exposure. Committee members can use their safety expertise to perform a more detailed analysis of these tasks.

1439 **Create and maintain a districtwide return to work program.** After your districtwide return to work program is up and running, the committee can be a great tool to monitor the progress of injured employees as well as the overall program.

1440 **Develop and maintain contractor/vendor safety procedures.** On a daily basis, your school district utilizes contractors/vendors ranging from food service delivery personnel to construction workers involved in remodeling or new construction projects. It is important to ensure that all of these non-employees follow the school district's safety and security procedures to protect themselves, your students and staff, and your school facilities.

1441 **Review and maintain the district's emergency preparedness and crisis plans.** Your school district's emergency preparedness is a never ending process. Working with your school district's crisis committee, the safety committee can provide valuable assistance in ensuring that plans are up-to-date, employees are trained, and the plans are ready to implement.

1442 **Develop, update, and implement school staff and student safety procedures.** Review unique safety protocols associated with playgrounds, technology education, art class, and home economics, just to name a few.

1443 **Review and evaluate work related accidents, near misses, injuries, and illnesses.** The committee can discuss past accidents, incidents, and near misses to ensure they have been adequately investigated and proper corrective action has been taken to reduce or eliminate future exposure or risk.

When working with a school district's safety committee, I stress the importance of contacting your insurance carrier to receive up-to-date loss history information. This information will be provided to all committee members a few weeks prior to the meeting, for their review. Safety committee members can then come prepared to discuss the status of your claims, accidents, and incidents.

1444 Discuss and evaluate employee safety suggestions and recommendations. If your school employees offer safety ideas, suggestions, or recommendations, the safety committee can review them to determine if further action will be taken. The risk assessment process (discussed later in this chapter) is a great method to categorically rank safety concerns based on their potential frequency, severity, and consequences.

1445 Discuss and evaluate safety recommendations submitted by your insurance carrier. On occasion, the insurance carrier will submit recommendations regarding your school district operations. The safety committee can review these recommendations to ensure they have been properly addressed and a response has been provided to the insurance carrier.

1446 Review upcoming risk management concerns (seasonal exposures). Your safety committee can be a great avenue to review upcoming or seasonal risk management concerns. For example, extremely warm weather during the spring and summer months may contribute to heat exhaustion — the committee can provide information and resources to the various departments. A school sponsored activity involving the public such as a large theater production, a festival, a bonfire, a parade, or a homecoming dance may present unique safety and security exposures due to the number of people that will be present. The safety committee can review the exposure and proposed controls to minimize the chance of an accident or injury.

1447 Your district safety committee should include at least one administrator and representative supervisors and employees from your various schools. 'Stack the deck' with employees who care about the overall safety and security culture of the school district. This is not the place for negative employees who will slow your efforts.

1448 **Your district administrator must grant the safety committee the authority to make change.** If your committee does not have the authority to expect their edicts to be carried out, your committee may be worthless. Safety committees that lack administration support are very often ineffective.

1449 **Your safety committee should meet on a frequent basis — preferably not less than once a month.** When meetings are held on a quarterly or biannual basis, it often leads to a loss of interest and deterioration of the safety committee.

1450 **School safety committee meetings should have a definitive agenda performed in a scheduled time frame.** Don't allow your committee to drift, with members discussing random items. Develop a definitive agenda a few weeks before the meeting and provide this information to your committee members so they can come prepared to discuss.

1451 **Rotate your safety committee members.** A self-perpetuating group of committee members tends to get stagnant and ineffective. Rotating your committee members (such as a two on and one off format) may make the best use of the knowledge and talent of your employees. By staggering your member's tenure, the safety committee will always have experienced and inexperienced members working together.

1452 **Develop a safety suggestion process that instructs staff and students as to how they can submit safety ideas, suggestions, or recommendations for the safety committee to review.** Your district's employees and students may have valuable ideas about making your schools safer and more secure. Develop a process where anyone can submit their ideas, have their ideas reviewed by the safety committee, and receive feedback on the validity of their ideas. The risk assessment form is a great tool to evaluate safety and security concerns.

1453

Utilize the risk assessment process to evaluate identified accident, incident, or near miss exposures. I have included the risk assessment form for your use. Here's how it works:

Any identified safety or security exposure can be reviewed by the safety committee to determine if it warrants follow up action or improvement.

1. In the first section, **'Describe hazard in detail,'** the identified hazard or exposure is explained.

2. In the second section **'Consequences — What can happen?'** the committee determines a numerical rating for the consequences of the discussed hazard or exposure. (Circle the highest number of corresponding consequence.)

3. In the third section — **'Severity — How bad could it be?'** the committee determines the numerical rating of the potential severity of the hazard or exposure. (Circle the highest number of the corresponding severity.)

4. In the fourth section **'Frequency — How often could in happen?'** the committee determines the numerical rating as to the potential frequency of the hazard or exposure. (Circle the number of the corresponding frequency.)

5. Multiply the **Consequence score** times the **Severity score** times the **Frequency score** to obtain the **Total Risk Index score**.

6. If the Total Risk Index score is 100 or greater, the hazard or exposure warrants immediate attention to address the seriousness of the potential accident or injury concern.

7. It is now time to develop the **Risk Management Plan**. As a group, the committee decides whether to 'terminate,' 'treat,' or 'tolerate' the risk. If the risk score is around 100 or greater, your objective should always be to treat the risk.

8. Through committee discussion, determine how, when, and by whom the risk will be addressed. Remember, the higher the risk score, the shorter the completion time.

9. The **Follow up Action table** is used to keep track of the various hazards and risks discussed. I suggest that you rank the risks with the highest risk score items appearing first — they warrant immediate attention.

Your committee can use this table meeting after meeting to monitor risk scores, assign tasks, register completion dates, etc. This table can be shared with your employees so they can see how much your safety committee has accomplished.

School District Risk Assessment

Describe hazard in detail:

_____

_____

_____

_____

Consequences — What can happen?

Damage	Fire	Explosion	Injury	Catastrophe	Disaster
1	2	3	4	5	6

Severity — How bad could it be?

Minor Injury	Disabling	Lost TIme Disability	Permanent Disability	Multiple	Death	Multiple Deaths
1	2	3	4	5	6	7

Frequency — How often could it happen?

Anytime	Hourly	Weekly	Monthly	Quarterly	Annually	Less Often
8	7	6	4	3	2	1

Evaluate the Risk:

Consequence Score x Severity Score x Frequency Score =
Total Risk Index

Rank the Risk:

Any Total Risk Index score of 100 or greater warrants
immediate attention!

Risk Management Plan:

TERMINATE	**TREAT**	**TOLERATE**
Get Rid of It!	Fix It!	Live With It!

Follow up Action: Explain How/Who/When

Item	Risk Score	Action Needed	By Whom and When	Date Completed

Skateboard Parks

Over the years, I have consulted with a number of school districts that were interested in building a skateboard park on school property. Some of the common issues that need to be addressed include:

1454 **Skateboard ramps must be well constructed.** If made of wood, skateboard ramps will require constant attention and maintenance. Watch for nails popping up that have to be nailed down again, warping boards, warping seams, bee/hornet hives beneath the ramps, and cracking blacktop around the ramp areas.

If wooden ramps are used, your maintenance personnel will be inspecting the ramps on a more frequent basis than playgrounds. Repairs tend to be more costly as well — you almost always have to replace something — it probably can't be 'fixed.'

1455 **Have participants and their parents/guardians sign a release of liability form.** It may be a nightmare to enforce, but I would push for the use of the liability form as well as a sticker badge that goes on the helmet denoting that the participant has signed a waiver form.

1456 **Post skate park rules and hours of operation.** I don't care for hours that state 'from dawn to dusk.' Rather, clearly define the hours (during daylight) when the park is accessible. Also you will want to list calendar dates as to when the park is open and closed — closed during the winter months, school vacations, etc.

1457 **Age requirements to use the park should be strictly enforced.**

1458 **The use of proper personal protective equipment should be required.** This includes the use of a helmet, elbow pads, and knee pads at a minimum.

1459 **No food, drink, or glass containers should ever be allowed in the skateboard park area.**

1460 Contact your local law enforcement to conduct additional patrols of the area if possible.

1461 Fence in the skateboard park if possible. This is the best method to control the safe use of the skateboard park.

Slip/Trip/Fall Prevention

Various insurance company studies indicate that slips/trips/falls are one of the top two exposures for a school district in frequency and severity. On a positive note, the slip/trip/fall exposure is one of the easiest to identify and correct.

Consider these best practices to reduce your school's slip/trip/fall exposure:

1462 Require good housekeeping practices both inside and outside your school buildings and facilities. Encourage all staff members to do their part by reporting or correcting slip/trip/fall exposures whenever they are observed.

1463 Ensure a slip resistant surface is present on all ramps, stairs and stairways throughout your school. Your insurance company's loss control services may be able to provide slip testing throughout your facilities to assist you in identifying your major slippery areas.

1464 Ensure that handrails are used on all stairways with four (4) or more steps.

1465 Make sure there is at least a 1.5" clearance between the handrails and the wall surface. A stair walker will not use the handrail if they can't grasp it.

1466 Post warnings at exit doors where staff or students could exit into the path of vehicular or pedestrian traffic.

1467 Highlight — better yet repair — any deviations in the height of concrete sidewalks or paths at your school entrance ways.

1468 On a periodic basis, inspect the rugs, carpets, and tile floors in your school. It's important to periodically check for tears and height deviations that could contribute to a trip and fall.

1469 Ensure floor mats are provided at entrance ways during the snow and ice months.

1470 Inspect your school's entrance floor mats, at least twice a day, during the snow and ice months. During winter, entrance mats in high pedestrian traffic areas soak up water very rapidly. When this occurs, water can easily be carried by a person's shoes throughout your school creating additional slip and fall exposure.

1471 Use 'Caution-Wet Floor' signs when appropriate. These signs should be used to indicate that someone is addressing the slip concern as soon as possible.

1472 Keep all extension cords off the floor to prevent trips and falls.

1473 Instruct all school employees to enter your school only through designated entrances. Especially during the winter months, employees must enter through those entrances that have been cleared of ice or snow.

1474 Require your school employees to wear proper non-slip footwear when entering or exiting the school — especially during winter conditions. Teachers can change to their dress shoes once they are in their classroom.

1475 Flip-flops and open toed sandals should never be allowed as acceptable footwear for your school staff members. Footwear of this type provides little ankle support and usually does not have an acceptable non-slip sole.

1476 Instruct your teachers to never stand on tables, desks, or chairs in the classroom. I would venture to say that every school district has had a costly workers' compensation claim where a teacher fell from an elevated height while hanging something from the ceiling or reaching for an item on a high book shelf.

1477 If teachers need to access something at an elevated height, call a custodian — they have the proper ladder.

1478 Don't allow your teachers to hang items from the ceiling or on the walls higher than their arm's reach.

1479 Require your technology education teachers to have students clean the floor of the shop work area every day. If your technology education shop areas have wood/metal shavings, oil, or other liquids on the floor, these materials can easily be transported by student's footwear throughout the school.

Substitute Teachers

Substitute teachers are important to the success of your school district, making it possible to continue the educational process in the absence of a teacher. Substitute teachers are 'temporary' employees of the school district and there are a number of important security and safety concerns that must be addressed.

1480 Conduct thorough background and criminal history checks on all substitute teachers. Background checks should be conducted to verify other schools where they have been employed and to ensure there is no criminal history that would prevent them from being a substitute teacher.

1481 Determine if classroom keys need to be issued to your substitute teachers. If a classroom cannot be secured from the inside, the substitute teachers may need to be issued the appropriate room key so they can execute a lockdown if necessary.

1482 Require substitute teachers to exchange their car keys for the classroom keys when they report for work. This will ensure the substitute teacher returns to the office at the end of the day to turn in the classroom keys.

1483 Do not allow substitute teachers to unlock rooms other than their own for any reason without the knowledge of the principal or the teacher responsible for that room.

1484 A list of important contact people should be provided to all substitute teachers. Substitute teachers need to know the names of the teachers in adjoining classrooms and know how to contact the main office as well.

1485 Ensure your emergency action plans are reviewed with all substitute teachers. This includes but is not limited to:

• Tornado Drills — substitute teachers must be familiar with your school's tornado evacuation plan.

• Fire Drills — substitute teachers must understand the layout of the school building and know where to immediately evacuate students.

• Crisis Plans (code for lockdown, evacuation, etc.) — ensure substitute teachers are familiar with your school's crisis plan. When seconds count, they must be able to immediately implement the plan.

• Early Dismissal.

1486 Do not allow substitute teachers to administer any medication to students — this is the duty of the school nurse. Even if the regular classroom teacher has left information about students with special needs, the substitute teacher must always check with the school principal.

1487 Instruct substitute teachers that they are to never harm or physically strike a student. As simple as this may sound, there have been a number of incidents where a substitute teacher physically confronted a child who was misbehaving in the classroom.

1488 Instruct substitute teachers that any confidential information learned at school is never to be shared in the community.

1489 Instruct substitute teachers to never leave students unattended for any reason. If there is an emergency or the substitute teacher must take a restroom break, call the office or send a student to the office with a note that you need another adult present in the classroom.

Take a few minutes at the beginning of the school day to ensure your substitute teachers have received proper safety and security training. During an emergency or crisis situation, seconds count; that's why it's important to ensure your substitute teachers are properly trained.

Teacher/Coach Athletic Participation

Every year, many teachers and coaches suffer injuries at school, usually to their back, shoulders, and knees, when participating in physical education or sports activities with their students. Besides the very real teacher/coach injury considerations, your school district's workers' compensation costs can skyrocket when costly debilitating injuries of this type escalate your experience modification factor.

Consider the following steps to address the teacher/coach participation exposure:

1490 Decide if your school district will allow teachers and coaches to participate in physical education and sports activities with students. This entails:

- Holding a meeting with school administration, building principals, and your athletic director to discuss the potential concerns — the frequency (number of claims) and the severity (workers' compensation dollars paid) of the claims related to teacher/coach participation in athletic events.

- Asking your teachers and coaches if they are physically involved with students, such as demonstrating wrestling moves.

- Determining if your teachers and coaches are involved in physical demonstrations which require rapid acceleration and stopping.

- Focusing your discussions on those activities that present injury exposure to physical education teachers and coaches.

1491 Within each school, require building principals to review the curriculum of their physical education classes. Determine which activities, sports, and games are taking place, the type of instruction involved, how physically involved the students are, and how physically involved teachers are in the activity.

1492 Try to uncover those activities which should be eliminated or at least modified for the protection of students. Over the years, I have assisted school districts in recognizing potentially dangerous activities such as dodge ball being played with leather soccer balls, gym hockey where too heavy a puck was used, students wearing inappropriate eyewear in certain activities, students climbing too high without proper fall protection or matting, etc.

Technology Education

1493 At the beginning of the school year, provide all technology education students with a written safety guidebook and require the teacher to review all relevant safety rules.

1494 During the first day of class, all students should have a tour of the technology education shop area. The teacher should point out the location of all fire extinguishers, fire blankets, eye wash stations, emergency power shut-off switches, and any other emergency equipment available to the students.

1495 All students must receive proper instruction regarding the safe use of tools, equipment, and material used in technology education classes. Teachers should have a documented, ongoing safety program reminding students of safety and safe use of tools and equipment.

1496 Students must be given safety instruction and tested each year they participate in any technology education class.

1497 Students should demonstrate their knowledge of the safety rules and guidelines by taking a safety examination with a 100% passing grade required. Allow your students to take the exam as many times as necessary or allow students to miss 10% of the questions and have them accurately write the complete question and correct answer, either on the back of the original answer sheet or on a separate sheet of paper.

1498 Both the original safety test and any correction sheets should be signed and dated by the student and retained on file for a minimum of four years. These safety tests should be maintained for the duration of the student's high school years.

1499 Loose fitting and/or unbuttoned clothing and open toed footwear are never to be allowed in the technology education area.

1500 Students with long hair should wear suitable protective and restraining headgear while working in the technology education shop area. Hair must be tied up or worn underneath a hard hat to prevent it from getting caught in rotating machinery.

1501 **Require students to wear appropriate personal protective equipment.** Many times over the years, I have observed students (and some instructors) not wearing safety glasses when walking through the shop area while other students were operating machinery.

1502 **Unsafe equipment must be locked out to prevent use by students and reported for immediate repair or replacement.** Students should never be allowed to repair a piece of equipment without the approval of the instructor.

1503 **All compressed gas cylinders not in use must be properly secured and chained.** Oxygen and acetylene cylinders must be kept separate by a distance of thirty lineal feet. Empty compressed gas cylinders should be tagged immediately to avoid confusion with other cylinders in use.

1504 **Maintain good housekeeping conditions throughout your technology education shop areas.** Serious slip, trip, and fall hazards are created when the shop areas are not kept clean at all times.

Flammable Storage

1505 **All varnishes, paint thinners, and other flammables must be kept in the flammable storage cabinet when not in use.**

1506 **Store only flammable liquids in any securable flammable storage cabinet.** Don't allow a flammable storage cabinet to be used to store paper, tools, lunches, etc.

1507 **Flammable cabinet doors must be closed and secured when not being accessed.** Don't hesitate to place padlocks on your flammable storage cabinets to prevent unauthorized access to these potentially explosive materials.

Auto Shop Safety Controls

🔑 **1508** Students should never be allowed to work on any vehicle that does not pertain to the instructor's assignment, without the instructor's prior approval.

🔑 **1509** All vehicle owners who agree to allow students to work on their vehicles must sign a 'work order' form, including a 'hold harmless' agreement. It is important that your school is held harmless for any repairs performed on vehicles.

1510 Only instructors and students who have the instructor's approval may drive a vehicle into or out of the auto shop. No one else should be allowed to drive vehicles within the auto shop.

1511 Instruct students to stand to the side of the vehicle when guiding it into the lift area or a parking space. Students have been struck and run over when standing in front of the vehicle while guiding it into the auto shop.

1512 Never bring a vehicle into the auto shop if it has a gasoline leak or defective brakes.

1513 Students should never be allowed to work early or continue after the regular class time without the instructor's approval and supervision. Vehicle work should be completed during the regular class time.

1514 Loose clothing and long hair should not be permitted since it could get caught in rotating parts of the engine. When working under the hood, always watch out for rotating parts.

1515 Require students to remove rings, watches, and jewelry when working on vehicles.

1516 **A fire extinguisher should be placed next to the vehicle if the work performed presents a fire danger.** The fire extinguisher must be returned to its proper location after the work is completed.

1517 **Before using any vehicle hoist, lift, or jack, your students must obtain proper permission and instruction from the instructor.** The auto shop instructor should supervise these activities to ensure that students do not create a falling vehicle hazard.

1518 **Car hoist inspections must be conducted on a frequent basis by the school district.** On a yearly basis, the hoist is to be inspected by a certified inspector.

Theater Safety

Anyone who has visited a school theater during performance preparation can relate to the fact that it often looks like organized chaos — no surprise, it often is.

Sets are being constructed, props and costumes are being designed, and cast members are working on their lines and choreography. Along with the excitement of an upcoming theater production is the very real concern of serious injury to those involved.

Before any theater activity is allowed to take place, consider the following best practices:

1519 **Prior to each performance, review your theater seating and circulation layouts.** This is important to reduce or eliminate the traffic flow problems that could be created by wheelchairs or props in the aisles.

1520 **Policies/procedures for use of equipment and machinery during set construction, play practice, and performances need to be in place and followed.** These policies should address the required safety training that must be provided for students and volunteers as well as the safety rules that must be followed by all.

1521 Before any theater production begins, adequate training must be provided to all staff, students, and volunteers so they understand the expectations and policy/procedure requirements of the school district. Ensure that all affected personnel sign off that they understand and will follow your requirements.

1522 Provide special markings to Identify orchestra pit openings. An orchestra pit cover should be in place whenever the pit is not being used. You may want to consider using a removable guardrail before and after performances until the pit cover is reinstalled. Additionally the stair landing leading to the pit area may need to be guarded to prevent someone from accidentally falling down the dark stairwell.

1523 A low voltage rope light or reflective tape may be needed to identify where the stage ends. Many performers have fallen off the stage because the edge of the stage was not clearly marked.

1524 At all times, all aisles and passageways must remain unobstructed for pedestrian access. Ensure that props and stage scenery never obstruct these areas at any time.

1525 Before any trap doors are used in any theater productions, ensure that your district safety coordinator has approved their use.

1526 Lock all trap doors when they are not in use. Other than the actual use of the trap door during a performance, the trap door must remain closed when the activity involving the trap door is completed.

1527 Your instructor should be the only person allowed to remove the padlock on a trap door.

1528 Line all stage trap doors and floor openings with yellow reflective safety tape to increase visibility during low light conditions.

1529 Provide protective railings for all runways, stairs, platforms, and trap doors. The railings must have a top rail, a mid rail, and a toe board. A vertical height of 42 inches from the upper surface to the top rail must always be maintained.

1530 Safety cables must always be used to attach light fixtures to the catwalk frame.

1531 Scenery hoisting equipment, suspended lighting equipment, and cabling must be inspected on a regularly scheduled basis.

1532 Ensure all stage lighting and electrical equipment controls are located in locked panels.

1533 Access to your catwalks must be strictly controlled. Only approved school employees should be allowed to access the catwalk area.

1534 Catwalks must be equipped with appropriate handrail and guardrail protection.

1535 Never allow materials to be stored on the catwalk. If materials were to be stored on the catwalk, a serious trip and fall accident could occur.

1536 Every stairway having four or more risers must be protected with a standard railing on all open sides.

1537 Handrails need to be provided on at least one side of every open stairway.

1538 If stairways are constructed in-house, they should be inspected and approved by your district safety coordinator and your maintenance supervisor prior to any use.

1539 If your theater uses a fire drop curtain, paint a reflective line on the stage floor to indicate the curtain drop area. This drop area must be kept clear at all times.

1540 Drop testing of the curtain must be conducted yearly by a certified contractor.

1541 Stage and other draperies or hangings must be non-flammable or fire-retardant.

1542 Before any special props are used, they should be approved at least 30 days prior to the theater production. The use of open flames must be strictly monitored.

1543 If a stage prop presents the risk of fire or injury, it should be fire proofed and approved by school administration and your local fire department.

1544 If multi-level structures are used in theater productions, plans must be submitted and approved by school administration before construction begins.

1545 Always use a fixed stairway when access between stage structures on different levels is needed.

1546 At all times, prohibit any props that are gasoline fueled or powered by combustible material.

1547 Authentic weapons, such as knives and guns should never be allowed.

1548 **Prohibit pyrotechnics and other potentially dangerous special effects.** The best practice is to always prohibit pyrotechnics on all school property. If your school district does allow the use of pyrotechnics, they should be used outdoors and only operated by a licensed pyrotechnic technician.

1549 **Make sure the pyrotechnic technician provides a certificate of insurance to your school district.**

1550 **Only those trained by a qualified instructor shall be allowed to use or operate hand or power tools.**

1551 **All operators of any power tools should be required to read and understand, prior to operation, the operating manual and safety requirements related to the particular tool they will operate.**

1552 **Power tool safety guards shall never be removed, by-passed, or altered for any reason.**

Storage and Work Areas

1553 **Maintain good housekeeping practices in your storage areas to prevent the accumulation of materials that present tripping exposures and fire concerns.**

1554 **Uniformly stack, block, or interlock all stored materials to prevent them from sliding or collapsing.**

1555 **Limit the height of all stored materials to prevent them from tipping over onto someone.**

1556 **Store all combustible and flammable materials in a fireproof cabinet or room.**

Student Concerns

1557 All students participating in a theatrical production should be required to review and sign a 'Student Safety Contract' prior to the start of each production. These signed safety contracts should be kept on file by the instructor.

1558 Adequate supervision is a key element in maintaining a safe theater environment. No potentially dangerous activities should take place unless proper adult supervision is present.

1559 Students should never be allowed to work unsupervised during or after school hours. I don't know of many theater volunteers who clearly understand the liability concerns associated with a lack of supervision.

1560 Never allow any students to perform electrical activities. A student's electrical involvement should be restricted to changing a light bulb or using an extension cord. Students should never be allowed to perform any type of electrical wiring activities; a master electrician should be the only one to perform these duties.

1561 Closely monitor any students who use ladders. A student should never be allowed to climb a ladder more than three feet.

1562 If you make the decision to allow students on a catwalk, they should only be there when the instructor is present.

1563 Do not allow students to operate any type of aerial lifts during theater production set up. Refer to the chapter regarding aerial lift safety for recommended risk management best practices.

1564 Never allow students to build or use scaffolding. As the old saying goes, 'gravity always wins.' A student falling off an improperly erected scaffold could suffer devastating injuries.

Tornado Safety

I know of many school districts that share tornado safety plans — the old 'one size fits all' approach. The problem with implementing such a generic tornado safety plan is that it does not account for the specific features, modifications, or additions that exist in your school.

1565 **Your tornado safety plan must be tailored to your specific school building design and focused on your staff's ability and resources to quickly move people.** It is critical that your school district develops a comprehensive tornado safety plan.

1566 **Always plan for the worst — if there are reports of tornados in nearby areas, enact your tornado plan immediately.**

1567 **When a tornado warning is issued, seconds count.** Your customized school tornado plan must be enacted quickly and efficiently.

1568 **When your tornado plan is activated within the school building, the biggest concern for a school administrator is ensuring that all students and staff are accounted for.** If a number of students are outside the school building, others may be put in danger ensuring these students and staff are in a safe location.

1569 **Instruct teachers to remain calm with their voice and visible with their hand motions when leading students to the designated safe areas.** Calmly inform students to remain quiet, crouch low, and keep their head down, protecting the head with their hands and arms.

1570 **Develop a tornado action plan which includes frequent drills.** Review the plan annually and whenever changes are made to your building, shelters, or classroom sizes. A good time to practice is during the annual statewide tornado drill held in April of each year.

1571 Determine if all students from the upper levels of your schools can be safely and quickly moved to the lower levels. Handicapped or special needs students may require additional assistance and time to move them to the lower levels of your school building.

1572 Practice your procedures to move disabled or special needs students. When a stairwell is full of students it is not the time to try to move a student who cannot walk as quickly as other students.

1573 Determine if your school's lowest level can accommodate all students and staff in a minimal amount of time. The lead time of tornado warnings issued by the National Weather Service has increased over the years; unfortunately many tornados still touch down with little warning or lead time.

1574 Ensure your tornado plan addresses how to move students out of portable classrooms as quickly as possible. Portable classrooms provide little or no protection during a tornado. The best plan is to evacuate your students when the weather is threatening; don't wait for the tornado warning to be issued.

1575 Ensure your students know the 'protection position.' It doesn't matter if the students face the wall or put their backs to the wall, as long as they cover their head.

1576 Always attempt to keep students and staff away from hallways, doors, and classroom walls that present a high exposure to flying glass. Flying debris caused by the tornado is your biggest concern.

1577 When the weather is threatening, avoid large open areas such as auditoriums, gymnasiums, and field houses. These areas may have inherent structural weaknesses and may collapse during a tornado.

1578 **Delay lunches or assemblies in large rooms if severe weather is anticipated.** Your gymnasiums, cafeterias, and auditoriums offer little or no protection from tornado strength winds.

1579 **Cancel any class activity outside of your school building when the weather conditions are threatening.** Field trips, physical education activities, etc. should be cancelled if warranted.

1580 **A registered engineer or architect should be used to designate and inspect the shelter areas in each of your schools.**

1581 **Basements offer the best protection during a tornado.**

1582 **Schools without basements should use interior rooms and hallways on the lowest floor and away from windows.** Put as many walls as possible between the students and the storm.

1583 **Each school should have a NOAA Weather Radio All Hazards (NWR) with battery back-up.** NOAA Weather Radio All Hazards is a nationwide network of radio stations broadcasting continuous weather information directly from the nearest National Weather Service office. NWR broadcasts official Weather Service warnings, watches, forecasts, and other hazard information 24 hours a day, 7 days a week.

1584 **Make sure the weather radio or other source of weather news is available during, before, and after school activities and events.**

1585 **If the school's alarm system relies on electricity, have an alternate method (air horn or megaphone) to notify teachers and students in case of power failure.** Make sure everyone understands your school's notification signal.

1586 Have a communication plan to contact staff and students who are away from the school (field trips) when your tornado plan is put into effect.

1587 During threatening weather, keep students at school beyond regular hours until the storms pass. Students are safer at school than in a bus or car.

Trampolines in School

During the 1980s and 1990s, the use of trampolines in schools was strictly taboo. Over the past 10-15 years this has changed; more and more school districts are inquiring about the use of trampolines.

1588 Simply stated, due to the significant number of injuries and liability exposures presented by the use of trampolines, their use should be prohibited in your schools. Check with your liability insurance carrier — they may not even allow the use of a trampoline in your school.

Though trampolines are not recommended, if your school district uses a trampoline, strict safety and security controls must be in place. These controls may include:

1589 A safety pad should cover all portions of the steel frame and springs.

1590 The surface around the trampoline should have an impact-absorbing safety surface material.

1591 The condition of the trampoline should be regularly checked for tears, rust, and detachments.

1592 Safety harnesses and spotting belts, when appropriately used, may offer added protection for athletes learning or practicing more challenging skills on the trampoline.

1593 Consider setting the trampoline in a pit so the mat is at ground level.

1594 Be careful, ladders may provide unintended access to the trampoline by small children and should not be used.

1595 Only one person should use the trampoline at a time.

1596 In supervised settings, the user of the trampoline should be at the center of the mat.

1597 The user of the trampoline should never attempt maneuvers beyond their capability or training, thereby putting them at risk for injury.

1598 Personnel trained in trampoline safety and competent spotters should always be present whenever the trampoline is in use.

1599 Even in supervised training programs, the use of trampolines for children younger than 6 years of age should be prohibited.

1600 The trampoline must be secured and not accessible when not in use.

Mini Trampolines

1601 Mini-trampolines (in the classroom) are to be used only by students for whom a school-based physical or occupational therapist has made a written recommendation.

1602 Qualifying students may use the mini-trampoline only when directly supervised by the therapist or classroom staff who have been trained and authorized by the therapist.

1603 Mini-trampolines may not be used:

• By a student who does not have a signed recommendation.

• By a student when not directly supervised.

• By any student or staff for recreational purposes (i.e. acrobatics).

Weight Room Safety

The risk of injury from weight training can be minimized by requiring proper instruction (teaching proper lifting techniques) and adult supervision.

To provide a safe experience in your school weight room, a plan should be developed that addresses the following four concerns: equipment, maintenance, instruction, and supervision.

Equipment Concerns

1604 Never assume that weight machines are safer than free weights. Weight machines have moving parts that can cause serious injury if they are not used correctly. Both weight machines and free weights present accident exposures that must be addressed.

1605 All stationary weight room equipment must be installed according to manufacturer's specifications. Always attempt to contact the equipment manufacturer for specific set up guidelines.

1606 If no equipment manufacturer specifications are provided, care must be taken to secure the apparatus so the equipment won't tip over during use. Bolting your equipment to the floor is a great option.

1607 If a piece of equipment malfunctions or is broken, remove it from service until it is repaired or replaced.

1608 Your weight room equipment must be properly spaced to allow lifters ample space for lifting and provide spotters ample room for spotting.

1609 All of the free weights must be held in place on the bar with clamps. Free weights being used without clamps can cause injury to the lifter and to those around if the bar 'unloads' all or part of the weight plates.

Maintenance Concerns

1610 On a regular basis, inspect all of your weight room equipment for broken or malfunctioning parts. Cables, clamps, pulleys, bearings, weight plates, channels, swivels, hangers, bars, and benches should be integrated into your periodic inspection program.

1611 Maintain written records of inspections, broken equipment and repair records.

1612 Contact the original equipment manufacturer for inspection forms relative to their equipment. If it is not possible to obtain these forms, use a generic inspection form, many of which can be found on the internet.

1613 Inspections should take place more frequently if the weight room is used on a more frequent basis. It is especially important to increase the frequency of inspections if the community uses the facility.

1614 Any damaged fabric on the apparatus should be sealed immediately to stop the contamination of the foam and padding from sweat and body fluids. Use non-porous tape, like wrestling mat tape, as a temporary seal until permanent repairs can be completed. When permanent repairs are made, if the foam or padding is contaminated, replace the material before reupholstering the bench or apparatus.

1615 Clean and disinfect all fabric and equipment padding on a regular basis. This is an especially important personal hygiene concern. There have been many reported cases of ringworm and other skin diseases transmitted by weight equipment padding that is in poor condition or isn't sanitized appropriately.

1616 All moving equipment joints must be lubricated on a regular basis according to manufacturers' specifications.

1617 On a quarterly basis, all bolted frames should be inspected and retightened if necessary. If a bolted frame is moved, check all joints for stability before allowing the apparatus to be used.

1618 To prevent damage caused by free weights striking the floor, cover the floor with shock absorption mats.

Instruction Concerns

1619 Post weight room rules and regulations in your weight room. Clear, concise rules must be posted and followed by all participants. Many examples of weight room rules can be found on the internet.

1620 Provide students with a written instruction sheet for each lift. Visual reminders such as wall charts help to reinforce proper lifting techniques.

1621 **Never allow anyone to attempt their maximum weight lift if proper training hasn't been provided.** Lifters should be taught the safe method of each lift.

1622 **Lifters must wear appropriate footwear while lifting.** Loose fitting shoes are not appropriate nor are sandals, flip flops, open-toed shoes, or shoes with high or modified high heels. Proper fitting shoes provide good arch, foot, and ankle support.

1623 **Lifters should always use weight belts as directed by the weight room instructor.**

1624 **Lifters should be instructed when to use spotters and spotters must be trained to perform their duties correctly.** Spotters must be physically strong enough to provide lifters a safe 'spot.'

1625 **The use of free weights requires the use of spotters — no exceptions.** Supervisors in the weight room can act as spotters.

1626 **If the instructor does not have a background in progressive weight training, schools should provide this training or provide additional personnel who are trained to assist the instructor.** Weight training should be progressive in nature and designed to help each lifter progress from their current lifting ability to a defined goal. Certified progressive weight training programs are available from many commercial sources as well as from colleges and other training institutions.

1627 **Never allow student lifters to attempt their maximum lift or lift more weight than they can safely handle.**

1628 **Instructors must stop any incorrect lifting technique and make the necessary adjustments in form, weight, etc.**

1629 Use wall mirrors to assist with teaching correct lifting technique. If mirrors are used, they should be non-breakable and secured to the wall.

1630 To help avoid injuries, instructors should require student lifters to warm up and stretch before lifting and cool down and stretch at the end of each session.

1631 When 'maximum' lifts are taking place, extra care must be given to provide adequate spotters and instruction as to how to perform maximum lifts. Instructors should be cautioned to examine the benefit of less weight and more repetitions as opposed to more weight and fewer repetitions when 'maximums' are attempted.

1632 All free weights must be returned to the storage rack after each use and at the end of the lifting session.

1633 Providing lifters with a written daily lifting plan is essential in keeping the lifters focused on their individual efforts as opposed to a free-lance program where the lifters decide how much to lift and how many repetitions to attempt.

1634 All lifters must be instructed in the emergency plan for the weight facility before starting lifting exercises.

1635 Post maps indicating emergency exits. Determine how weight room participants will be moved or secured during lockdown and evacuation drills.

Supervision Concerns

1636 Instructors and supervisors must be present at any time students are in the weight room. Instructors must move around the weight room to supervise.

1637 No students should ever be left alone in the weight room unsupervised.

1638 Students should never be allowed key access to the weight room if a qualified instructor is not present.

1639 If you open your weight room to the community, trained supervision must be present at all times the facility is open to the public. Students should not be allowed to be supervisors.

1640 Your instructors and supervisors should be the last ones to leave your weight room and make sure the facility is locked and secured.

1641 Strict weight room key control must be maintained. Keys to the weight room should never be provided to community members, students, or a staff member who is not qualified to use the equipment.

1642 If an instructor observes an unsafe lifting technique, the instructor must immediately stop the lift and correct the technique. The instructor is there to prevent injury to the lifter or those around them.

1643 Instructors and supervisors should never try to supervise other areas, in addition to the weight room area. Weight room supervisors should never leave the area when lifters are present. If your weight facility is a divided room, the supervisor should review the supervision expectations with their immediate supervisor before starting any lifting session.

1644 Instructors and supervisors should never be lifting weights when their duty is to supervise. Supervisors can't work out and supervise others at the same time — it's either one or the other.

1645 Instructors and supervisors should not provide any dietary advice to student-athletes. Leave the dietary advice to be provided by a trained nutritionist.

1646 **Do not allow too many lifters in the weight room at one time.** Due to the inherent dangers of free weights and weight machines, your school should determine the maximum number of lifters who can use the equipment at any one time.

1647 **Bystanders and friends are not allowed in the weight room.** Your weight room should never become an area for non-lifters, visitors, or spectators to congregate. Oftentimes, when the community is allowed to use the facility, their children are brought along to save the cost of a babysitter — this practice should never be allowed.

1648 **Consider having all weight room participants sign a waiver to provide liability protection to your school district.** All participants must be provided the rules and regulations of the weight room. It is important to understand that waivers often do not hold up in the court of law; they simply indicate the individual involved in the activity understands the risks that are inherent to the activity.

1649 **If community members are allowed to use the weight room, they need to sign a participant waiver.**

1650 **All weight room participants must sign in and sign out, including the date and time when they are in the weight room.**

1651 **Community members entering your school to use the weight room must follow your school's visitor control policy.** There may be potential problems if visitors must walk through the school to get to the weight room.

There are a number of concerns that your school must address if the public is allowed to use the weight room during normal school hours, including:

• Who will check these visitors in to the school?

• How will you ensure they go directly to the weight room?

• How can you ensure they leave the weight room and immediately leave the school building?

Worst case scenario, a visitor with bad intentions enters your school with the intention of using the weight room; instead they are 'allowed' to freely walk around your school, with access to students and staff.

As you can see, equipment maintenance, supervision, and instruction are critical factors. No student or athlete should be allowed to use a weight room if they have not been properly trained in the use of the equipment. Additionally, supervisors must be ever present, ensuring lifters are using the equipment properly and ensuring that horseplay and bystanders are barred from the weight room.

Wintertime Safety

Long before wintertime approaches is the time for your school district to ensure your snow and ice removal program is in place. Make sure these best practices are part of your snow and ice removal plan:

1652 Prepare all equipment for readiness condition long before the snow and ice season begins.

1653 Develop an action plan that addresses snow and ice removal from building entrances, sidewalks, parking lots, etc. Develop guidelines for when snow and ice must be removed from your entrances (main entrances first), walkways, and parking areas.

1654 Use your website and local radio/television stations for weather reports and school closing information.

1655 Develop a snow storage plan for each school facility. Heights of snow piles should be reduced in those areas where they could create traffic or pedestrian blind spots.

1656 Instruct playground supervisors to keep children off snow piles whenever possible.

1657 Especially at elementary schools, level off snow piles to reduce the 'attractive nuisance' exposure whereby children view these snow piles as a play area.

1558 Obtain written agreements and certificates of insurance from the subcontractors your school district uses for snow and ice removal.

1559 Ensure that subcontractors responsible for snow removal clearly understand the 'time of day' your snow removal is to take place.

1560 Publish bulletin reminders of snow and Ice safety, parking regulations, etc., for staff members and students to review.

1561 Require building and grounds personnel wear proper personal protective equipment (boots, gloves, hearing protection, etc.) when operating snow removal equipment, such as a snow blower.

1662 Clearly mark hydrants and other fixtures that need to be protected.

1663 Clean leaves from drainage paths and pedestrian areas to allow for snow/ice handling and melting of pathways.

1564 Develop 'spot salting' procedures for trouble areas such as around stop signs, curves, building entrances, etc.

1565 Instruct your building principals to monitor snow accumulation throughout the day which may require additional snow removal.

1566 Maintain a daily log of conditions and treatments. This is especially important for your building's main entrances, exterior walking areas, etc.

1667 Instruct school employees to use designated entrances during snow and ice conditions. At most school districts, there are a select number of entrance ways that are cleared first after a snowfall. Many slip and fall accidents occur when school employees choose to enter the school where the snow and ice has not been removed.

1668 Instruct all school employees to wear slip resistant shoes during snow and icy conditions. They can change to their dress shoes once they enter the school building.

1669 Periodically clean and replace entrance door rugs and mats to reduce the amount of water brought into your school.

1670 Develop a procedure to quickly respond to complaints and problems of slippery walking areas.

1671 Develop a plan to remove overhanging snow and icicles. This is especially important around entrance ways where a falling icicle could injure someone.

1672 Make sure a plan is in place to remove heavy snow and ice loads from school building roofs. You may want to subcontract this job to a professional to eliminate the exposure of your employees falling off your building's roof.

1673 If school employees are involved in removing snow and ice from roofs, ensure that proper fall protection controls are in place.

1674 Locate your building's downspouts in a position that does not direct water over walk ways.

Volunteers in School

Whether they are used for classroom instruction or activity supervision, volunteers play an important role in your school. Ensure your school makes the most educated and safest decisions when using volunteers in your school.

1675 **All volunteer activities should be conducted under supervision of school staff.** Your principal should review and approve the schedule, work location, and duties of volunteers.

1676 **Learn the many volunteer activities that may require background checks, review of criminal records, or fingerprinting.** This list includes but is not limited to:

• Coaching activities.

• One-on-one tutoring or mentoring outside the classroom or other supervised school setting.

• Attending or chaperoning overnight school-sponsored trips.

• Any volunteer activity where there is a possibility of unsupervised contact with children.

• Any additional activities as defined by your school district.

1677 **Your school district should reserve the right to require background checks and/or fingerprinting of any prospective or current volunteer.** This includes any parents, legal guardians, step parents, and grandparents serving as volunteers.

Your superintendent or principal should determine the circumstances that support a background check or fingerprinting of volunteers.

1678 **Utilize your state's Public Sex Offender Registry to screen all your school volunteers.**

"Have a plan. Follow the plan, and you'll be surprised how successful you can be. Most people don't have a plan, that's why it is easy to beat most folks."

– Paul "Bear" Bryant
legendary football coach

SCHOOL **LIABILITY** BEST PRACTICES

Athletic Liability

With athletic seasons taking place throughout the entire school year, there are a number of athletic liability concerns that should be addressed by your school district:

1679 **Athlete's parents/guardians must be made aware of the inherent risks and dangers of their student's sport, prior to the first practice of that sport.** A presentation by your coaches and athletic director that requires mandatory parent/guardian attendance is the best time to review inherent risks of the sport. Review appropriate safety controls, answer questions, and have parents/guardians sign the required athletic participation release forms. Make sure that your school documents the date and content of this meeting.

1680 **With the chance of serious injury occurring in any sport, use waivers and liability releases in an attempt to release the school district from liability which may result from an athletic injury.** These forms explain the risks and dangers involved in the activity, the training rules of the activity, and the need to follow the coaches' instructions. If the parent/guardian and students sign these forms, they agree to assume the risks of the sport or activity.

1681 **A parent/guardian may waive their own rights by signing a waiver or liability release form; a minor student cannot.** Understand that the use of a waiver or liability release will not always protect your school district from injuries resulting from negligence.

1682 **Develop a risk statement that clearly outlines the inherent risks of the sport or activity.** This risk statement provides parents/guardians with full knowledge of:

• The risks associated with the sport/activity.

• The importance of following instruction and the rules of the sport/activity.

The goal of the risk statement is to ensure the student and their parent/guardian voluntarily assumes the risk of the sport or activity.

1683 Prior to the first practice of any sport, coaches must be made aware of the student-athlete's medical background and any physical limitations they may have. This includes knowledge of health concerns such as asthma, heart disorders, severe allergies, epilepsy, diabetes, etc. Again, ensure that documentation is maintained regarding a student-athlete's medical background.

1684 For students with identified medical conditions, ensure that special precautions have been reviewed with all coaches. This includes:

• In case of emergency, a medical action plan is in place.

• Ensuring medical support aids are available (such as an epinephrine auto injector for severe allergies, a blood testing kit/fast acting sugar for diabetes, or relief medications for allergies).

1685 Before involving student-athletes in outdoor sports, consider how physically strenuous the sport will be, the maximum temperature for the day, and how long will the athletes be physically active. When it is 95 degrees outside with 90% humidity, a rigorous football practice should probably be cancelled.

1686 The more dangerous the sport, the greater responsibility of your coaching staff. Your coaches must:

• Understand their duty to provide proper supervision, training and instruction.

• Take measures to ensure that student-athletes follow the rules of the athletic contest to avoid injuries.

• Warn against all known dangers that should have or could have been discovered in the exercise of reasonable care.

• Supervise their players in proportion to how dangerous the activity is.

Proper supervision and instruction are the key components to reduce your school's athletic liability exposure.

1687 **All coaches must understand their duty to take reasonable precautions.** Coaches have a duty to their student-athletes and must do everything practical (what a prudent parent would do) to minimize the risk of injury to student-athletes under their control.

A coach may breach their duty to a student-athlete if the coach "intentionally injures the student or engages in conduct that is reckless in the sense that it is 'totally outside the range of the ordinary activity' involved in teaching or coaching the sport."

1688 **Your coaches must ensure proper protective equipment is provided for your student-athletes.** Coaches may be found liable if an injured athlete was not provided with the proper protective and safety equipment.

1689 **Your coaches must ensure the student-athlete is properly instructed as to the appropriate use of protective equipment.** A coach must also ensure that the equipment is properly maintained so that its effectiveness is maximized.

1690 **Students and parents/guardians must be made aware that any equipment brought from home must be in safe playing condition (hockey helmets, hockey sticks, racquets, golf clubs, etc.).**

1691 **Teach your coaches how to foresee accidents before they occur.** This means eliminating dangerous conditions or behaviors as soon as the coach becomes aware of them. Horseplay, hazing, bullying, harassment, or the use of unsafe practice drills must be strictly monitored and barred.

1692 **Ensure that all of your coaches understand basic first aid procedures.** Carrying a cell phone with '911' on speed dial should be required for all coaches.

1693 **Coaches must use common sense when matching and selecting competitors in athletic competitions.** Do not allow mismatched student-athletes to compete or practice against each other if there is a chance of injury due to the discrepancy in their athletic skills. Don't ever teach a student-athlete 'a lesson' by having them compete against someone who is significantly bigger, stronger, or faster, when your only goal is to humiliate that individual.

1594 **Strongly discourage the practice of having your student-athletes run or sprint in school hallways as part of their training.** From the student-athlete's perspective, hallway floors are hard and shin splints commonly occur. A more serious injury exposure exists for those students, teachers, or bystanders who may be walking down a hallway, rounding a corner, or exiting a classroom door and are struck by a sprinting student-athlete.

I understand that some northern climate schools have no alternative but to run in their hallways. If this is the case, precautions must be taken to protect both the student-athlete and any bystanders. Some athletic supply companies manufacturer 'sprint strips' which allow athletes to run indoors with their running spikes. Additionally, various types of protective padding and mats are available to protect student-athletes from hitting the wall or obstacles in the hallway.

1595 **It is critical that the hallway used for running be shut down to pedestrian traffic.** Observers on both ends of the course should be in place. Classroom and other doors leading to the running area should be secured to prevent accidental access to the running area.

1696 **Instruct your student-athletes to never share their water bottles, towels, or athletic equipment.** The risk of infection increases if you allow athletic equipment to be shared between athletes.

1697 **Develop a policy that addresses spectators who are close to the field, court, or athletic event.** From a risk management standpoint, there are a number of exposures the school should address when allowing spectators on the sidelines of an athletic event.

1698 Your best and safest option is to keep all spectators off the sidelines.

1699 If spectators are allowed on the sidelines, restrict the spectators to one identified designated area where they will not be allowed to move around, especially up and down the sidelines.

1700 Ensure adequate distance is maintained between the athletic event and the spectator area. It goes without saying that the spectator area should not be close enough to the sidelines that a spectator or athlete could be injured in a collision.

1701 Limit the number of spectators allowed on the sidelines at any one time.

1702 Do not allow your spectators to be mobile or moving (with the possible exception of pre-approved photographers).

1703 Small children should never be allowed on the sidelines. This is often seen when the coach's young son is the water boy during a football game or the bat boy during a baseball game. Accidents and injuries have occurred when children cannot get out of the way soon enough and are struck by running athletes.

1704 Use extra precautions (and distance) if any spectators are on crutches or use a wheelchair. Besides the obvious injury exposure to the spectator, athletes could be seriously injured if they were to collide with someone in a wheelchair.

1705 Consider using a field pass waiver if spectators are to be allowed on the sidelines of your athletic events. Examples of good field pass waivers can be found on the internet. Consult with your school district's legal counsel before developing your own waiver form.

1706 **Never allow activities where balls or other objects are thrown at students.** If kickball is played as part of your physical education class, softball rules should apply, where a runner is thrown out by throwing the ball to the base and not at the runner.

The purpose of dodge ball is to throw a ball at another student. A number of school districts are viewing dodge ball as a bullying activity, where a number of stronger students can 'gang up' on a weaker student.

1707 **Thoroughly review all new athletic programs, training drills, physical education activities, etc. for safety concerns prior to recommending them for implementation.**

1708 **Require your physical education teachers and athletic coaches to periodically conduct documented safety inspections of your equipment and facilities and report any concerns to the athletic director.**

1709 **Educate your coaches on the importance of preventing hazing from ever occurring.** Hazing prevention controls include:

1710 **Don't encourage hazing by providing privileges to one group over another (varsity over junior varsity, seniors get to sit where they want on the bus) that the students may use to haze others.**

1711 **As a coach, never tell students about the initiations or hazing that you participated in when you were in school.**

1712 **Never minimize the importance of any reports or investigations that involve hazing incidents.**

1713 **During bus trips, require the coaches to walk throughout the bus at random times, paying special attention to what's going on between the students.**

1714 If more than one coach (or adult) is on the school bus, don't allow them to sit together. Instead, have one adult sit in back of the bus and one in the middle of the bus.

1715 Your coach is the supervisor on the bus — don't fall asleep or become involved in another activity or distraction.

Attractive Nuisance Doctrine

Though it's application may vary from state to state, the attractive nuisance doctrine states that a property owner, in your case the school district, may have liability for injuries to children trespassing on school property if the injury is caused by a hazardous object or condition on the property that is likely to attract children who are unable to appreciate the risk posed by the object or condition.

The attractive nuisance doctrine has been applied to hold property owners liable for injuries caused by large snow piles, sports equipment such as blocking sleds and baseball hitting cages, abandoned vehicles, piles of lumber or debris, trampolines, and swimming pools. However, it may be applied to virtually anything on the property of the school district.

In most cases, a possessor of property is not liable to a trespasser for physical harm caused by the failure to exercise reasonable care to make the land reasonably safe.

However when the trespasser is a child, the doctrine of attractive nuisance imposes on the possessor of land a duty to exercise reasonable care when certain special conditions exist.

In general, five conditions must be met for the property owner (school district) to possibly have liability:

• The location where the condition exists is one where the school district knows or has reason to know that children are likely to trespass.

• The condition is one of which the school district knows or has reason to know and which they realize or should realize will involve an unreasonable risk of death or serious bodily harm to children.

- The children, because of their youth, do not discover the condition or realize the risk involved in intermeddling with it or coming within the area made dangerous by it.

- The utility to the school district of maintaining the condition and the burden of eliminating the danger are slight as compared with the risk to children involved, and

- The school district fails to exercise reasonable care to eliminate the danger or otherwise to protect the children.

Focus on what a 'reasonable prudent person' would do in this situation. Consider controls such as:

1716 **During school hours, do not allow children to play on equipment or items that are not considered playground equipment.** Ensure that playground supervisors are mobile and moving, keeping your students in pre-designated play areas that are off limits to these items.

1717 **Determine the best area where equipment and items should be stored.** Any piece of equipment left out in the middle of a field will draw attention to itself — for example a football blocking sled left on the practice field near the playground.

1718 **If possible, locate and secure your outdoor equipment and items against a fence.**

1719 **Turn over and cover your outdoor equipment so it cannot be accessed.**

1720 **Consider placing signage around the perimeter area stating "No Trespassing."** Signage does not provide significant protection in a potential liability suit. The placement of signs may not work in all situations — especially for small children who cannot read the sign.

1721
Level off or remove large snow, dirt or gravel piles that your students may view as a play area.

1722
Ask law enforcement to patrol your school grounds — especially during after school hours.

Concussion Injury Control

Concussions are a hot topic beyond the playing field and locker room. Concussion issues are being addressed in the corridors and meeting rooms of our state capitols as lawmakers advocate the importance of concussion management for youth athletes. If your state hasn't already passed legislation, it's likely coming. You will note three common elements in the majority of laws:

• Education.

• Removal from play.

• A qualified medical provider makes the return-to-play decision.

In turn, interscholastic associations are creating concussion policies that support their state laws. For instance, the Wisconsin Interscholastic Athlete Association's rule states:

> "A student who displays symptoms of concussion and/or is rendered unconscious may not return to practice or competition during the same day. The student may not return to practice or competition until approved in writing by an appropriate health care professional."

1723
School districts may be held responsible for providing educational materials for athletic trainers, coaches, parents, and student-athletes as well as enforcing the removal and return-to-play guidelines.

When an athlete receives a head injury, other than a teammate, the first person they generally come into contact with is the coach or athletic trainer. The coach's or trainer's responsibilities may include evaluating the condition and informing the student/parents of the assessment.

1724 In addition to awareness and education, one method school districts can use to address their concussion exposure is to provide computerized cognitive testing in conjunction with their athletic programs. There are several tools on the market to choose from. For instance, Axon Sports has developed a web-based tool that can assist qualified medical providers in facilitating the safe return of student-athletes to the field and the classroom.

1725 Have your student-athletes take an initial 'baseline test,' before the first contact practice of the season. The medical provider can compare these results to an after-injury test. This information, along with the medical providers' clinical assessment aids decisions about returning the individual to the classroom, practice, and competitive play.

1726 Develop a Concussion Management Plan for your school district. Make sure this plan is reviewed with all of the personnel responsible for the care and treatment of student-athletes.

1727 A copy of your Concussion Management Plan should also be provided to the parents/guardians, the students engaged in competitive athletics, and the faculty/administrators of your school.

1728 All of your student-athletes, coaches, athletic trainers, guidance counselors, and school nurses should be required to attend annual general presentations on the symptoms and signs of concussion.

1729 Your coaches, athletic trainers, and other support personnel should be required to attend additional educational sessions on the diagnoses and management of student-athletes suspected of having a concussive head injury.

1730 Athletic directors, coaches, and athletic trainers should become proficient in the proper selection and fitting of protective head gear (where appropriate), and proper maintenance and safety of athletic facilities in an effort to reduce and prevent concussive brain injury.

1731 Every student-athlete should complete a baseline test and a baseline symptom questionnaire before starting any sporting activity for that academic year. Results of the test and the questionnaire should be kept on file with the student-athlete's sport physical exam.

If a student-athlete is involved in an athletic event where a concussion is suspected, the following controls should be implemented:

1732 All student-athletes exhibiting signs and symptoms of suspected concussion will be removed from play for the remainder of that day.

1733 Any student-athlete suspected of concussive head injury who exhibits deteriorating and worsening symptoms will be transported by ambulance to the nearest hospital.

1734 Student-athletes with suspected concussion but stable symptoms may be released to the custody of their parents for further medical evaluation. No student-athlete with suspected concussion may leave the school grounds without adult supervision.

After Injury Care controls (usually seven to 10 days) include:

1735 No athlete diagnosed with a suspected concussion may return to the activity without an evaluation and signed permission document from a qualified medical provider. To aid diagnosis and return-to-play decisions, a qualified medical provider should ask the student-athlete to complete an After Injury Test and/or undergo further testing and evaluation.

1736 A student-athlete returning to activity following a concussion must follow a gradual plan. This includes:

a. No activity until all concussion symptoms are gone.

b. Light aerobic activity followed by increased intensity of activity until full return to competition.

c. Light contact progressing to full contact.

d. Full return to competition.

• If the student-athlete experiences any recurrence of symptoms during the recovery stages, the activity level should revert to the previous level until symptoms subside.

• It is generally recommended that activity levels be progressed no faster than one level per 24 hours.

1737 All records of after injury care including the return-to-play document signed by a qualified medical provider and the after injury test result shall remain in the student-athlete's file.

1738 School nurses, guidance counselors, and athletic trainers should be involved in after injury management recommendations for students requiring accommodations in academic and physical activity. This is especially necessary for students with prolonged concussive symptoms.

Thank you to Axon Sports for providing information in the development of these concussion management controls. Axon Sports can be contacted at customerservice@axonsports.com or by calling (715)-848-1024.

School Construction Concerns

New school construction or renovation to your existing buildings can be costly — very costly. During construction projects, your school administration is seeking to ensure that your school facilities fully support future educational and community needs, provide a healthful and safe learning environment, and fit harmoniously into your community.

1739
It is the duty of your school administration to protect the school's property interest during all phases of the construction project.

Such interests may include, but are not limited to:

- A review of the existing insurance policies for coverage of new construction and preparation of such policies for conversion upon completion of the construction project.
- Liability insurance for design errors, code violations, or lack of adherence to appropriate construction standards.
- A duty to protect school employees, students and the general public from exposures inherent to the new construction project.

With these concerns in mind, consider the following risk management best practices when new construction or building renovation takes place:

1740
Although the school is not liable for the actions of the contractor, the school must show due diligence and reasonable care when selecting contractors. First of all, check the safety record of all contractors. Request your contractors provide their workers' compensation experience modification factor. Also ask if they perform daily job site safety training (toolbox talks) for their employees.

1741
At the beginning of all construction projects, require that as part of the work being performed and the contracts entered into, all general contractors, subcontractors, etc., maintain up-to-date insurance coverage. This includes workers' compensation coverage.

1742
Require a certificate of insurance evidencing coverage from each and every contractor. Failure to obtain the certificate of insurance evidencing workers' compensation coverage can result in an additional premium on your school district's workers' compensation policy.

1743 **Ensure that the contractor is adequately insured.** Ensure that the limits of coverage are at least $1 million for general liability and the school district is named as an additional insured on the contractor's policy. Confirm a contractor's pollution liability policy is in place for all work completed.

1744 **Obtain builder's risk coverage for new construction as well as any renovation projects.** The standard property policy does not provide coverage for buildings under construction or the materials being used to complete the project.

1745 **Ensure that your school district doesn't use an owner (school) — construction contractor contract that transfers liability from the construction company to your school district.**

1746 **During the construction project, regularly meet with the general contractor to evaluate the workmanship, the quality of materials, safety and security controls, and project progress.** From day one, set up regularly scheduled meetings with the contractor where you will discuss job progress, problems, etc. Any changes to the original plan must be approved by the school district.

1747 **When developing your construction contract, state that the contractor must follow the safety regulations of OSHA 1926.** These are the OSHA construction safety regulations.

1748 **Insist that the contractor conducts daily, pre-job safety inspections and that a copy of this inspection is posted daily on the job site.** A representative from the school should be able to go out to the job site at any time and review this posted inspection.

1749 **Ask contractors if background checks have been conducted on their employees.** This is especially important when construction workers are working within your school and may have contact with students.

1750 **Limit the number of school personnel and community members on the job site.** There are always school board members who want to tour the job site. Keep people out of the construction area if at all possible — if they must go on the job site, they must be escorted and wear appropriate personal protective equipment such as safety glasses, hard hats, boots, etc.

🔑**1751** **Keep children and students out of the job site at all times.**

1752 **Work with the contractor to determine how the job site is going to be barricaded or fenced. Post appropriate** signage stating "No Trespassing."

1753 **Ask your police department to patrol the construction area during non-school hours such as evenings and** weekends.

🔑**1754** **Never loan any school equipment to contractors.** If a contractor would fall or be injured on borrowed equipment — usually ladders, man lifts, scaffolding, etc., the school may be liable for the accident.

1755 **Notify parents of a new construction project if it will affect building entrances, visitor parking areas, student** drop off/pick up areas, etc.

1756 **Update your school's crisis plan if the construction process involves temporary exits, alterations to hallways** or classrooms, etc.

1757 **Make sure that all construction materials are properly stored and secured.** This may entail fences placed around construction supplies with gates that are always secured unless a construction worker is present in the area.

1758 Ensure that students and staff are never allowed to drive or walk through an ongoing school construction project.

1759 If an exterior construction project is taking place, determine if overhead protection is needed for sidewalks, walkways, or any other areas beneath the work site. These areas should be fenced off to prevent staff and student access.

1760 Ensure the construction contractor has taken appropriate controls to prevent dust and other air contaminants from passing to areas occupied by your students and staff.

1761 Use Gypsum board in exit areas that require fire separation. Heavy duty plastic should only be used to contain air contaminants, not as a means to separate occupied areas from construction areas.

1762 Designate hallways, stairwells, and elevators to be used by the construction workers during school hours. It is important to separate students and staff from construction workers whenever possible.

1763 Construction workers should be required to wear photo identification badges at all times when working within one of your schools.

1764 Require construction debris be removed from the school in a timely manner. Debris piles are danger zones — they can be viewed as play areas by small children.

1765 Never allow construction materials or debris to be dropped out of windows or off roof tops. If this practice must take place, such as removing worn roof shingles, it should take place after normal school hours when students are not present. An adequate number of supervisors should be on the ground to keep others away from the area.

1766 Ensure that fire alarm systems and fire extinguishers are maintained on the construction project at all times.

1767 Know where the construction contractors are venting fumes produced by welding, painting, and other operations. Take precautions to ensure these fumes are not drawn into your school building by the fresh air intakes.

1768 At the conclusion of the construction project, conduct a safety survey of the project to ensure that all areas are ready for school use.

As you can see, there are many liability and risk management concerns associated with a new construction project at your school district.

Sexual Harassment or Accusations

Sexual harassment is often defined as an unwelcomed behavior of a sexual nature that interferes with your student's ability to learn or to participate in school activities. Sexual harassment may range from a mildly annoying behavior to something as serious as a sexual assault.

The allegation of a sexual harassment incident can be extremely damaging to your school district. Even if the allegations prove to be false, reputations and careers may be permanently damaged and bad feelings may develop between the school district and your community.

For these reasons, it is critically important that all of your school employees clearly understand what may constitute sexual harassment and what controls must be in place to prevent it from occurring in any of your schools.

🔑**1769** **Ensure that all school staff (including part-time employees, substitute teachers and volunteers) understand what constitutes sexual harassment.** Some examples of sexual harassment acts include:

- Touching a student's clothing or placing your hands in a student's pocket.
- Unwelcome physical contact or gestures.
- Offensive communications via letters, emails, phone calls.
- Displaying offensive materials such as posters, emails, cartoons.
- Asking questions of a sexual nature.
- Sexual jokes or comments.

1770 **Designate a school district coordinator to address complaints of sexual harassment related to your students.**

1771 **Review your school district's sexual harassment policy with your employees throughout the school year.**

🔑**1772** **Outside of the normal school day, avoid being alone with students in your classroom — especially opposite sex students.** If a teacher must be alone with a student before or especially after school, ensure that your school's administration is aware of this meeting.

1773 **Never meet with a student alone, behind a closed door.** If your door window is covered with paper or decorations, remove them.

1774 **Keep the meeting room door open whenever possible.** If there are privacy or confidentiality concerns, move the meeting to the office area where other school employees are present.

1775 **Meet with students in open areas whenever possible.** Hold your meeting in a conference room in the main office area, the cafeteria, or a classroom that has an adjoining door to another classroom.

1776 Don't ever physically touch a student in a way that could be viewed as inappropriate by others. This includes rubbing a student's neck or shoulders, tickling, hugging, or any other body contact.

1777 Never display sexually suggestive materials in the classroom such as videos or internet images.

1778 Don't make sexually suggestive comments or tell inappropriate jokes at any time.

1779 Don't make sexually or physically suggestive gestures about anyone in front of students.

1780 Avoid personal meetings with students off school grounds. It's just not a good practice to meet with students for a meal, even in a public restaurant setting.

1781 As a teacher, refrain from counseling students in non-academic or personal matters. Don't ever have conversations with students that are considered romantic or sexual in nature.

1782 As a school employee, don't ever discuss your personal problems with your students.

1783 Don't lend your vehicle to students or transport students in your personal vehicle without the knowledge of school administration and the permission of the student's parent/guardian.

1784 Never give students hall passes to come to your classroom for non-school related matters.

1785 Never entertain students in your home unless it is an approved school-sponsored activity. The student's parents/guardian must have full knowledge of the activity. Additionally, it is never a good idea to have a student come to your home alone.

Teacher Instruction Concerns

An important teacher's liability concern relates to providing proper 'instructions, warnings, and equipment inspections.'

In many school liability cases, recovery will be attempted to show that your school district and/or teacher failed to properly instruct or warn students of a hazard or danger.

Additionally, the recovery may also attempt to show that a piece of equipment failed and that failure was because your school district and/or teacher failed to properly inspect or maintain the equipment to ensure that it was in proper working condition.

The following instructional liability best practices should be reviewed with your teachers and coaches:

1786 **Ensure your instructors provide accurate and complete instructions to students.** It doesn't matter if it is a simple classroom activity, a school sponsored sport, or a student using a table saw — proper and thorough instructions must be given to all students involved.

....

1787 **Determine which books, manuals, and instructional papers need to be used to provide proper instruction to your students.** If the activity involves using a piece of equipment or machinery, always attempt to use the instructional materials provided by the equipment manufacturer.

....

1788 **Require students taking safety tests to obtain a mandatory 100% passing grade.** Only when students answer all questions correctly can they be allowed to use certain types of equipment or machinery. This is primarily applicable in your technology education classes.

....

1789 **Post written instructions and rules on and around all equipment or machinery used by your students.** Again, this is primarily applicable to the equipment or machinery used in your technology education classes.

1790 **Determine if the school activity is too advanced or too complicated for the age or nature of your students.** Understand the nature of the activity relative to the students who are to perform it.

1791 **Before any student activity begins, determine if it is safe.** Contact your insurance company's loss control consultant to review safety controls associated with a questionable activity.

1792 **Ensure that all recommended safety measures have been implemented.** For example, in your technology education class this means that all equipment guards are always in place and are being used.

1793 **Never force a student to do something they are scared of or do not want to do.** Students in technology education classes may be hesitant to operate certain pieces of equipment. Students in physical education classes may be scared to ascend the climbing wall. If this is this case, don't ridicule the student for their apprehension and don't 'force' them to be involved in the activity.

As you can see, proper instruction is important for all school activities. I strongly encourage your school district to constantly review your instructional procedures throughout the year.

Teacher Supervision Concerns

If a student is injured on school premises or during a school sponsored event, that student, their parents/guardian, or both can initiate a lawsuit to recover medical costs as a result of the student's injuries. The suit may also include a request for payment for pain and suffering as a result of the injury.

The suit can be made against your school district and oftentimes the teacher is named in the lawsuit. Attorneys representing the injured student/parents will attempt to show that your school district and/or the teacher 'allowed' the injury to occur or the school district and/or teacher failed to do something that resulted in the injury. This is known as acts of commission or acts of omission.

An important area of concern when dealing with teacher liability is proper supervision. Supervision is the first area and generally the most common area where recovery is sought. An attempt may be made to show that the school district and/or teacher failed to adequately supervise the student's activity. This may entail determining that not enough supervisors were present or the supervisor(s) were performing an inadequate job of supervision.

The following concerns should be addressed when developing your school district's supervision guidelines:

1794 **Supervise students accordingly.** There is no magic number as to how many students one teacher may adequately supervise. Understand that when the number of students increases, so should the number of supervisors.

1795 **Clearly understand the size of the area to be supervised.** Are your teachers supervising a small classroom or a large outdoor play area? Larger areas usually require more supervisors.

1796 **Supervise according to the age of your students.** Younger students may require more supervision simply because of their age. Older students may require more supervision because of the complexity or danger of the activity (using power equipment in the technology education class).

1797 **Supervise according to the nature of your students.** Special needs or handicapped students may require additional supervision.

1798 **Understand the nature of the activity.** Are the students quietly working at their desks or are they using power tools in a technology class? More supervision may be needed if the activity is more complex.

1799 Teachers should always try to be positioned so they can see their entire area of concern. Whenever possible, avoid turning your back to the majority of the students (for example, a teacher who positions their classroom desk to face away from the students).

1800 In a potentially hazardous area, never leave students unsupervised for any amount of time. Unfortunately I have visited many schools where students are allowed to operate machinery in a technology education class when no supervisor is present.

1801 Keep your supervisors mobile and moving around the supervised area.

1802 Instruct teachers to supervise student movement in the hallways between classes.

"Prediction is difficult, especially about the future."

– Yogi Berra

SCHOOL **INSURANCE** BEST PRACTICES

Claims Management

1803

Your frequency of claims is an effective indicator of the future severity of claims. When I meet with administrators to review their past workers' compensation loss history, I am amazed by the excessive attention given to the few high dollar (severity) workers' compensation claims that have occurred. I agree that it's important to review these claims, but don't forget to focus your efforts on reviewing those trends that are occurring at your school district — the types of claims that occur again and again over the years (frequency).

My review of the loss history of hundreds of school districts over the past 25 years and has determined the major school loss drivers to be:

Teachers:

- Elevation injuries from falls caused by standing on tables, chairs and desks in the classroom.

- Manual material handling injuries from lifting improperly or lifting too much weight.

- Injuries as a result of slips/trips/falls caused by wearing improper footwear when walking in and out of the school during bad weather conditions and by not entering and exiting through the proper school entrances. Additionally, many teachers wear footwear that contributes to accidents — flip flops, high heels, etc.

- Injuries as a result of physical confrontations with combative or special needs students.

Food Service Employees:

- Manual material handling injuries from repeatedly handling boxes and food product.

- Injuries from slips/trips/falls on slippery surfaces when walking or pushing carts.

- Knife cut injuries.

Custodians:

- Manual material handling injuries from lifting a variety of objects throughout the school day.
- Slip/trip/fall injuries both inside and outside the school building.

Physical Education/Athletic Coaches:

- Teachers and coaches injured when physically involved in a sports activity with students and athletes (wrestling, football, volleyball, tennis, etc.).

Keep these claims management best practices in mind:

1804 **Periodically review your school district's open claims and reserves with your workers' compensation insurance carrier.** Excessive time lags in medical care or claim activity may indicate that a workers' compensation case may be spiraling out of control. At a minimum, your school district's claim management team should review open claims and reserves on a quarterly basis.

1805 **Understand how many of your workers' compensation claims are litigated.** A recent insurance study stated that a 5% litigation rate is very good, a 10-15% rate is good and anything over 20% should be considered a 'red flag' warranting further analysis.

In my opinion, these percentages seem extremely high — many school districts will never have a litigated workers' compensation claim for many years. I don't believe it's so much a percentage you need to be concerned about but rather the extremes. If your workers' compensation insurance carrier isn't litigating any claims, it may mean that they are merely paying everything or 'playing the insurance game' of taking the best and worst case scenario and settling for 50% of the claim cost.

1806 Each of your school's workers' compensation cases should be evaluated on its own merits — but be aware of the extremes of all or none. At a minimum, your school district should understand the insurance company's attorney's thoughts on the chances of prevailing, the worst case scenario, the settlement value with the facts as they appear to be, the additional work needed to strengthen the defense position, and the anticipated defense costs.

1807 Department supervisors should frequently communicate with their injured employees. It's important to check on their well-being and to ensure they have received their workers' compensation payment on a timely basis. Injured employees who feel neglected or hopelessly lost in the system are fodder for hungry attorneys.

1808 Ensure your employees know what they are entitled to under the workers' compensation system. Insurance studies indicate that injured workers seek attorneys for information when they feel lost in the system, not because they want to punish their employer.

1809 Effectively control your medical costs. While state statutes differ with respect to the extent to which employers can direct injured workers to certain medical providers, the medical management of a workers' compensation claim is essential to reducing costs.

1810 Evaluate your relationships with medical providers and medical bill review processes to be sure they are working for your school district and the injured employee. Medical costs now account for over 60% of a workers' compensation claim. Employers who only focus on return to work efforts as a way to reduce their workers' compensation premiums may struggle to see a significant reduction.

1811 Develop a positive working relationship with local doctors and clinics. Developing a relationship with local medical providers helps them understand the work restrictions and available light duty opportunities at your school. This helps to return the employee to work safely and reduce or eliminate the potential for indemnity payments on a workers' compensation claim.

1812 Talk to your insurance company about developing a districtwide wellness program. If you don't have a wellness program, now is the time to explore the options. While a wellness program is often lumped in as part of the school district's health insurance program, the overall health of your employees can dramatically affect your workers' compensation results.

Studies show that injured workers who are diabetic, obese, or in overall poor health can have longer healing periods from work related injuries increasing the cost of the claim and ultimately your workers' compensation insurance premium.

Facility Use Agreements

1813 Simply stated, any organization or outside group using your school district facilities (gym, pool, auditorium, classroom, etc.) or grounds should sign a facility use agreement. This agreement outlines the responsibility of the school and the organization/group using your facility. It also requires the organization to provide evidence of insurance coverage and list your school district as an additional insured on the general liability policy. This creates a layer of primary protection for the school district in the event of a claim.

1814 Facility use agreements should be used for meetings, luncheons, conferences, concerts, recreational activities, or other special events that take place on school property.

In general, there are two types of facility use agreements that will involve your school district:

• Outside groups asking permission to use your school district's facilities or property.

• Your request to another school district or nearby business to use their facilities or property during an emergency such as an evacuation.

If an outside group requests use of your school facilities or property to host an activity or event, consider the following controls:

1815 As a general rule, insurance should be required for any event that is deemed high-risk to your school district. This includes but is not limited to the rental of a school's recreational facility (excluding use of its meeting room) for outdoor activities and overnight activities. Meetings, luncheons, etc. will ordinarily not require proof of insurance.

1816 Develop clear guidelines regarding the type of activities or groups that can use your school's facilities or property. Dangerous activities such as fireworks, the use of combustible or flammable materials, overcrowding, and the presence of dangerous animals should never be allowed in your school under any circumstances.

1817 No amusement rides or attractions, trampolines of any type, enclosed or air supported structures of any type, climbing walls, climbing ropes, firearms or shooting (including bow and arrow), should be allowed to be brought onto the your school premises or used in any manner.

1818 Before any facility use takes place, ensure a written agreement is in place that lists the parties, date and time of activities, number of people attending, the identified facility or property, and any restrictions that are to be enforced.

1819 The outside group (facility user) should take out an insurance policy with a reputable insurer, having an A.M. Best rating of A- or better.

1820 The outside group(s) should agree to indemnify and hold harmless everyone associated with the school district. This includes the school, school board, school board elected and appointed officials, administrators, principals, teachers and all other school employees, volunteers or representatives, and all persons and bodies corporate acting for or on behalf of the school district.

1821 Ensure the approved facility use applicant holds the school district harmless for all accidents and incidents. The applicant should assume all liability responsibilities arising from any accidents or incidents arising from the occupancy/use of the school district facility.

1822 The school district should be indemnified in an amount not less than $2 million for any claims (including injury to persons or damage to property) arising out of the use of the school premises by the outside group.

1823 The school district should be named as an 'additional insured' under the general liability policy.

1824 The outside group must provide the insurance policy or a certificate of insurance prior to use of the school facilities or grounds.

1825 The outside group must agree that their insurance policies are primary and non-contributory. Any policies procured by the school district that might happen to provide protection or benefits to the school district arising out of the outside group's use of the school facilities must be excess.

1826 Restrict access to your school facilities. Only those areas identified in the facilities use agreement should be available to the applicant. Use physical barriers such as gates, locked doors, or increased supervision to prevent access to restricted areas of your school.

1827 Consider the use of additional supervisors or security personnel if a large number of attendees are present.

1828 Develop your school district's facility use policies and agreements with the advice of your district's legal counsel. Many good examples of facility use agreements can be found on the internet.

1829 Ensure that any furniture or equipment that is moved during use of your premises is replaced.

1830 A school representative should be present at any significant event and the school custodial or maintenance department should be responsible for inspection and any clean up not performed by the user(s) after the event.

1831 The person receiving the permit shall obtain permission from the school district to decorate, using only materials acceptable to the local fire marshal. All decorations should be removed before the group leaves your school building or property.

1832 All decorations must be removed by the outside group before they leave your school building or property. If the decorations are not removed the school district should consider a fee that addresses decoration removal should be considered.

1833 Reserve the right to terminate the agreement immediately by notice in writing.

1834 Require the outside group (facility user) to provide written notice of any incident or accident that results in bodily injury or damage to school facilities or property. This notice should be provided within 24 hours of the incident or accident. The notice must include details of the time, place, circumstances, and the names and addresses of any person(s) witnessing the accident.

1835 The building administrator should forward the facility use application to the necessary personnel. This may include your superintendent, maintenance supervisor, activities director, and the kitchen supervisor.

1836 Require check in and check out procedures with your building administrator and/or maintenance supervisor.

1837 Do not rent your school facilities or equipment to any profit-making individuals or organizations for private or commercial use not directly associated with your school district.

1838 Never loan your school equipment to individuals or organizations unless the loan is part of the agreement for rental or use of your district facilities.

1839 Develop a list of facilities and classrooms that are not for rent except under special conditions.

1840 Clearly define the activities which will not be allowed on school district property. This includes but is not limited to gambling or games of chance, and promoting any activity that damages the school district.

1841 Clearly state that the possession or use of alcoholic beverages, illegal substances, tobacco products, and weapons in and on all the school district property, including all district buildings, district grounds, district owned and leased vehicles, and sites leased by the district is prohibited.

1842 The selling or consuming of food or drink in auditoriums, gymnasiums, or other sitting areas must be approved by the school district.

1843 The use of any special equipment must be identified in the application and, if necessary, may require district personnel to operate. Any overtime compensation will be paid by the applicant.

1844 The applicant should understand they may be required to provide supervision and security depending on the activity.

1845 Damages or destruction to any facility and/or premises is not permitted and the cost of all repairs will be charged to the applicant.

1846 Never allow outside groups to exceed room capacity.

1847 Restrict outside groups from making temporary electrical or mechanical modifications.

1848 Do not allow outside groups to use open flame, candles, or fire on or around school district property at any time.

1849 Do not allow individuals into the building if they appear to have partaken of alcoholic beverages and/or illegal substances, etc.

1850 If your school district requests the use of facilities or property of another school district or nearby business in cases such as emergency evacuation, a formal written facility use agreement should be reviewed and signed by all concerned parties.

The following is an example of the language that could be used in a facility use agreement (ensure your legal counsel reviews and approves any agreement of this type):

> At any given time, a situation can occur which requires the off campus evacuation of school staff and students. (The School District) and the (Party owning building or property) have entered into this mutual agreement to provide access to their facilities and property should the other party require an off campus evacuation.
>
> The (school district) is ultimately responsible for ensuring appropriate care, supervision, and services for its staff and students in the event of an off campus evacuation. All costs incurred for care and services provided are the responsibility of the evacuating facility.
>
> The **Evacuating Facility responsibilities** include, but are not limited to:
>
> • Promptly notify the Sheltering Facility of the potential to evacuate and/or active evacuation.

- Evacuate students and staff, utilizing their own resources, to the Sheltering Facility.
- Supplement the Sheltering Facility's staff.
- Provide emergency supplies and family contact information.

The **Sheltering Facility responsibilities** include, but are not limited to:

- Provide a contact person upon notification of evacuation.
- Receive students and staff and direct them to the area where they will be sheltered.

By the signing of this agreement by the representative of each respective school, they agree to the above stipulations; however, the representative of either school may revoke this agreement at anytime.

Goal Setting

There are many methods to determine the effectiveness of your school district's risk management efforts — measuring your safety activities, incident rates, or frequency/severity of claims, just to name a few. To develop a good overall picture of the effectiveness of your school safety program, I suggest that you use a measurement combination of incident rates, frequency rates, and severity rates.

Your school district's incident rate of injuries and illnesses may be computed using the following formula: (number of injuries and illnesses x 200,000 / employee hours worked.)

If not interpreted correctly incident rates as a single safety goal can be very deceiving.

....

1851 Simply stated, measure yourself against yourself — your school district's incident rate vs. your school district's **incident rate — on a periodic basis.** Measure your incident rate year vs. year (school district as a whole, department) and time periods — 4, 6, 8, 12 month marks (school district as a whole, department).

Stand alone frequency rates are not good measures of an effective safety program. A frequency rate that increases may simply indicate the commitment to better accident investigation, prompt claim reporting, etc.

1852 Consider drilling down the frequency rates to focus on specific high frequency schools, departments, or specific accident types such as manual material handling, slips/trips/falls or repetitive motion injuries. In very general terms, most schools have a frequency concern with their custodial employees, due to the variety of tasks they perform.

As a stand-alone measurement, severity rates are not a good indicator of an effective risk management program. Your school district cannot control medical costs or medical inflation so attempting to measure this year's severity with that of years past is difficult to do.

1853 Measure severity rates in very 'ballpark' terms, drilling down to specific schools, occupations, or accident exposures. For example, if your district has experienced monumental dollar losses associated with custodial workers' compensation claims, a realistic goal may be to reduce the number of custodial material handling claims by 25-30% during the coming year.

1854 Share your risk management goals with department heads and building principals throughout the school year. It's wise for your administrative team to know which schools have the greatest exposure, the highest frequency of claims, and the most workers' compensation loss dollars associated with their claims.

Insurance Coverage Concerns

The goal of an effective property and casualty insurance program is to ensure accidental losses are efficiently mitigated with minimal disruption to your school district's learning environment. Consider addressing these important school insurance best practices:

1855 Ensure your school district's liability limit is sufficient, including the umbrella coverage. The negative impact a catastrophic claim would have on your school district is much more costly than the premium associated with additional limits of liability. Be sure to review your exposures to determine a worst case scenario and purchase adequate limits to protect your school district.

1856 Ask your insurance carrier to remove the deductible to your umbrella policy. Many carriers will honor that request for no additional premium.

1857 Ensure your district's umbrella policy covers your educator's legal liability and employee benefit liability coverages. Occasionally, these lines of coverage are not included in the umbrella policy especially if the actual educator's legal liability policy is written by a different insurance company than the insurance company writing the others lines of coverage. Do not assume that because you are getting an option from an insurance company that they are the insurance company on each line of coverage being presented by your agent. Make sure you know the names of insurance carriers writing each line of coverage and their financial ratings, that the coverages are structured properly, and that the limits are adequate.

1858 Determine if adding a deductible or increasing existing deductibles will result in significant changes for your school district. Deductibles exist or can be added to the district's general liability, employee benefits liability, automobile (liability/physical damage), umbrella, and property coverages. In some cases, the premium savings may not warrant the district taking on the potential added expense should a loss occur but in other cases, the premium savings can be significant. Do not hesitate to ask your insurance agent to provide a variety of options.

1859 Monitor your Workers' Compensation experience modification calculation. This is typically issued 4-6 months prior to the effective date of your workers' compensation policy. Insurance companies report your loss data six months prior to your effective date. Claims can close for less than when the data was reported. In these situations, the data for the calculation can be updated resulting in a lower experience modification factor and ultimately lower premium. Much can occur between when the data is reported and your effective date.

1860 Request a loss report from your agent thirty days prior to your effective date and compare those losses with the worksheet provided with your experience modification calculation. If a discrepancy exists, ask that the insurance carrier issue a revised unit stat card to the state for each claim where the loss run demonstrates incurred cost less than what was initially reported to the state.

1861 If you have students in work study programs, ensure the workers' compensation coverage includes an alternate employer endorsement. Providing the workers' compensation coverage for students involved in work study programs reduces the potential impact of the participating employer. This may be a great way to help promote the program in the community. An employer may not be willing to participate in the work study program if they know there may be a negative impact on their own workers' compensation program.

1862 Determine if your school district's insurance provides coverage for foreign trips. If a staff member is injured outside of the United States, your workers' compensation policy may not respond with coverage until the staff member is back in the United States; this means that any medical costs or repatriation expenses incurred would not be covered. In addition, most general liability policies will only respond to suits brought in the United States. There are policies and endorsements available to cover districts' foreign exposures if they are needed.

1863 Determine if you want to add volunteers to your crime policy. The Crime policy can easily be extended to include coverage for volunteers handling money within the school district, i.e. ticket sales, concession workers, etc. Before making this decision, consider your current deductible and the frequency that a volunteer would handle money exceeding that amount.

1864 If your parent-teacher organization is a separate organization, ensure they are carrying their own Directors and Officers Liability coverage. The school district's Educators Legal Liability policy does not extend to the board of that organization. If the organization isn't purchasing their own coverage, the personal assets of the board members are at risk. This risk can be avoided by purchasing a separate Directors and Officers Liability policy.

1865 If your school has an auto shop class, ensure that your current policy will respond to claims arising out of Garage Liability and Garagekeepers Liability. Most General Liability policies exclude coverage for property in your care, custody, and control which arguably includes vehicles left at the school for service. Not only can the district be responsible for damage to vehicles left in their care, but there are inherent risks associated with a garage operation that are not routinely found in a school setting, requiring specialized coverage.

1866 Delete the fellow employee exclusion from the school district's automobile policy. If two school district employees are driving together in the same vehicle and are involved in an accident, the injured employee may attempt to personally sue the employee who was driving the vehicle. Removing this exclusion from the automobile liability policy extends coverage to the employee driving the vehicle at the time of the accident.

1867 Determine your district's need for flood coverage. Flood coverage is not typically covered under most property policies and if it is, the extension the property policy offers provides a sub-limit that is usually not adequate to meet the district's exposures. Flood zones were remapped in 2010 so if you have not conducted a review of your exposures since then, it is suggested that you do.

1868 Determine if earthquake coverage should be maintained on the school property. If the school district is located in an area susceptible to earthquakes, adequate coverage for the buildings, contents, and business interruption/added expense should be maintained.

1869 Include a joint loss agreement for your property and equipment breakdown coverage if it is provided by separate insurance carriers. If a loss were to occur, this endorsement will assist the school district in receiving payment for the loss first. It is the insurance carriers responsibility to determine who is responsible and for how much. The joint loss agreement avoids any potential delay in payment to the school district.

1870 Insure your fiber optic cables on the property policy, both above and underground. On occasion, a school district will own their fiber optic cables; it is important to ensure the property policy has been amended to cover overhead transmission lines as well as underground cables or coverage is provided on a separate policy for fiber optic cables.

1871 Determine if your school district has coverage for abuse and molestation and corporal punishment on the General Liability policy. If a teacher or school district employee abuses, molests, or physically punishes a student, the General Liability policy needs to afford coverage for the school district. Standard General Liability policies need to be endorsed to include these coverages. Some policies will cover this under their Educator's Legal Liability policy and thus will likely have lower limits and a deductible. Know where this exposure is covered under your current insurance policy.

1872 Ensure additional insured status is extended to school sponsored organizations, booster clubs, PTO, PTA, etc. School sponsored organizations may not be large enough to purchase insurance coverage. Your school district should be able to add them as additional insureds on the school district's general liability policy to ensure these organizations continue to operate and provide benefit to the school district.

1873 Understand what the 'trigger' is on your Educator's legal liability policy — lawsuit or compliant. Some Educators Legal Liability policies will only respond when a lawsuit is filed, not when the complaint is initially received by the district which requires the district in some cases to incur expenses they thought would be covered. Another important factor to keep in mind is that virtually all Educator Legal Liability policies contain a provision that allows the insurance carrier to select legal representation for the district and the policy specifically states that they will not be responsible for defense costs incurred prior to their having notice of the claim. If the district assigns counsel, they do so at their expense. Any time you receive notice of a claim falling under your Educators Legal Liability policy, your first call should be to your insurance agent who can provide you with the 'next steps' and prevent the district from incurring unnecessary expense.

Return to Work Programs

The development of an effective return to work program will benefit your school district and the injured employee in a variety of ways.

From a monetary standpoint, the use of a return to work program will:

- Save the school district lost time (indemnity) expenses in temporary disability payments.

- Provide the school district some work production for the wages being paid to the injured employee.

- Save the costs of hiring/training replacement employees.

- May save the costs associated with overtime.

Additionally, proactive return to work programs will:

- Reduce the likelihood of fraudulent or malingering claims.

- Encourage school district and injured employee contact, often providing the school district more control and direction of the claim, leading to a more positive resolution.

- Speed healing and save on medical expenses of a prolonged disability claim.

Your school district return to work program will also benefit the injured employee in a number of ways, including:

- Improving the injured employee's self-esteem, possibly minimizing the concerns of being injured.

- Promoting positive morale among all employees.

- Contributing to a quicker recovery by keeping the injured employee involved in a regular work schedule.

- Reducing the negative financial impact an injured employee might experience due to a loss time injury.

1874 Your district's top administration must show their commitment by endorsing a formal return to work policy statement.

1875 Develop a list of light duty jobs relevant to your school. An important part of your school district's return to work program is to identify medically authorized alternate jobs for the injured worker to perform. These jobs are intended to be time-limited, temporary, productive, and meaningful.

The following is a partial list of school related light duty jobs:

General light duty jobs could include:

• Hall duty — extra eyes and ears to assist monitoring student conduct.

• Playground supervisor.

• Bus drop off/pick up area supervisor.

• Shredding documents and making copies.

• Parking lot security — eyes and ears using a walkie-talkie.

• Picking up trash with a stick.

• Monitoring video cameras.

• Cafeteria monitor — helping young students open milk cartons and juice boxes.

• Escorting students and visitors within the school when they arrive late or leave early for appointments.

• 'Fetch and carry' for front office and guidance office.

• Stuffing envelopes, answering the phone, distributing flyers.

• Filing paperwork.

• Placing purchase orders by phone, fax, e-mail etc.

• Computer data entry work.

• Outgoing mail stuffing, applying postage.

• Incoming mail opening, mail bin distribution.

• Making photocopies.

- Taking inventory (but not physically moving inventory stock).
- Inspecting for safety hazards, document hazards, complete work orders, report hazards to the school safety committee.

Teacher/administrator light duty jobs:
- Grading papers and proofreading.
- Tutoring students on a one to one basis.
- Developing lesson plans.
- Signing in visitors and volunteers.
- Assisting substitute teachers — remain in class with students and have the substitute teacher perform the majority of the work.
- Making phone calls such as setting up teacher parent conferences for guidance.
- Inventory athletic equipment for the athletic director.
- Assemble statistics for athletic director; make flyers for upcoming games, dances, events.
- Inspect physical education fields and playgrounds for hazards, note hazards, complete work orders.

Custodial/food service light duty jobs:
- Light dusting.
- Light sweeping.
- Picking up trash with a spear/stick.
- Tool room/storage checkout.
- Using spray cleaner to wipe down desks and cafeteria tables.
- Emptying trash containers (comply with lifting restrictions).
- Clean the sinks in the classrooms, fill soap dispensers.
- Light stocking of supplies for bathrooms/kitchen areas.
- Clean every water fountain, wipe down computer screens.
- Dust books in the media center.
- Wash windows- bucket can be placed on a cart to comply with bending/twisting restrictions.
- Remove gum from under desks and counter tops.
- Inspecting fire extinguishers on a monthly basis.

1876 Schedule a meeting of department heads and employees to discuss and develop a list of alternate duty jobs. Encourage everyone to come up with as many suggestions as possible, even if they may think their ideas are unrealistic. The way to come up with a couple good ideas is to have a lot of possible ideas. Be creative and look at what meaningful work/job tasks need to be performed within your school district.

1877 Develop job descriptions that accurately reflect the essential functions of your school's various occupations and jobs. List the physical activities required of each task as this will assist the physician in understanding the work.

1878 Always remember to treat all your injured workers who are on a transitional duty job assignment with respect and care. Never make a return-to-work job demeaning or meaningless.

A school district's return to work program can be a win-win proposition for everyone involved. The school district wins by minimizing workers' compensation insurance costs while retaining the use of valuable employees and the employee wins by returning to work and avoiding the negative effects of a long-term absence.

Managing Your Workers Compensation Claims

Simply stated, many school districts do not have a good understanding of the importance of a structured claims management system that requires prompt claim reporting, implementation of an effective return to work program, and subsequent monitoring of the program.

I would like to share with you an effective return to work program that can be instituted by your school district.

1879 The first step in this process is to develop a specific list of light duty jobs for each school related occupation. Rather than just listing 'custodial duties', develop a more definitive list of jobs such as 'cleaning toilets, wiping tables, dry sweeping, etc.' Working with other school districts, I sat down with the various department heads and asked them to begin developing this specific light duty list. The building principal should also contribute to making this list as he or she may have interesting ideas for light duty jobs that cross departments.

1880 The second step is to ensure that your medical providers have this light duty list on file and understand the physical capabilities and restrictions of each of these jobs. Don't be afraid to invite the medical provider to come out to see your operation, to understand your commitment to light duty work.

The third step is where we really begin this process.

1881 Inform all employees that they must report all workers' compensation claims immediately.

1882 Inform all employees that they must obtain and use a "Return to Doctor" form prior to any follow up or subsequent doctor visits. This is the most important step of this return to work process. You are asking all employees who have follow up doctor visits to contact a designated representative of the school district to obtain this form. The employee will then give this form to their doctor or medical provider at their next visit. The medical provider will be asked to fill out the section regarding light duty restrictions and return dates.

1883 Ask the medical provider to cross off the jobs that the injured employee cannot perform; that way, you have a definitive list of jobs that the employee can perform. This process eliminates confusion if the employee later says that they were asked to do more than their restrictions allowed.

I suggest you ask the medical provider to place the completed form in a sealed envelope so it cannot be altered by the employee.

1884
Require the employee to return the form to the school district immediately after their doctor visit. At this point, the school district representative can review the restrictions assigned by the medical provider. Oftentimes, you will see one of the following:

- The doctor will not list any light duty jobs because they don't know what light duty jobs the district has that would fit within their restrictions, or

- The doctor is generous with the number of days off they recommend. For example, if an injury occurs on a Tuesday doctors will often advise the employee to go back to work the following Monday. If you can get that employee back on Thursday or Friday, there are no workers' compensation payments to address.

This process will assist the school district in addressing those claimants who don't have much say in the process and just go along with whatever the doctor says as well as those employees who are trying to take advantage of the system. Additionally, the word gets out quickly that the school district wants fair and prompt medical service for their employees but will be watching every part of the process. Unnecessary doctor and emergency room visits decrease when an injured employee knows they are being monitored.

"Organizing is what you do before you do something, so that when you do it, it is not all mixed up."

— A.A. Milne

SCHOOL
FLEET LIABILITY
BEST PRACTICES

Your district has a number of employees who drive school owned, leased, rental, or personal vehicles as part of their school duties. School employees should be expected to operate vehicles safely, to prevent accidents which may result in injuries or property loss.

1885 **Develop a formal school district vehicle safety policy.** Your school district should develop a motor vehicle safety policy that is reviewed, signed, and followed by all drivers. Some significant components of the vehicle safety policy are:

- Assigning responsibilities at all levels of employment.
- Vehicle use and insurance requirements.
- Employee driver's license checks and identification of high risk drivers.
- Accident reporting and investigation.
- Company Accident Review Board.
- Vehicle selection and maintenance.
- Training standards.
- Safety regulations.

1886 **Assign a school district fleet safety coordinator.** This individual will be responsible for:

- Issuing periodic reports of losses/accidents for the administrator and school board to review.
- Reviewing motor vehicle accident reports as part of the school district's Accident Review Board.
- Revising the Vehicle Safety Program as necessary and distributing the new version to school drivers.
- Maintaining appropriate fleet safety records.

Vehicle Use Controls

1887 Only school employees authorized by the school district should be permitted to operate a school district vehicle.

1888 Do not allow employees to drive school vehicles for personal use. In the past, I have consulted with school districts that allowed employees to use school vehicles for moving firewood and other personal items.

1889 No one under the age of 21 should be permitted to drive a school vehicle.

1890 Develop protocols for employees who use their personal vehicles for school-related business. Employees who drive their personal vehicles for school-related business should:

- Maintain a valid driver's license.
- Maintain appropriate auto liability insurance for bodily injury and property damage.
- Provide proof of insurance (copy of declaration page) to the school district.
- Maintain an acceptable Motor Vehicle Report (MVR).
- Not have a 'business use' exclusion on personal insurance policy.
- Maintain current state vehicle inspections when required.
- Maintain their vehicle in a safe operating condition when driven for school related business.

1891 Develop a fleet policy that addresses 'unauthorized use of school vehicles.' Assigned drivers and other authorized school employees should never allow an unauthorized individual to operate a school vehicle. There should be no exceptions to this policy. Additionally, if unauthorized use results in an accident, the responsible employee should be required to make restitution for the damages.

1892 Develop 'driver selection' criteria for all employees driving school vehicles. To evaluate your school employees as drivers, your administration should:

- Review past driving performance and work experience through previous employer's reference checks.

- Review the employee's Motor Vehicle Record (MVR) annually (more frequently if circumstances warrant).

- Ensure the employee has a valid driver's license.

1893 Where applicable, your drivers must comply with DOT Commercial Driver License (CDL) regulations.

1894 Develop criteria for identifying high risk drivers. High risk driver criteria may include but is not limited to:

- Driving under the influence of alcohol or drugs (DUI).

- Involvement in a hit and run accident.

- Failure to report a vehicle accident.

- Negligent homicide arising out of the use of a vehicle.

- Driving during a period of suspension or revocation.

- Use of a motor vehicle during commission of a felony.

- Operating a motor vehicle without the school's permission.

- Permitting an unlicensed or unauthorized person to drive.

- Reckless driving.

- Speeding (three or more speeding tickets in a three year period).

- Two or more preventable vehicular accidents in a 12 month period.

1895 Develop protocols for addressing drivers identified as high risk or in violation of your school district's fleet policy. Several actions may be warranted including:

- Suspending or revoking driving privileges.

- Requiring drivers to operate their own vehicle for district business.

- Requiring drivers to attend a defensive driving course on their own time and expense.

1896 Require that all accidents, no matter how minor, are reported to the school district. All vehicle accidents involving school employees, school vehicles, or school property should be promptly investigated and reviewed by your district's fleet accident review committee.

1897 Develop formal vehicle accident investigation procedures. Motor vehicle accident record keeping procedures should consist of the following components:

• Documentation of causes and corrective action.

• Management review to expedite corrective action.

• Analysis of accidents to determine trends, recurring problems and the need for further control measures.

1898 Develop school employee accident reporting procedures. An example of employee accident reporting procedures is as follows:

• If possible, move the vehicle to a safe location out of the way of traffic.

• Call for medical attention if anyone is hurt.

• Secure the names and addresses of drivers and occupants of any vehicles involved, their operator's license numbers, insurance company names and policy numbers, as well as the names and addresses of injured persons and witnesses.

• Record this information on the school district accident report form.

• Do not discuss fault with or sign anything for anyone except an authorized representative of the school district, a police officer, or a representative of the school district's insurance company.

• Immediately notify the school district's fleet safety coordinator.

• If any injuries were involved and the district's fleet safety coordinator is not available, contact your supervisor immediately.

• Do not have the vehicle repaired until you receive authorization from the school district.

1899 Implement a school district fleet accident review board that will review all accidents to determine preventability. For reference purposes, the following definitions relate to motor vehicle accidents:

- A motor vehicle accident is defined as "any occurrence involving a motor vehicle which results in injury, death, or property damage unless the vehicle is properly parked. Who was injured, what property was damaged and to what extent, where the accident occurred, or who was responsible, are not relevant factors."

- A preventable accident is defined as "any accident involving the vehicle, unless properly parked, which results in property damage or personal injury and in which the driver failed to do everything he/she reasonably could have done to prevent or avoid the accident."

1900 Develop a school district theft and vehicle damage policy. Remember these key points:

- If you did not witness the theft or damage to the vehicle, you must notify the local police department immediately.

- Immediately notify the district's fleet safety coordinator.

- Provide a copy of the police report along with a memo outlining any additional information to the district's fleet safety coordinator.

1901 Equip all of your school vehicles with an accident reporting kit that is kept in the glove box. This kit should include the accident report form, a pen or pencil, and a disposable camera.

Driver Training

Drivers hired by your school district to operate a motor vehicle will have the basic skills and credentials necessary to perform this function as confirmed through your district's driver selection process.

1902 All school employees who drive school district vehicles should receive a copy of your district's fleet safety policy.

1903 Keep a copy of the district's fleet safety program in each vehicle.

1904
A fleet in-service training program should be conducted to assure all drivers are presented with the district's fleet policy, understand their responsibilities, and are familiar with the vehicles.

Areas that should be reviewed with all drivers include:

- An understanding of the district's fleet safety program.
- An understanding of the vehicle assignment agreement which should then be signed.
- A review of the driver's motor vehicle report (MVR).
- An understanding of the district's accident reporting and emergency procedures.
- A review of the operation and controls of the district vehicles.
- How to conduct an inspection using the vehicle inspection form.

1905
Drivers must notify the district's vehicle safety coordinator immediately if their license is suspended or revoked.

1906
The best and safest policy is to ban the use of all cell phones and electronic devices when driving. The following is an example of a procedure that you may want to apply with employees driving on school business and who use a cell phone in the vehicle:

- An external speaker and microphone must be available to allow hands-free operation.
- The cell phone must have phone number memory and programming capabilities.
- Drivers must refrain from placing outgoing calls or responding to pagers while the vehicle is in motion.
- Incoming calls should be limited.
- For any vehicle equipped with a cellular phone that does not meet the above equipment specifications, use of the phone or pager is authorized only when the vehicle is safely parked.
- Employees are prohibited from using a headset or similar device while operating a motor vehicle.

1907 Employees should be prohibited from using motorcycles when traveling on school-related business.

General Fleet Safety Rules

1908 School drivers should:

- Never pick up hitchhikers.
- Never accept payment for carrying passengers or materials.
- Never use any radar detector, laser detector, or similar device.
- Never push or pull another vehicle or tow a trailer.
- Never transport flammable liquids or gases unless a DOT or Underwriters' Laboratories (UL) approved container is used, and only then in limited quantities.
- Never assist disabled motorists or accident victims beyond your level of medical expertise. If a driver is unable to provide the proper medical care, he/she must restrict their assistance to calling the proper authorities.

1909 Employees are responsible for school property such as computers, school papers, and equipment under their **control.** Your school district should never reimburse the employee for stolen personal property.

Transportation to Events

1910 Your school board should develop a specific policy for transporting students.

1911 Your best policy is to never allow teachers to use their private vehicles to transport students **for school-related activities.** Always use alternative methods of transportation.

1912 All transportation must stay within the scope of the school employee's employment with the school district and within the scope of the insurance coverage.

1913 Athletes and students should travel to and from events with the school group unless prior approval is obtained from the athletic director or administration. No spur of the moment, driving home from events with friends or other parents should be allowed.

1914 If alternative transportation is allowed, a "Transportation Waiver Form" must be signed by a parent or guardian. The parent or guardian must come to the school office and sign the form — don't allow the student/athlete to simply take home a note and have the parent or guardian sign it.

1915 Under no circumstances should a coach arrange transportation by directly contacting a transportation vendor. All transportation contracts must be reviewed and approved by your school district's administration.

1916 All coaches and teachers must travel to and from contests with the team unless prior approval is obtained from the athletic director or administration. Coaches and teachers are needed as supervisors during the transportation of a group of students/athletes.

1917 Instruct your coaches and teachers to refrain from transporting athletes or students to or from practices or events in their private vehicle unless prior authorization has been obtained. This authorization should be provided only when there is no other method to transport the student/athlete.

1918 Always obtain written permission from school administration and parents before transporting students off school grounds, especially if using personal vehicles.

1919 Understand that the teacher's private automobile insurance would provide the primary coverage in these situations and the school district's automobile policy would provide the excess coverage. If your staff members must transport students in their personal vehicles, written authorization should be obtained and the staff member should consult with his/her automobile insurance agent about coverage. In some instances, teachers have negotiated with their school district to pay any additional auto liability premium costs.

1920 Opposite sex transportation (male coach/female athlete, female teacher/male student) should be strongly discouraged.

1921 Develop a specific policy if your school district will allow athletes and students to return home from an 'away' event with their parents or guardians. If your school district does allow this practice, ensure prior approval has been obtained from the school district administration and the appropriate waiver has been signed. These permission slips should be received by the school district at least 2-3 days prior to the event.

In these cases, the coach is often responsible for ensuring that the athlete leaves the contest with his or her parent or guardian. Coaches may not want this responsibility and simply require all athletes to ride 'home' in the school sponsored vehicle.

1922 Never allow an athlete to ride to or from an 'away' sporting event with another athlete or go home with another student. It's just not a wise decision to approve and allow athletes and students to ride together to or from an event. If an accident were to occur, the liability ramifications could be huge.

Bus Safety

Backing a School Bus

🔑 **1923** **The best control is to avoid backing the school bus if at all possible.** The best way to eliminate backing accidents is to eliminate backing.

1924 **Review each and any situation requiring a bus to back up, rather than assuming that situation will exist for the entire school year.** Work with the student's parents to find an alternative to backing the bus, such as asking the student to go to another pick up point.

1925 **When route conditions necessitate daily backing in order to pick up a student, contact the parents in the area to alert them that a bus will be backing up on their street.**

1926 **Instruct bus drivers to drive around the block instead of turning around in the street.**

1927 **When backing a school bus cannot be avoided, institute strict driver safety controls.** These controls include:

1928 **Make sure your bus drivers practice backing their school bus.** No amount of forward driving experience can help you in backing your bus.

1929 **Back the school bus slowly.** Never back up faster than two to three miles per hour. Backing slowly gives someone behind you a chance to get out of the way.

1930 **Back up the bus for the shortest possible distance.** This distance should be just enough to enable the driver to proceed forward.

1931 **The bus driver must keep their eyes constantly moving.** A parent may have driven up behind the bus or a child may have walked up behind the bus since the driver last looked — everyday reasons to avoid backing whenever possible.

1932 **If backing in a loading or unloading zone is unavoidable, provide an adult spotter to assist the driver from outside the bus to complete the backing maneuver before children are present.**

1933 **Always be able to see the entire body of the spotter in the mirrors.** Ensure spotters stand off to one side and warn others that the bus is backing up. Never depend solely on a spotter to ensure it is safe to back up.

1934 **Never depend solely on your mirrors when backing the bus.** A school bus has blind spots up to 20 feet in front of and 200 feet behind the bus. Keep in mind that mirrors can't provide the driver the whole picture.

1935 **Activate attention-getting devices such as back-up alarms, four-way hazard lights, and horns before backing the bus.** To signal backing, use four short blasts of the horn. Leaning out the window and looking back will assist in notifying the bus driver behind you.

1936 **The driver should request silence on the bus during the backing maneuver.** The bus driver will be able to more easily hear any warning from outside the bus, such as another vehicle's horn.

1937 **Adjust the mirrors on a daily basis.** Before any trip begins, the bus driver must adjust the mirrors accordingly.

1938 **Use the flat driving mirrors to back in a straight line or make steering corrections as needed.** Instruct bus drivers to not twist around in their seat to look behind you as they back up — this is ineffective in a school bus.

1939 Use the overhead mirrors only if you are backing up to something which is not visible in your driving mirrors. This includes objects such as trees, light poles, etc.

1940 Watch for the front end swing of the school bus. In tight spaces, ensure that the front end of the bus does not swing out and strike someone or something.

1941 When backing is unavoidable on the route, a spotter is recommended. If a spotter is not available, the driver must exercise extreme caution. Depending upon the ages of the students on the bus, it might be possible to use an older, more responsible student inside the bus as a spotter.

1942 Design your bus routes to load children before turnarounds and unload them after turnarounds.

Develop Bus Rider Rules

1943 Review student bus behavior rules with students and parents throughout the school year. Home mailings, emails, and parent-teacher conferences are great ways to stress these behavior rules with parents.

1944 Implement and enforce strict 'student conduct on bus' rules regarding student behavior on the school bus. These rules may include:

1945 Students should be seated immediately and always remain seated when the bus is in motion.

1946 Students must always obey the driver's instructions. The bus driver is in complete control of the passengers on their school bus.

1947 Educate students to speak in a quiet voice so the bus driver will not be distracted.

1948 Educate students to keep their hands to themselves at all times when on the bus. Fighting, bullying and picking on others creates a dangerous bus ride.

1949 Educate students to always be silent when their bus approaches a railroad crossing. A bus driver must be able to hear if a train is approaching.

1950 Instruct students to never throw things out of the school bus windows.

1951 Students must be instructed to keep the bus aisles and emergency exits clear at all times. Large objects such as band instruments or sports equipment should never block the aisles or emergency exits of the bus. Unobstructed aisles are important if the bus must be evacuated quickly.

1952 Instruct students to never tamper with the emergency door, the fire extinguisher, or any other equipment on the school bus.

1953 Never vandalize or deface the school bus. Anyone caught damaging bus equipment should be subject to disciplinary action by the school district and be required to pay restitution.

1954 Using profanity or obscene gestures on the school bus is never permitted.

Preventing Stranded Students

In northern climates, leaving a child on a school bus can be a life-threatening situation, especially when temperatures drop during the winter months.

A variety of electronic devices and signs are available to ensure the bus driver walks to the back of the bus after each route; however, the bus driver is still the most important control in preventing stranded students on your school buses.

1955 At the conclusion of each bus trip, walking through the entire bus must become part of the regular routine of the bus driver.

1956 Develop a zero tolerance policy for drivers who leave a child stranded on a school bus.

1957 Bus drivers should not be given a second chance if a stranded student incident takes place. After one incident where the bus driver fails to check their bus and a student needs to be recovered, the driver should be terminated. New bus driver training is the time to discuss your driver's post-trip inspection. Educate drivers that termination will follow if a student is stranded and that there is no room for discussion if this occurs.

1958 Require bus drivers to place an "Empty Bus" placard in the back of the bus each and every time the bus is used. This will help to reinforce the fact that the bus driver must walk to the back of the bus at the conclusion of each trip.

1959 The "Empty Bus" placard system is an easy way for your transportation manager to walk or drive your bus parking area to determine which buses have been walked through by observing the placards. Keep in mind this system is not foolproof; a bus driver could place the placard in the back of the bus and never visually check the bus.

1960 If the "Empty Bus" placard system is used, a bus that is missing the placard should be inspected immediately. The bus driver should also receive a stern warning about their actions.

1961 During bus evacuation drills, educate students about how to use the bus horn to get someone's attention in case they are ever accidentally locked in on a school bus.

1962 Your bus transportation manager should frequently conduct spot checks of drivers when they complete their route to ensure drivers are looking for stranded students on their bus.

1963 During monthly bus safety meetings with drivers, always review the procedures for conducting their post trip inspection as well as all other emergency protocols.

Unfortunately no checking system is completely foolproof. If a student is scared or falls asleep, they may easily end up under the bus seat. Unless your bus drivers are always attentive, the child may be missed with potentially serious consequences.

Bus Drop-Off Area Concerns

1964 The best control is to design your school's bus pick up and drop off areas to permit only one way traffic by the school bus.

1965 Always attempt to segregate parents' vehicle access from bus traffic.

1966 If your bus pick up or drop off area cannot be segregated from the parent/student pick up and drop off areas, the entrances and exits of these areas should be closed off to all pedestrian and vehicle traffic.

1967 Consider posting supervisors at the bus entrances to ensure parents and visitors do not drive into this area during designated times.

1968 Ensure supervisors wear highly reflective vests so they are clearly visible to students, parents, and visitors.

1969 Ask your local law enforcement to park or patrol the area during drop off and pick up times.

1970 Post signage that lists the time of the day that these areas are closed to others. I must admit, signage does little to stop a parent from driving into a restricted area.

1971 Post brightly colored barricades to prevent anyone from driving into these areas during designated times. Barricades must be erected to ensure that parents or visitors cannot simply drive around the barricade.

1972 Staff and other school vehicles must have designated parking which is separate from the school bus loading zone. Install highly visible signage directing parking traffic to these areas.

1973 Design your pedestrian walkways so they do not intersect with the bus loading zone.

1974 Never allow students to cross between buses if they are walking away from the school to be picked up. Students should be instructed to walk around the back of the last school bus — supervisors can play a key role in ensuring that this takes place.

1975 Parents approaching the school to drop off their children should have a separate traffic area which separates their entrance from the school bus entrance. This will prevent the dangerous exposure of a vehicle attempting to drive around a school bus while students are present. It will also prevent children from walking around or between school buses when entering or exiting the school.

1976 Load students on school buses using scheduled 'waves.' Only when the school buses have entered the loading zone should students walk out of the school to enter the bus.

1977 Instruct your bus loading supervisors to give a clear signal to bus drivers that the area is 'all clear' — a visual message indicating that no students are walking in or around the loading zone area. This process should be repeated until all buses have loaded students and left on their routes.

1978 Consequences should be developed for parents, suppliers, or visitors who attempt to violate the traffic pattern parking rules developed by your school district. Law enforcement should be contacted to become involved in these situations.

Video Cameras on School Buses

Many school districts approve the use of video cameras for the purpose of reducing vandalism and disciplinary problems on the school bus. The ultimate goal is to allow the driver to focus on driving the bus, providing safer transportation for your students.

When developing your district's policy regarding the use of bus video cameras, keep the following considerations in mind:

1979 Your school district should notify parents at the beginning of the school year that video cameras are being used on the buses. Notification can include inclusion in the student handbook, via a school newsletter/email, and during discussions at parent-teacher conferences.

1980

Clearly state the purpose of your bus videotaping is to document student misconduct and determine which student(s) may be involved. The use of video cameras on your buses is authorized for the purpose of maintaining order, preventing vandalism, or other illegal activities, and ensuring that all students have a safe and positive experience while riding on the bus. Also stress that your school district may take disciplinary action with students based on the video documentation.

1981

The only individuals authorized to view videotapes should be your district's transportation director, bus drivers, principals, board members, and the district administrator.

When a videotape is used as a disciplinary tool, your school district should adhere to the following provisions:

1982

Only adult students (those at least 18 years old) and the parents/guardian of minor students can have access to the videotape.

1983

Minor students should not have access to the videotape. Access does not mean an adult student or parent/guardian has permission to remove the videotape from the school district premises. Rather, all viewing should be performed with the business administrator or administrator's designee in attendance.

1984

The videotapes shall not be available for viewing by the general public, the media, or other individuals. The district administrator or transportation director may authorize a teacher or school guidance counselor, social worker, school board members, transportation committee members, or other pupil services professionals to view segments of a specific tape if:

• Such individuals are working with the student on the videotape because of a behavior, emotional or learning problem; and

• Viewing the videotape would be beneficial to their role in assisting the student.

1985 If more than one student is identifiable in a given frame or series of frames, neither the student to be disciplined (regardless of age) nor their parent/guardian will be able to view the tape unless special precautions are taken. These include:

- The tape can be edited or altered so as to render all other students unrecognizable or;

- Written consents are obtained from the other adult students and the parents/guardians of the other minor students. Consents must be signed, dated, and must specify the records to be disclosed, the purpose of the disclosure and the party or parties to whom disclosure may be made.

1986 Develop timelines as to when bus videotapes can be deleted. For example, if there are no bus problems pertaining to the date a videotape was taped, the videotape may be erased or reused after three (3) student school days or ten (10) calendar days, whichever occurs first.

1987 Stress in your policy that the district recognizes the confidentiality of student records pursuant to state and federal law. The school district must also recognize that any videotapes created are student records and subject to the protection of state and federal pupil records laws. As pupil records, these video-tapes are confidential; disclosure or review is limited to those persons authorized by law to inspect pupil records.

1988 Your school district should reserve the right to introduce a videotape at any disciplinary hearing involving student misconduct or rule violations on the school bus, but only as permitted under applicable state and federal law.

1989 The building principal should maintain a log regarding all requests to use a videotape, including the date(s) of request and the names of all individuals who viewed the videotape.

1990 Your district administrator or his/her designee shall approve the rotation schedule of the cameras and maintain a log which includes the date, bus number, and driver. Bus drivers may not be informed as to the placement of the video camera. Individual drivers and principals may request that the video camera be on a specific bus on designated dates.

1991 The video tapes shall not be available for viewing by the public in general, employees in general, media, or other individuals.

1992 The principals or district administrator may authorize other individuals, such as the guidance counselor, school psychologist, or social worker, to view segments of a specific video tape, if such individuals are working with the student on the video tape because of a behavior, emotional, or learning problem, and viewing the video tape is beneficial to their role in assisting the student. A log shall be kept of the date and names of the individuals viewing the video tape.

"Let our advance worrying become advance thinking and planning."

– Winston Churchill

CONCLUSION

Conclusion

I have to believe that my safety and security consulting efforts over the past 25+ years have educated thousands of school employees, made hundreds of schools safer, and possibly prevented a number of violent acts from occurring.

My objective for writing this book was simple — to share with your school staff, law enforcement, and emergency medical services personnel the thousands of safety and security best practices that I have gathered over the years. My sincere wish is that these best practices will make your schools safer and more secure... end of story... or so I thought.

The entire world of school safety and security was turned upside down with the December 14, 2012 shooting massacre in Newtown, Connecticut. No one wanted to believe that a lone deranged individual was able to carry out such a horrific act — especially one involving such small innocent children. In an instant, this one tragic act of school violence opened our eyes as to just how vulnerable our schools (and children) may be in our nation's schools.

Since that terrible day, I have repeatedly asked myself, "Can a totally senseless act of violence, like the one that occurred in Newtown, ever be prevented?" My heartfelt answer is 'no.' No matter what security protocols your school district, law enforcement, and emergency medical services implement, a bad person with bad intentions will be able to get weapons in to your schools and do terrible things.

This is not to say that you should lose hope; that there is nothing that can be done to prevent or reduce violent acts from occurring. When meeting with school district administrators to review their safety and security controls, I often refer to the development and implementation of safety and security 'barriers' that create an atmosphere of 'perception and deception.'

Create a perception that your school is safe and secure by developing and implementing a variety of 'barriers' — policies, procedures, physical controls, and building modifications that will significantly increase safety as well as reduce the chance of a violent act from occurring in one of your schools. Create 'deception' by never playing your hand — don't let the bad guys comprehend your various security protocols.

Preventing school violence is an 'all or nothing' proposition. We can't develop visitor control policies for some and not for all. We can't attack the ever present problem of bullying and harassment just some of the time. And we can't involve law enforcement in our schools when it satisfies our fancy.

Sadly, we as a school community, continue to focus too much of our time, efforts, and dollars not on developing pro-active security controls to protect our students and school employees, but rather on discussions regarding the never ending gun control debate as a way to prevent school violence.

For a long time to come, politicians on both sides of the aisle will call for or against strict gun control laws — laws in my opinion that will only take guns out of the hands of law abiding citizens and not out of the hands of criminals or deranged individuals with serious psychological problems. Wherever you stand on the gun control issue, one thing is for certain, we as a society must rethink if we are doing everything possible to provide maximum safety and security for all of our school employees and our children.

On a personal note, this tragedy has affected me greatly. I am the proud father of three beautiful teenage daughters — Alexa, Mikala and Madeline. I am also an avid outdoorsman; an owner of multiple firearms and hundreds of rounds of ammunition that are safely secured in my home. My daughters have all learned to safely shoot a variety of guns; it was always my intention for my daughters to have a healthy and safe appreciation for guns — I have accomplished this goal.

For as long as I've been consulting to ensure our schools are safe and secure, I will never understand how a 'troubled individual' can brazenly walk in to a school and murder defenseless small children. I will never understand... that's for psychologists and psychiatrists of this world to figure out.

What I do know is that I am concerned more than ever for my daughters and their teachers while they are in school. No one should ever have to daily face the verbal and physical abuse or the threat of being injured that has become too commonplace in many schools throughout our country. Yet too many school districts still are hesitant to step up and do everything possible to develop and implement maximum safety and security controls.

I have my opinion as to why safety and security is not a top priority at many school districts. The answer is two-fold:

- Schools throughout our country continue to believe that a tragic and deadly act of school violence 'cannot happen here.' In reality, your school district will never be immune to the deadly consequences of school violence.

- Schools are scared to admit to their community that they just aren't prepared to deal with violence issues. Too often, I hear that making drastic safety or security improvements will scare our children or are just too costly to implement.

Nothing could be further from the truth.

Contrary to what you may wish to believe, school shootings are a rare occurrence in our schools. School crises and emergencies are not. It goes without saying that a deadly school shooting will always receive more national media attention due to the horrendous nature of the incident than the thousands of acts of bullying and harassment that take place every day — precursors to school violence.

Always remind yourself to not lose focus on the big picture — it's important that your policy development, crisis plan implementation, employee training and new building construction/modifications always plan for the variety of violent acts that can occur in your school. Don't exclusively focus your safety and security efforts on the prevention of school shootings.

Right now is the time for your school district to get serious about developing a comprehensive school risk management program that addresses the critical controls of safety and security. Implementing critical safety and security controls is hard work. But the implementation of these controls will reduce your school's exposure to accidents, injuries, and a tragic act of violence.

It's time to stop believing that your school is a public facility. The days are gone when your exterior doors are left open day and night for everyone to use to access your school. Become diligent in your efforts to secure your school building, have a clear understanding of who is using your school, and don't be afraid to say 'no' to those who aren't willing to follow your security protocols.

In summary, I would like to conclude this book with those best practices that in my opinion, will have the greatest impact on enhancing the overall safety and security of your school. So here they are in no particular order:

1993 **Ensure your efforts also address the spectrum of school crises — weapon possession, hostage situations, trespassers, custody disputes, kidnappings, bomb threats, utility intrusions, terrorism, and all other man-made and natural emergencies.** Preventing school shootings is only part of your crisis plan development efforts.

....

1994 **Develop school security controls for everyone.** If you are a parent, don't be offended when your school requires you to follow stricter visitor controls by not allowing you to simply walk down to your child's classroom. Support teachers when it comes to the discipline issues that involve your child — not every child is innocent nor an angel. But most importantly, give the time to become involved in your child's school. Assist in the classroom, be a walking supervisor in the hallways, offer to perform periodic security checks of the buildings/grounds, and supervise dances and other events.

....

1995 **If you are a school administrator, require your teachers to follow your school's safety and security protocols.** Throughout the school year, make time to educate, make time to train. There are countless topics that should be frequently visited with your staff including: lockdown and evacuation procedures, how to confront strangers and visitors, self-defense training, facility security controls, supervision requirements, etc.

....

1996 **Teach teachers to 'act not react.'** When hearing a loud bang down the hallway, don't go to the source to see if it was actually a gunshot — go into 'rapid response' lockdown. When an emergency announcement is made, immediately follow your security protocols. People die when teachers make the poor decision to determine if the emergency or crisis is real. If it's not, you'll know soon enough.

1997 If you are a teacher, clearly understand your role in preventing violence. Don't assume that violence will never occur in your school. Be vigilant for bullying and harassment, and never forget to act on rumors.

1998 If you are a police officer, make it a point to stop by your schools throughout the day and 'rattle your saber.' Walk the hallways, stay for a free hot lunch, and make yourself available for student presentations, parent in-service programs, and parent/teacher conferences. Let it be known to all parents and students — there is a highly visible law enforcement presence in your school.

1999 If you are a fire department official, hold your schools accountable for adhering to strict life safety controls. Too many times over the years, I have witnessed fire inspectors who said nothing when too much combustible material was covering a classroom wall, too many flammables were unsecured in the technology education shop, exits and hallways were blocked or classroom door windows were covered with paper.

2000 If you are a member of the media, take the initiative to meet with your school administrators and law enforcement officials to determine what you can do to assist before, during and after a crisis occurs. I realize that the media always wants their story (and will always get their story) but sometimes I think the media's 'reporting' is actually detrimental in preventing future school violence acts. I find it very interesting that a few days after a school shooting occurs, most people will be able to provide the first and last names of the shooter, but would have a difficult time in remembering the names of any of the victims. Maybe I am wrong, but something tells me that the emphasis the media places on the shooter, simply fuels the fire of the next deranged individual out there who is intent on shooting up a school.

2001 Your police and sheriff's department provide a distinctive perspective on how to address the safety and security concerns of your schools. **Listen to them, they've done this before, you haven't.** Work with your emergency services. Staff members must understand how to act when law enforcement responds to your school during an emergency or crisis. This means that school employees must understand how law enforcement will respond to a crisis or emergency.

2002 Get a school resource officer in your school. Do everything possible to find the funds to support a police presence in your schools. A school resource officer will evaluate your safety and security procedures, conduct physical security assessments of your buildings, and talk with students on a daily basis to diffuse potentially violent situations. Bad guys don't want confrontation — a school resource officer is their worst nightmare.

2003 Begin the discussion of arming a select number of highly trained school staff members. The day is coming when the need for armed teachers will be discussed in your school district. Whether that weapon is a firearm, a taser, or pepper spray, protocols must be in place to keep the weapon away from your students.

2004 Supervise — supervise — supervise. Bad things occur when there is little or no supervision. Educate your teachers to make supervision a top priority each and every day. Walk the hallways, monitor parking lots, and check secluded areas like bathrooms.

2005 Stop bullying and harassment whenever it is observed or brought to the attention of school staff. The majority of violent incidents center on an individual who has been bullied or harassed in school.

2006 Lock all your doors — inside doors, outside doors, all of your doors, all of the time. Bad things take place in secluded areas — they can't occur if the room is locked when it is not occupied by a staff member.

2007 During the planning of new school construction or modifications, budget dollars for safety and violence prevention systems. Every year, schools throughout this country spend millions of dollars on improving their fire prevention systems. Yes it's important, but there haven't been any fire deaths in our nation's schools for many, many years. Yet, hundreds of students and staff are injured and even killed on school grounds — it's time to take your school violence prevention more seriously.

School administrators are being pressured to 'do something' to further protect our students from violent incidents. Nevertheless, school administrators should avoid spending dollars on security before researching the various options. Have a school safety and security consultant conduct a detailed risk assessment of your safety and security programs to determine your specific areas of strength and weakness.

The tragic event in Newtown, Connecticut has awakened us all. Now is the time for all of us to act. Don't continue to be in denial to do what is needed to protect our students and school staff.

"People often complain about lack of time when the lack of direction is the real problem."

– Zig Zigler

ABOUT THE AUTHOR

For the past 27 years, Ted Hayes has served as a safety and security consultant to school districts and municipalities in Wisconsin and throughout the United States.

From 1994 to 1996, Ted served as the president of the Wisconsin School Safety Coordinators Association (WSSCA). In 2001, Hayes and Waukesha County (WI) Sheriff Bill Kruziki authored the book, *Not In MY School! A Pro-Active Guide to School Violence Prevention*.

During the fall of 1998, Hayes was a featured presenter at the Wisconsin School Safety Summit hosted by Attorney General James Doyle.

Additionally, Ted has been a featured speaker for the:
- **National Sheriffs Association**
- **National Association of Pupil Transportation**
- **Kansas DARE Officers Association**
- **Law Enforcement Training Network**
- **Wisconsin Attorney Generals conference**
- **Wisconsin School Counselors Association**
- **Wisconsin Association of School Boards**
- **Wisconsin Association of School Business Officials**

Currently, Hayes is a member of the Wisconsin Association of School Business Officials (WASBO) Safety and Risk Management Committee.

Hayes continues to author articles on school safety, security, and violence prevention and consult with school districts and municipalities throughout Wisconsin.

For more information, please email Ted at: **hayes.schoolsafety@gmail.com**.